One Thing Leads To Another

Promoting Industrialisation by Making the Most of the Commodity Boom in Sub-Saharan Africa

One Thing Leads To Another

Promoting Industrialisation by Making the Most of the Commodity Boom in Sub-Saharan Africa

Mike Morris
University of Cape Town, South Africa

Raphael Kaplinsky,
The Open University, UK

David Kaplan,
University of Cape Town, South Africa

Copyright © 2012, Mike Morris, Raphael Kaplinsky and David Kaplan

All rights reserved. No part of this book may be reproduced, stored, or transmitted by any means—whether auditory, graphic, mechanical, or electronic—without written permission of both publisher and author, except in the case of brief excerpts used in critical articles and reviews. Unauthorized reproduction of any part of this work is illegal and is punishable by law.

ISBN 978-1-4717-8188-9

Preface

Over the past four decades, the authors of this book have wrestled with the challenges of promoting industrial development in low and middle-income economies in general, and in Sub-Saharan African (SSA) economies in particular. We have witnessed a series of changes in the framing conditions for industrial development, and in the associated policy agendas and fashions. These include the rise and fall of protectionist *dirigiste* import-substituting policies (which initially fostered the building of domestic capabilities, but then often led to low productivity and internationally uncompetitive industries), their supplanting by structural adjustment policies (which generally eroded many of the industrial capabilities built in the preceding era), and more recently, the hopeful promise that SSA economies could emulate the export oriented success of various generations of East Asian economies. During the course of these four decades, SSA's industrial development stagnated and the continent's share of global manufacturing value added fell. Moreover, unlike some other regions of the world, Africa did not experience an increase in knowledge intensive service sectors. It is not surprising therefore, that per capita incomes stagnated in much of the continent in the 1980s and the 1990s.

However, after the turn of the millennium, there were signs of change, both in the continent's general economic performance and in the external conditions framing SSA's industrial development. SSA's GDP growth performance improved dramatically, rising from 2.0 per cent per annum in 1990-1999 to 4.7 per cent per annum between 2000 and 2010. (During the same periods, global GDP growth rates were 2.7 and 2.5 per cent respectively). From the mid-1980s, China's rapid economic growth (followed by that of India from the early 1990s) meant that there was an increasing shift in the trajectory of global GDP from industrialised high income northern economies to low and middle income southern economies in general and to the two giant Asian Driver economies (China and India) in particular.

Responding to the rapid rise of the Asian Driver economies a network of global researchers began to focus on the impact of China (in particular) and India on the economic growth of low and middle-income economies. This included a large research programme undertaken by the African Economic Research Consortium (the AERC) (http://www.aercafrica.org/publications) in which a distinction was made between the complementary and competitive impacts and the direct and indirect impacts of the Asian Driver economies. The first generation of these studies in the African and Latin American contexts was suggestive of a negative impact on industrialisation (see, for example, the Special Issue of World Development, Vol. 36, No. 2, 2008). It was widely concluded that the competitiveness of China and other East Asian economies in global markets created major problems for African economies seeking to emulate the export oriented industrialisation success of East Asia.

Moreover, the combination of rising commodity prices after 2002 and often stagnant and falling prices of manufactures was leading to changes in the commodities-manufactures terms of trade. The received wisdom on the consequences of rising commodities prices for the industrial and traded services sectors in commodity exporting developing countries was overwhelmingly gloomy – they represented a Resource Curse. For a combination of economic reasons (notably rising exchange rates), policy failures (the inefficient use of resource rents) and political factors (the kleptocracy associated with commodity intensive economies), it was widely considered that the expansion of the commodities sectors would undermine industrial development.

When we first considered working on the impact of the commodities price boom on industrial development in SSA, our intention was to focus on these Resource Curse issues. Although we felt uncomfortable with this half-empty and negative perspective, which left SSA in a policy *cul de sac*, it seemed as if the outcome was determined. And then we stumbled across an article written by Wright and Czelusta (*'The Myth of the Resource Curse'*). It argued that the development of industry in many of the currently industrialised northern economies occurred in close synergy with the growing exploitation of natural resources. The more we picked away at the literatures on the historical experiences of countries such as the United States, Canada, Sweden, Norway and Australia, the more evident it became that far from the commodities sectors undermining industrial development, the growth of the two sectors was positively interrelated in these countries. We had moved from a half-empty to a half-full perspective, and the task was to develop a policy agenda designed to *Make the Most from Commodities*. This focus was not to deny the continuing challenges posed to macroeconomic management by rising commodity prices, but we were conscious of a major research and associated policy gap on the promotion of industrial development in the context of expanded commodities production.

Fortuitously midway through the AERC's Asian Drivers research programme, we mentioned these conclusions to Basil Jones of the Canadian International Development Research Centre and he suggested that we build a research programme to inform SSA policy makers of the potential that the commodities price boom held for the promotion of industrial development and the growth of knowledge intensive services. Soon after we engaged with the William and Flora Hewlett Foundation who were interested in research designed to promote the growth of SSA's infrastructural corridors.

Together, with complementary funding from the Open University in the UK and the Harry Oppenheimer Centre for African Studies at the University of Cape Town in South Africa, this led to a three year research programme, the predominant part of the funding coming from the IDRC. The Making the Most of Commodities Programme (MMCP) was designed to explore the nature and determinants of linkages from the commodities sector for industry and knowledge intensive services (http://commodities.open.ac.uk/discussionpapers or http://www.prism.uct.ac.za). Crucially, all funders were simultaneously concerned to build African based research capabilities, and thus at the heart of the MMCP was the promotion of PhD researchers (leading to six successful doctorates). The fact that much of the research involved doctoral students meant that we had unique access to qualitatively rich (and often messy) primary material which made it possible to push the analysis and policy discussion well beyond the existing knowledge frontier which is overwhelmingly based on a combination of hearsay, casual empiricism and secondary data.

Although from the outset our intent was to deliver policy relevant conclusions from the research, it rapidly became clear that our conception of dialogue with policy makers was hopelessly flawed. (In fact, given our experience, this should have been obvious from the onset of the research). We had initially conceived of this policy dialogue in the conventional manner as consisting of a final grand 'multi-stakeholder' workshop in which we passed on the wisdom of our research to an assembly of policymakers. However, we quickly came to realise that we needed deep policymaker involvement (from both the public and private sectors, as well as international development agencies) in order to undertake the research. At the same time, unless policymakers were involved throughout the research process, then it would be unlikely that the research results would be incorporated in policies. As a consequence, throughout the multi-year programme and the subsequent period of write-up, there was interaction with, and presentation to, African and internationally based policymakers through participation (and follow up discussions) in forums hosted by the African Development Bank, UNCTAD, UNIDO, Afreximbank, the World Bank, the International Council on Mining and Metals (ICMM), The Common Fund for Commodities, World Economic Forum, and the AERC, as well as with large TNCs and smaller firms in the private sector. It is gratifying that as this book is being published, these links are deepening as the policy conclusions are being picked up by these various stakeholders.

It is this desire to build capabilities and to deepen the dialogue with policymakers which explains the unusual route we have adopted for the publication of this book. We have been approached by a number of publishers wishing to place this book in their portfolios. But at what price? And with what delay? Our recent experience in publishing with one 'first league' publisher resulted in a book selling at a 'discounted price' of $112/£68, and with a nine month delay for publication. This is a form of publication which limits the spread of information particularly in cash-strapped SSA. Our intent, by contrast, has been to maximise the capacity of researchers to aid policy development. We have therefore proactively chosen the open-access route as a way of maximising the social utility of academic endeavour. We are gratified to note that an increasing number of academics are similarly challenging the knowledge-limiting historic trajectory of academic publishing. Having said this, we have not completely withdrawn from the traditional academic route and a collection of (blind peer reviewed) articles drawn from the MMCP programme will be published in a Special Issue of Resources Policy in 2012 and a number of individual researchers are publishing in other journals and edited volumes.

Finally, we would like to offer our thanks to all of those who have made this book possible. Our primary debt is owed to the long suffering family and friends of the researchers. Next in line are the researchers themselves who struggled to document the nature and determinants of linkages in the commodities sectors under review, as well as the many respondents who generously gave their valuable time and without whom research could not have been undertaken. Similarly, without the generous funding of the IDRC, the Hewlett Foundation, the Harry Oppenheimer Foundation and the Open University, none of this would be possible.

It is invidious to name individuals, since so many people contributed in so many large and small ways to the research programme. Having said this, there is little doubt that without the intelligence, diligence and energy of Judith Fessehaie and Masuma Farooki, this book would not have emerged from the wealth of empirical material and detailed analysis contained in the individual research reports.

About the Authors:

Prof. Mike Morris is Director of the Policy Research on International Services and Manufacturing (PRISM), and Professor of Economics, University of Cape Town, South Africa

Prof. Raphael Kaplinsky is a Professor of International Development at the Development Policy and Practice unit at The Open University, UK

Prof. David Kaplan is Professor of Business Government Relations and Professor of Economics, University of Cape Town, South Africa

Contents

Chapter 1. Beyond Resource Pessimism 1

    The fulcrum: rising commodity prices 1

    Why has resource pessimism become the conventional wisdom? 3

        Declining commodities-manufactures terms of trade and the price volatility of commodities 4

        The Resource Curse and the Dutch Disease – Resource intensity undermines growth in general and industrial growth in particular 6

        The enclave economy – Resource exploitation has limited linkages 8

        The demonstration effect – the close association between per capita incomes and industrial development 10

    Blocked routes to industrial development 12

    The challenge to industrialise development are increasing 16

Chapter 2. 'One Thing Leads to Another' – Why Local Linkages may Become the Norm Rather than the Exception 21

    A taxonomy of commodity sectors and types of linkages 22

    'Staples Theory' – the experience of industrialised economies with significant resource sectors 27

"One thing leads to another" – Hirschman's framework of linkages from the commodities sector 29

A model of linkage development from the resource sector 31

    Intrinsic determinants of linkage development 35

    Contextual determinants of linkage development 38

    Speeding up and slowing down linkage development 43

In conclusion 45

Chapter 3. Data and Methodology 47

    Core research questions 48

    Sectoral coverage and resource dependence in the sample economies 49

Chapter 4. The Breadth and Depth of Linkages 57

    Backward linkages into offshore oil production in Angola 58

    Forward linkages in the diamond sector in Botswana 64

    Forward linkages into the timber sector in Gabon 73

    Backward linkages into the gold sector in Ghana 79

    Backward linkages into the oil sector in Nigeria 87

    Backward linkages into mining equipment and services in South Africa 94

    Backward linkages into the gold sector in Tanzania 101

    Linkages into the copper sector in Zambia 111

Chapter 5. The Contextual Drivers of Linkages 121

    Ownership as a determinant of linkage development 122

    Buyers as a determinant of linkages 123

    Ownership of lead commodity firms as a determinant of linkages 126

    The origin of foreign ownership as a determinant of linkages 128

    Firm specific attributes and their impact on linkages 133

    Infrastructure as a determinant of linkage development 137

        Oil: enclave infrastructure with different linkage outcomes 139

        Corridor infrastructure in Zambia, Mozambique and Gabon 143

        Gold and diamonds 146

    Capabilities: skills and the National System of Innovation 149

        Skill as a constraint and an enabler of linkage capabilities 150

        Supportive institutions in the National Systems of Innovation 161

    Policy development, management and implementation 167

        Angola 167

        Botswana 170

        Gabon 174

        Ghana 175

        Nigeria 178

        South Africa 180

        Tanzania 182

Zambia 184

Chapter 6. Does One Thing Lead to Another and if Not, Why Not? 187

    Has one thing led to another? 188

    Why does one thing not always lead to another? 190

        The role of ownership in promoting linkages 191

        The role of infrastructure in linkage development 198

        The role of capabilities in linkage development 201

        The role of policy in linkage development 204

    How can policy help make one thing lead to another? 207

        Implications for government policy 210

        Implications for corporate policy 213

    Might one thing lead to another? 214

References 217

Figures

Figure 1.1 United Nations Conference on Trade and Development (UNCTAD) monthly average price index, 2000=100 (2000 to January 2012) 2

Figure 1.2 The 'normal' relationship between per capita incomes and share of manufacturing in GDP, Uganda, India, Korea, and the US (1970) and US (1980) 12

Figure 1.2 World transport costs as measured by CIF/FOB ratios (1948-1998) 14

Figure 1.3 Percentage of sectors with falling prices (1989-2007) 19

Figure 1.4 The commodities-manufactures terms of trade (1949-2008) 20

Figure 2.1 Backward, forward and horizontal linkages in the wood and timber sector 25

Figure 2.2 Market driven linkages over time 35

Figure 2.3 Different trajectories of linkage development 44

Figure 4.1 Angola annual GDP growth rate percentage (1986-2010) 60

Figure 4.2 Angola sectoral composition of GDP percentage (2003-2008) 60

Figure 4.3 Botswana annual percentage GDP growth (1971-2009) 65

Figure 4.4 Botswana sectoral contribution to GDP (2000-2009) ..66

Figure 4.5 Botswana composition of government revenue (2000-2009) 66

Figure 4.6 Botswana's downstream diamond value chain 69

Figure 4.7 Gabon's tropical timber value chain 76

Figure 4.8 Gabon export volumes of wood products in cubic meters (1961-2007) 77

Figure 4.9 Gabon intra-chain value-added distributions 79

Figure 4.10 Nigerian shares of oil in total revenue and GDP (1980-2010) 88

Figure 4.11 Alignment of perceptions on the frequency and quality of interchanges between lead oil firms and first tier suppliers in Nigeria 92

Figure 4.12 Tanzanian value of gold exports and percentage share of total exports (2000-2011) 102

Figure 4.13 Tanzanian gold mining value chain 104

Figure 4.14 Zambian copper value chain 113

Figure 4.15 Zambian copper exports by composition in $ '000 (2000-2009) 114

Figure 4.16 Comparative rating of supplier capabilities by northern buyers', Chinese buyers and by the supply chain itself in Zambia 119

Figure 5.1 A framework for assessing the impact of ownership on linkages 123

Figure 5.2 European and Chinese buyers' public and private standards in Gabon 125

Figure 5.3 Perception of Infrastructure performance in Nigeria . 142

Figure 5.4 Industry and government responses on government's policy in Botswana 172

Figure 5.5 Industry and government views on corporate beneficiation policies in Botswana 174

Figure 5.6 Newmont Ghana vision for backward linkage development 177

Figure 6.1 The trajectory of local supply 209

Tables

Table 1.1 Average percentage tariff levels for SSA imports from World (1990-2010).. 14

Table 1.2 Percentage change in value of clothing exports to the US (2004-2006) 16

Table 2.1 General characteristics of the three major families of commodities.. 22

Table 2.2 Three primary commodity families and their sector of use... 23

Table 3.1 Core characteristics of case studies 51

Table 3.2 Summary of sample size and composition for sectoral studies... 53

Table 4.1 Angolanisation targets 61

Table 4.2 Value and percentage share of investment in the offshore oil production sector (2004-2010) 62

Table 4.3 Percentage share of local content in domestic manufacture of flow lines, control lines 63

Table 4.4 Local labour content in manufacture in Angola (2003/4-2014) 64

Table 4.5 Industry and Botswana government estimates on the range of cost per carat in Botswana relative to some centres ($) .. 70

Table 4.6 Value addition in the diamond pipeline......................... 71

Table 4.7 Ownership and employment patterns in twelve cutting and polishing firms 72

Table 4.8 Direct employment, and wages and salaries in Botswana diamond cutting and polishing sector (2010)................. 73

Table 4.9 Gabon distribution, origin and cost of labour (%, Euro) 78

Table 4.10 Ghana gold mining production (1990 – 2009) 80
Table 4.11 Local linkages in Ghanaian gold mining: distribution of funds in Ghana chamber of mines producing members (2008) 83
Table 4.12 Ghanaian feasible products for future near term backward linkages 85
Table 4.13 GFG Foundation expenditure (%) on sectors and total contribution ($) on community development projects (2002-2009) 86
Table 4.14 Share of inputs from local suppliers/outputs sold to local processors 91
Table 4.15 Responses to supply chain development programmes 93
Table 4.16 Percentage share of local content in purchases by first tier suppliers to the oil and gas industry 93
Table 4.17 South African percentage share of mining and quarrying in GDP and exports (2000-2010) 95
Table 4.18 All patents and mining technology patents at the USPTO; South Africa and comparator countries (1976-2006) 97
Table 4.19 South African mining equipment exports and imports $'000 (2005 -2009) 99
Table 4.20 Outsourced and in-house activities in exploration sub-chain 105
Table 4.21 Gold exploration firms active in Tanzania 106
Table 4.22 Exploration geochemical works goods/services providers in Tanzania 108
Table 4.23 Geophysical work service providers active in Tanzania 110
Table 4.24 Local sourcing as percentage of total spending among selected mining companies in Zambia 116
Table 4.25 Key participants in the copper mining supply chain in Zambia 119
Table 5.1 Ownership and forward linkages in the Gabon timber sector sub-sector activities and final markets (n = 15) 124

Table 5.2 Selection of new entrants in the copper industry supply chain in Zambia..130

Table 5.3 Ownership characteristics of oil service suppliers in Nigeria 137

Table 5.4 Infrastructure performance assessment by oil firms in Nigeria 141

Table 5.5 Infrastructure performance assessment by suppliers to oil industry in Nigeria..142

Table 5.6 Percentage share of Angolans in skills in backward linkages feeding into the Angolan oil sector (2004-2014) 150

Table 5.7 Percentage share within employment categories and country of origin in Gabon's timber value chain (2009)..............152

Table 5.8 Perceptions of skill availability in firms supplying to the Nigerian oil industry (number and % of firms) 153

Table 5.9 Local content and intra-firm training in Angola (% of respondents)..154

Table 5.10 Skill spill-overs in backward linkages in the Nigerian oil sector (% of firms)..159

Table 5.11 Zambian suppliers employing ex-staff from the mines..160

Table 5.12 Angolan education expenditure and research output (2001-2009) 163

Table 5.13 Nigerian innovative activities amongst suppliers and the sources of innovative support (% within sector).............164

Table 5.14 Angolan categories of preferential products since 2003 169

Table 5.15 Industry and government responses on government's capacity (% response) in Botswana......................173

Table 5.16 Consistency of government regulations with meeting objective of increasing local content (%) in Nigeria 180

Table 6.1 Summary of findings on the breadth, depth, and trajectory in linkages from commodities to other sectors in eight SSA economies. 192

Acronyms

AGA	AngloGold Ashanti
AGOA	Africa Growth and Opportunity Act
ALP	Ahafo Linkages Program
ANIP	National Private Investment Agency
ASGISA	Accelerated and Shared Growth Initiative for South Africa
BDS	Business Development Service Centres
CAD	Computer Aided Design
CDC	Central Development Corridor
CENAREST	National Scientific and Technological Research Centre
CNC	Computer Numerically Controlled
CSF	Core Success Factors
CSIR	Council for Scientific and Industrial Research
CSR	Corporate Social Responsibility
DMR	Department of Mineral Resources
DRC	Democratic Republic of Congo
DST	Department of Science and Technology
DTC	Diamond Trading Company
EDTP	Engineering Design Training Programme
ENEF	National Water and Forestry School
EPCI	Engineering, Procurement, Construction and Installation
ER	Economic Recovery Programme

ES	Enterprise Survey
EU	European Union
FDI	Foreign Direct Investment
FOCAC	Forum on China Africa Co-operation
GAEC	Ghana Atomic Energy Commission
GCM	Ghana Chamber of Mines
GDP	Gross Domestic Product
GFG	Gold Field Ghana
GNP	Gross National Product
GSB	Ghana Standards Board
GSDF	Golden Star Development Foundation
GST	Geological Survey of Tanzania
ICMM	International Council on Mining and Metals
ICT	Information and communications technology
IFC	International Financial Corporation
ILO	International Labour Organisation
IMITT	Integrated Mining Technical Training
INP	National Petroleum Institute
IPAP	Industrial Policy Framework and in the Industrial Policy Action Plan
IPAP	Industrial Policy Action Plan
IRAF	Agricultural and Forestry Research Institute
ISO	International Standards Organisation
JOA	Joint Operating Agreements
LBDP	Local Business Development Programme
LSS	Local Scholarship Scheme
MDA	Mining Development Agreements
MMCP	Making the Most of Commodities Program
MVA	Manufacturing Value Added
NCPS	National College of Petroleum Studies

NNPC	Nigerian National Petroleum Company
NTBC	National Technology Business Centre
OECD	Organisation for Economic Co-operation and Development
OEM	Original Equipment Manufacturer
OLI	Ownership, Location and Internalisation
OSS	Overseas Scholarship Scheme
PML	Primary Mining Licences
PPL	Primary Prospecting Licences
PSC	Production Sharing Contract
PTDF	Petroleum Technology Development Fund
PTI	Petroleum Training Institute
RTO	Research and Technology Organisations
SACEC	The South African Capital Equipment Council
SADC	Southern African Development Community
SAP	Structural Adjustment Program
SDI	Spatial Development Initiatives
SEED	Sustainable Community Empowerment and Economic Development
SEPBG	Société des Parcs à Bois du Gabon
SETA	Skills Education Training Authorities
SME	Small and Medium Enterprises
SOE	State Owned Enterprises
SSA	Sub-Sahara Africa
SURF	Sub-Sea Umbilicals, Risers and Flow Lines
TCME	Tanzanian Chamber of Minerals and Energy
TIRDO	Tanzania Industrial Research and Development
TNC	Trans-National Corporation
UK	United Kingdom
UNDP	United Nations Development Programme

UNIDO	United Nations Industrial Development Organisation
US	United States
USPTO	United States Patent and Technology Office
VAT	Value Added tax
VETA	Vocational Education and Training Authority
WTCP	Welders Training and Certification Programme
ZCCM	Zambia Consolidated Copper Mines

Chapter 1

Beyond Resource Pessimism

The fulcrum: rising commodity prices

After five decades of post-war stability, since the turn of the millennium, the global economy has been shaken by a series of disruptive developments. These include major financial and economic crises and the very rapid growth in the share in global economic output and trade of the emerging economies in general, and China and India in particular. Accompanying these changes has been a rapid and sustained increase in the prices of commodities, beginning in 2002 (Figure 1.1). This price boom was particularly marked for oil and minerals as well as ores and metals, but after 2006 the prices of agricultural commodities also began to rise sharply. Although prices of all commodities fell back after the 2008 financial crisis, they soon resumed their rapid growth. Even at the depth of the post 2008 trough, the overall commodity price index was almost double that of 2002 and by May 2011 it was close to its 2008 peak, three times the level of prices in 2002. This price experience is distinctive in that the two previous commodity price booms (in the early 1950s and early 1970s respectively) were short lived.

The underlying fundamentals suggest that, notwithstanding price volatility, commodity prices will continue to be robust and in many cases be on a rising trend for some years to come (Farooki and Kaplinsky, 2012). What implications does this recent and expected price performance have for commodity intensive and commodity exporting economies, particularly in developing countries?

Figure 1.1 United Nations Conference on Trade and Development (UNCTAD) monthly average price index, 2000=100 (2000 to January 2012)

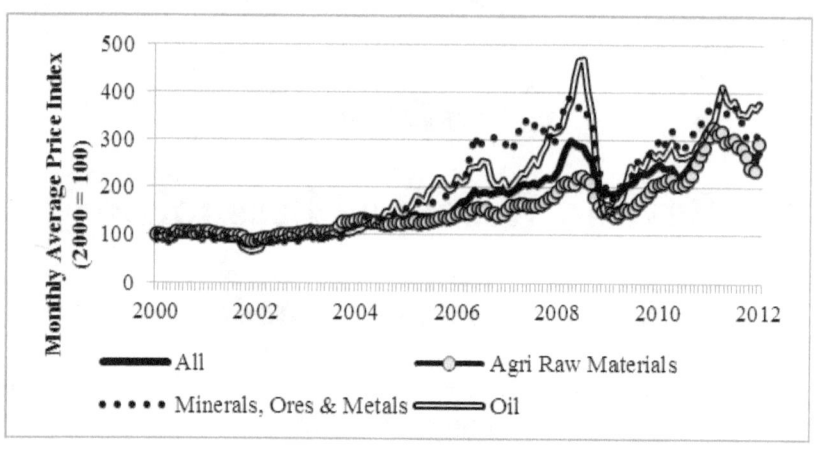

Source: Compiled from UNCTAD Stat. data. Online. <http://unctadstat.unctad.org> (accessed April 2012).

In this book, we examine one particular set of consequences—the impact on the manufacturing sector and those service sectors that feed into, and use the outputs of the commodities sector. We will argue that recent developments in the global economy open new opportunities for synergistic links between the commodity producing and related manufacturing and service sectors, but that the extent to which these opportunities are grasped will be a function of the responses of key public and private stakeholders. Our attention will be on low and middle-income economies in general and on Sub-Sahara Africa (SSA), in particular. Our analysis follows from eleven detailed research studies on the nature and determinants of linkages to the commodities sector in eight African economies (http://commodities.open.ac.uk/discussionpapers; www.cssr.uct.ac.za/prism/projects/mmcp).

We begin the analysis in the next section by reviewing the received wisdom on the impact of resources on economic and industrial growth, revisiting the reasons why it has been widely accepted that commodity exploitation undermines industrial and economic growth. Arising out of this resource pessimism is the need for countries to diversify their economic structures and to expand their industrial sector and knowledge intensive sectors in areas that are unrelated to their commodity specialisation.

However, as we show in the section after, the paths that successful late-industrialising economies followed are difficult to replicate. This does not remove the case for economic diversification in resource intensive low-income economies, but as we argue later, it does reframe the nature of the challenge. We will follow this conclusion in the following chapter when we consider the scope for a path of industrial diversification that feeds more centrally into and out of the resource sector, a path which is made more feasible by recent developments in the corporate strategy of leading commodity-producing firms. Then in subsequent chapters, we explore the extent to which these developments are evidenced in nine African resource-exploiting economies.

We argue that new opportunities are opened for low and middle-income economies to promote industrial and service sector development by 'making the most of commodities'. As a guide to achieving these ends, we present a model in chapter two, which we believe explains the development of linkages from the commodities sector to industry and related services. We believe that this model can be used to shape the actions of key stakeholders to broaden, deepen, and speed up these linkages and thus to 'make the most of commodities.' Our primary concern is thus to reframe the discussion of the role of commodities in development by refocusing the lens from resource pessimism to resource optimism.

Why has resource pessimism become the conventional wisdom?

Since the 1950s, it has been widely accepted that the promotion of sustainable economic growth and development in resource intensive economies requires diversification out of the commodities sector into industry and knowledge intensive services. This conventional wisdom has been built on four pillars – long-term trends in terms of trade and the volatility of commodity prices, the apparent negative correlation between resource intensity and growth in general (the 'Resource Curse') and industrial development in particular (the 'Dutch Disease'), the enclave nature of resource extraction, and the demonstrated association between high per capita incomes and industrial development. We briefly review each of these four developments.

Declining commodities-manufactures terms of trade and the price volatility of commodities

Until the end of the Second World War, it had generally been assumed that the commodities-manufactures terms of trade would move in favour of commodities. This view was challenged in 1950 by the combined writings of two pioneering development theorists – Raul Prebisch (1950) and Hans Singer (1950). Drawing on emerging empirical evidence on the character of United Kingdom (UK) trade, they argued that the long-term trend was in fact for the prices of commodities to fall relative to those of manufactures.

Prebisch and Singer provided a number of arguments to explain these long-term price trends. Central to their argument (although this is often glossed over in the current discussion on terms of trade) was the nature of labour markets in high-income and low-income economies. They believed that relatively full employment in the high-income manufacturing economies meant that cost-push pricing would result from the higher wages demanded by powerful trade unions. The prices of exports of these economies would consequently increase. By contrast, the surplus of labour and the weakness of trades unions in low-income economies would not be reflected in similar cost pressures and the prices of their exports would either remain stable or decrease. The logic of their argument would have been to compare the prices of high-income economy exports against low-income economy exports, since their argument hinged on the supply of labour in the two sets of countries.

However, given the paucity of trade data at that time, these prices could not be obtained. Hence, they chose commodities and manufactures as surrogates for these economies' exports and imports respectively, because low-income economies were predominantly exporting commodities and high-income economies were predominantly exporting manufactures. To evidence this they focused on the UK's trade between 1870 and 1938. Throughout this period, Britain had been a major exporter of manufactures and a major importer of raw materials, having few primary commodities of its own.

The difference in labour markets was not the only reason why Prebisch and Singer believed that the terms of trade would turn against commodities. They also marshalled their argument around the nature of demand for different products (as incomes grew the consumption of manufactures and services would be less commodities intensive) and the development of synthetic substitutes for natural resources when commodity prices rose. Moreover, Singer argued, manufacturing was more subject to Schumpeterian innovation rents (that is, difficult-to-copy technology) than were the commodities sectors and, as a consequence, the barriers to entry in manufacturing were relatively high, protecting the incomes of producers in these sectors. By contrast, barriers to entry in most primary commodity sectors were low, which meant that the incomes of producers in these sectors were subject to intense competitive pressures.

Since the seminal contributions of Singer and Prebisch, there has been an industry of very detailed research enquiry into the commodities-manufactures terms of trade. Notwithstanding two short-lived commodity price booms in the early 1950s and early 1970s, as a general long-term trend, the prices of commodities fell relative to those of manufactures. Although this conclusion is not without controversy, the balance of informed analysis supports this trend, not just for the post 1950 period, but for a much longer stretch of time. The original Singer-Prebisch pioneering analysis was based on the empirical work of Schlote who examined the terms of trade for the UK over the 1870-1938 period (Diakosavvas and Scandizzo, 1991). His study showed a 40 per cent improvement for the United Kingdom's terms of trade and therefore, by assumption, a decline in the terms of trade of commodity exporting developing countries. Most subsequent studies supported this conclusion, if not as a consistent phenomenon, then as a generalised long-term trend.

Some examples of these investigations are as follows. Sproas (1980) compared pre and post-World War II prices (1900-70) and found that although there were negative commodities-manufactures terms of trade trend before the war, this was not the case in the post war era. Going back over a longer period, Cashin and McDermott (2002) showed a downward trend in the terms of trade of around one per cent per year over the 140 year period between 1862 and 1999. Sapsford (1985) using 1900-80 data and excluding petroleum prices, estimated a decrease of 1.3 per cent per year in terms of trade for primary commodities, interrupted briefly by the 1951-53 commodity price boom. Bleaney and Greenaway (1993) focus on the 1900-91 period and estimate a downward trend of 0.5 per cent per year for non-fuel primary commodities. Grilli and Yang (1988) focused on the period 1900 to 1986 and found a 0.5 per cent fall per year for all commodities and a decrease of 0.6 per cent per year in the terms of trade of non-fuel commodities relative to manufactures.

However damaging the impact of a long-run decline in the commodities-manufactures terms of trade may be for the producers of commodities, this effect on commodity producers is compounded massively when one takes into account the impact on growth and development of short term variations in commodity prices, particularly when these price variations are frequent and large. The volatility of commodity prices is a well observed and uncontested phenomenon. In some extreme cases, commodity prices have varied by a 100 per cent on a year-to-year basis, affecting government budgets, employment, profitability and a country's foreign exchange reserves. A long-term study of the declining terms of trade between 1862 and 1999 concluded that volatility was a more damaging challenge to producers than a predictable and stable decline in commodity prices (Cashin and McDermott, 2002).

The Resource Curse and the Dutch Disease – Resource intensity undermines growth in general and industrial growth in particular

In a cross country regression analysis of the growth performance in 97 countries for the period 1970-1990, Sachs and Warner (1995) concluded that resource abundance, measured as the ratio of primary commodities exports to Gross Domestic Product (GDP), was negatively correlated with GDP growth. They estimated that a doubling of the share of primary products in total exports between

1970 and 1990 led to a reduction in the annual GDP growth rate of between 0.62 to 1.51 per cent. Their results were statistically significant after controlling for a variety of explanatory variables affecting growth rates. These were geography and climate, the presence of oil in exports, integration into the global economy, capital accumulation, institutional quality, commodity price shocks, and resource abundance (the ratio of mineral production to GDP, the share of primary exports in total exports and per capita land area).

In subsequent analysis, Sachs and Warner (1997, 2001) argued that the Dutch Disease was the major driver of this growth reducing resource curse. That is, robust commodity exports forced up the exchange rate which made it difficult for traded goods producers in other sectors to compete in export markets and with imports. First, they found services output to be higher than manufacturing output in resource rich countries. This, they believed, confirmed their hypothesis that the natural resource sector diverted capital and labour into the non-tradable sectors. Second, resource abundance was associated with a reduction in the growth of the manufacturing and services sectors and in the merchandise export sector. Third, almost all countries responded to the Dutch Disease with protectionist policies to promote industrialisation. This protective environment fostered inefficient firms and compounded the problems confronting the manufacturing sector.

However, although widely accepted, Sachs and Warner have been increasingly challenged. Davies (1995) examined the performance of mineral and non-mineral economies in relation to Gross National Product (GNP) per capita level and social indicators such as the Human Development Index. He concluded that there was no evidence to support the contention that commodity dependent economies had performed less well in respect of sustained growth or human development indices. To the contrary, oil producers achieved the highest growth increments and, in most cases, mineral economies outperformed non-mineral economies.

In a recent analysis, Lederman and Maloney employed additional estimation techniques using time series data that allowed for a more sophisticated analysis of the dynamic interrelationship between growth and the commodities sector (Lederman and

Maloney, 2007). They also adopted a different proxy for resource intensity that is, net resource exports per capita (rather than the share of natural resources in GDP adopted by Sachs and Warner). Utilising this definition of resource intensity, they concluded that Norway, New Zealand, Canada, Finland and Australia ranked as the most resource intensive economies rather than economies such as the DRC and Papua New Guinea in the Sachs and Warner analysis.

Other analytical adjustments were also made to the Sachs-Warner methodology, including using an average price over the period under analysis in order to take into account high price volatility. The consequence of these assumptions was not just that the natural resource curse found by Sachs and Warner disappeared, but that there was a mildly positive correlation between resource intensity and GDP growth (Lederman and Maloney, 2007). Similar conclusions were reached in econometric studies undertaken by Manzano and Rigobón (2007) and Bravo-Ortega and De Gregorio (2007). Brunnschweiler (2008) found a particularly positive relationship between resource abundance and economic growth for minerals and energy 'sub-surface' commodities.

Two major conclusions emerge from these various attempts to verify the Resource Curse theory. The first is that in some cases – countries such as the United States (US) and Sweden, and firms such as Nokia – there is demonstrated evidence of a positive synergy between commodities and manufacturing (Wright and Czelusta, 2004). Secondly, where commodity dependence is extreme, this is more often a result of the unrelated underdevelopment of the industrial sector rather than as the consequence of the destructive impact of commodities production on industry. Thus what shows up, and is interpreted as, a manufacturing sector weakened by a commodities specialisation, is in fact often a commodities specialisation in an economy with no or little history of industrial development.

The enclave economy – Resource exploitation has limited linkages

In 1950, Singer produced a seminal critique of the enclave nature of production in the commodities sector (Singer, 1950). In this analysis, he addressed the complexion of hard commodities production in low-income economies and argued that, as a rule, the extraction of these hard commodities occurred in isolation from the local economies in which the mines were based. As a consequence of their high capital intensity, few jobs were created, and there were weak linkages to local suppliers. Instead, as the title of his seminal paper implied ('The Distribution of Gains between Investing and Borrowing Countries') the beneficial spill-overs from commodity production were largely reaped in the high-income countries where the large foreign owned mining companies were based:

> *I would suggest that if the proper economic test of investment is the multiplier effect in the form of cumulative additions to income, employment, capital, technical knowledge, and growth of external economies, then a good deal of the investment in underdeveloped countries [hard commodities sectors] which we used to consider as 'foreign' [and taking place in low-income economies] should in fact be considered as domestic investment on the part of the industrialised countries. (Singer, 1950: 475)*

Closely linked to this argument by Singer was the assertion that the hard commodities sector offered little scope for technological progress and had few external economies. Singer (1950) asserted (since this was backed with little evidence), that the hard commodities sector was characterised by low technology, limiting the learning opportunities provided to the local economy. Further, Singer argued, specialisation in the export of raw materials diverted scarce entrepreneurial activity and domestic investment away from manufacturing. Whilst admitting that these speculations were a 'tantalizingly inconclusive business', Singer argued that in contrast to a specialisation in commodities, manufacturing provided greater scope for technological progress, for skills development, for the creation of new demand, and for the demonstration effect, which promoted diversified economic development. In summary, weak linkages would result from a combination of two factors. First, there was the sectoral effect, with commodities intrinsically having little scope for linkages and technological spill-overs. Secondly, linkages within the low-income producing economies would be limited, since whatever linkages did emerge would be reaped in the high-income home economies of the lead commodity firms.

The enclave character of commodity extraction in developing economies was reflected in and, to some extent, caused by the enclave oriented development of infrastructure in many developing economies in the postcolonial period. As a general rule, roads, ports, and often also power and water facilities were developed to facilitate the extraction of commodities, their transport to the coast and their shipping to final markets abroad. This restricted pattern of infrastructural development limited the development of industrial linkages, since commodity extraction generally took place in areas distant from settlement and the industrial sector.

The demonstration effect – the close association between per capita incomes and industrial development

It has long been recognised that there is a strong and positive relationship between per capita incomes and the share of industry in GDP. Although this relationship weakens as per capita incomes increase, it occurs at levels beyond those prevailing in most low and middle-income economies. Drawing on earlier analysis by Chenery (1960) and Taylor (1969), a UNIDO study undertaken in the late 1970s supported this correlation, taking account of country size (since countries with large populations in this period of shallow globalisation allowed for economies of scale in production) and for the share of natural resources in GDP (UNIDO, 1980). It was concluded from these comparative studies of industrial structure that a 'normal' growth path over time could be identified. This 'normal' pattern of structural transformation is shown in Figure 1.2, based on the relationship between Manufacturing Value Added (MVA) and GDP per capita in 1970 for Uganda, India, South Korea and the US (and, in the case of the US, for 1980 as well). At low levels of per capita income, industry accounted for only a small share of GDP – for example, Uganda (at 9.2 per cent). As per capita incomes rose, this share began to grow rapidly – as in the case of India (14.2 per cent) and south Korea (17.8 per cent).

Further up the per capita income scale, the share of MVA grew even higher, reaching its peak with the US share of 26.6 per cent in 1970. However, when incomes increased even further, the contribution of MVA to GDP began to fall back below its peak as the growth in demand switched from manufactured goods to services. This falling share (from 26.6 to 22.8 per cent) is indicated in Figure 1.2 for the US in 1980. (After 1980, the falling share of MVA in GDP in the US began to reflect the outsourcing of manufacturing to China and other low cost suppliers, hence exaggerating the fall in the contribution of MVA at very high levels of per capita income). Figure 1.2 presents a general story. More detailed analysis showed that the share of manufacturing in GDP is affected by two factors. The first is size – the larger the economy, the greater the share of manufacturing (which in general is characterised by scale economies). The second is that the greater the concentration of commodities in exports, the smaller the share. However, neither of these qualifications rules out the positive overall association between per capita incomes on the share of manufacturing in GDP.

Three primary reasons were provided to explain this 'normal' pattern of growth, away from resources towards industry, and within this, a gradual shift from light to heavy industry. The first was the elasticity of demand, that is, the intensity of consumption of particular types of goods at particular levels of income and prices. 'Engels Law' argued that at low per capita incomes, consumer demand would be concentrated on soft commodities (such as food) and industries using soft commodities (such as apparel, footwear and furniture). However, as incomes rose, so the demand for these products would expand less rapidly and demand for other more sophisticated industrial products and services would grow. It is important to bear in mind the period in which these strategic conclusions were developed, since in most cases, the economies whose structures were being measured were predominantly operating as relatively closed economies, selling into local markets. (Nowadays, with firms selling into global markets, the structure of domestic demand in any particular economy may be relatively unimportant, particularly in the case of small economies).

Figure 1.2 The 'normal' relationship between per capita incomes and share of manufacturing in GDP, Uganda, India, Korea, and the US (1970) and US (1980)

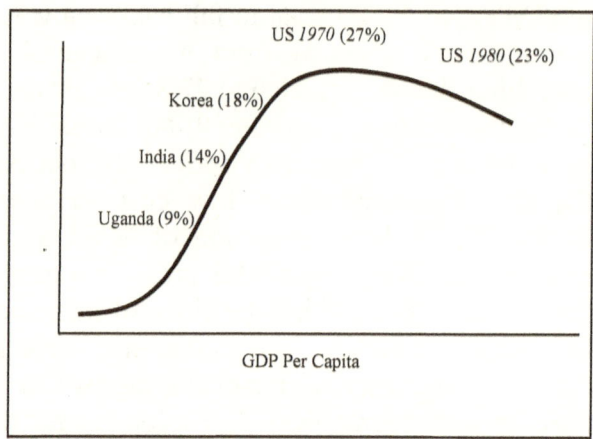

Source: Farooki and Kaplinsky (2012)

Second, closely related to this income elasticity of demand was the price elasticity of demand for natural commodities. The development of substitutes for many primary products (synthetic rubber for natural rubber, artificial sweeteners for sugar, fibre-optics for copper) meant that technological progress in other sectors dampened the demand for natural resources, particularly if the price of these natural resources grew.

Third, it was argued that the skill and technological barriers to entry in many commodity sectors, particularly those in agricultural commodities, were much lower than those in manufacturing were. Hence, economies would begin in low skill commodity sectors and then make a natural progression to higher skill – and higher wage – industrial sectors.

Blocked routes to industrial development

For the reasons discussed above, it is widely accepted that long-term and sustainable economic growth requires industrial development and an expansion of knowledge intensive service industries. The demonstrated success of the Gang of Four newly industrialising countries (Hong Kong, Korea, Singapore and

Taiwan) from the late 1960s followed by a clutch of rapidly growing emerging economies (particularly China) after the mid-1980s is an important exemplar of this path to sustained growth. It is not unnatural therefore that in the current period, resource rich low and middle-income economies seek to emulate their success, developing industries and services which are unrelated to the resource sector. However, unfortunately, emulating this well-trodden path of industrial development is not as simple as it seems, since in some critical respects the opportunities open to the 'late industrialisers' of the second half of the 20th century are no longer available to the same degree to the late-late-industrialising economies in the 21st century.

There are two reasons why this route may be difficult to follow. The first concerns the space available for import substituting industrialisation. As Chang (2002) has shown, following the early industrial development of the UK, each of the industrialised northern economies which caught up with (and many of which overtook) the UK achieved their success in an environment which protected their domestic industry from external competition. Much of this protection arose from the high cost of transport, which provided natural barriers of protection for domestic production.

Nevertheless, improvements in product design and logistics have reduced many of these natural barriers. An example of product design changes was the introduction of flat-pack furniture in the 1990s, which transformed location in the global furniture industry (Kaplinsky and Readman, 2005), shifting the centre of global furniture production from Italy, Germany, the UK and US to China and Eastern Europe. Another important development was the reduction in transport costs. Figure 1.3 reflects this by showing the ratio of CIF prices ('cost, insurance and freight', which includes the cost of transport) to fob prices ('free on board', which excludes transport and insurance costs) in global trade. This ratio fell steadily during the second half of the 20th century.

Import substituting industrialisation has also become less feasible because of the trade liberalisation policies, which have been pursued in many low and middle-income economies. This involved a reduction in tariffs, a trend towards the equalisation of tariffs cross sectors (disfavouring policies of selective industrialisation) and the removal of non-tariff barriers. Each of these trade policy instruments had played an important role in the industrialisation of northern economies and the newly industrialising economies. Table 1.1 shows how these protective barriers fell in SSA between 1990 and 2010. In the case of manufactures, average tariff levels fell by 45 per cent, from 21.8 per cent in 1990 to 12.4 per cent in 2010. A similar series of changes occurred with regard to industrial policies, with most low and middle-income economies sweeping away incentives and selective policies favouring industrial development.

Figure 1.2 World transport costs as measured by CIF/FOB ratios (1948-1998)

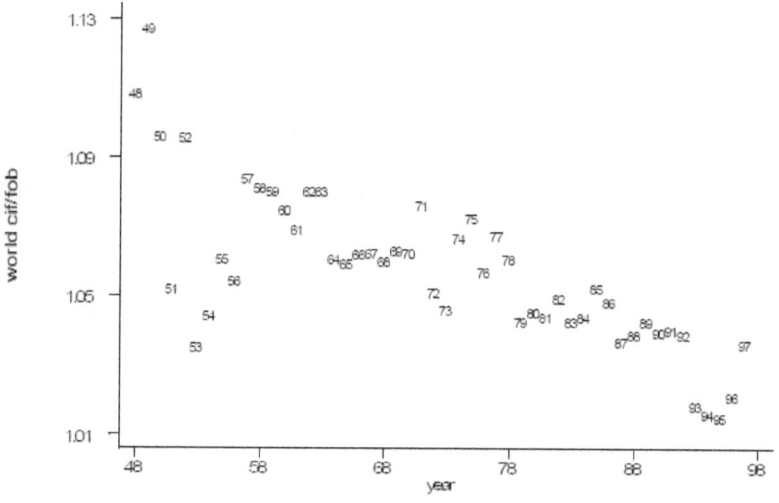

Source: Hummels (1999).

Table 1.1 Average percentage tariff levels for SSA imports from World (1990-2010)

Category	Sub-Saharan Africa				
	1990	1995	2000	2005	2010
Food	26.1	25.4	25.4	18.2	15.3
Fuels	10.9	10.3	17.6	7.7	5.4
Manufacturing	21.8	21.9	18.8	13.9	12.4
Ores and metals	15.3	12.1	14.3	6.8	5.9

Source: TRAINS accessed via WITS online < https://wits.worldbank.org/WITS > (accessed July 2011)

The second reason why industrial development is more difficult for late latecomer economies in the 21st century arises out of blockages in the route to export oriented industrial development. The very rapid growth of the newly industrialising economies in the 1970s and the second tier industrialising economies such as China after the 1990s, was based on the very rapid growth of manufactured exports. This structural transformation of global trade and exports by formerly low-income economies is widely seen to provide a path that currently low-income economies might emulate. There is, however, a fallacy of composition in this policy agenda that is often overlooked. That is, it is a path that may make sense for an individual economy, or a restricted set of economies to follow. However, once all economies take the same route, its attractiveness is diminished. This is particularly the case when a very large economy – such as China – becomes a major actor in international trade.

China's emergence as the manufacturing workshop of the world has had the effect of blocking the opportunities open to follower economies in many sectors, rendering export oriented industrialisation more difficult to achieve. This is particularly evident in the recent experience of SSA economies seeking to take advantage of trade preferences made available to them in the US by the African Growth and Opportunities Act (AGOA) scheme and the Everything but Arms preferential tariffs into the European Union (EU).

Until 2005, these trade preferences were supplemented by quantitative restrictions on Chinese exports of clothing to the US and the EU. Nevertheless, in January of that year, all quantitative restrictions were removed. The consequences for SSA's nascent clothing industry exporters of the removal of quantitative barriers on Chinese (and other Asian) exporters was near catastrophic.

As Table 1.2 shows, the results for the major exporters of clothing in SSA were that, in each case comparing the individual country's top 10 exports with those of China in the same product groups, the aggregate and unit value of Africa's exports fell, while those of China grew. It is also worth bearing in mind that the clothing sector is a key sector in early industrial development and that in 2005, clothing exports represented more than half of all SSA's (excluding South Africa) merchandise exports (Kaplinsky and Morris, 2008).

All of this is not to say that import substituting industrial development is impossible in low-income resource exporting economies. Nor does it mean that all routes to export oriented industrial development are blocked. However, what it does mean is that the routes to industrialisation pursued by now industrialised northern economies and by the late comer economies in Asia are increasingly difficult to replicate.

Table 1.2 Percentage change in value of clothing exports to the US (2004-2006)

Exporters	2005/2004		2006/2005		2006/04		Change in Unit Price of top 10 products 2005/04	
	SSA	China	SSA	China	SSA	China	SSA	China
All AGOA	-16.5	56.9	-11.2	17.8	-25.9	84.8	-0.9	-46
Kenya	-2.5	77.8	-2.7	18.7	-5.1	112.9	-1.9	-45
Lesotho	-14.3	110.8	-0.9	28.5	-15.1	170.9	-3.2	-46
Madagascar	-14.4	72.2	-13.9	21.0	-26.3	108.3	-9.5	-44
Mauritius	-26.4	73.2	-28.7	17.9	-47.6	104.2	-4.6	-45
Swaziland	-9.9	93.3	-16.0	22.1	-24.3	136.1	-2.7	-52
S Africa	-43.7	63.9	-17.0	15.4	-53.3	89.1	3.0	-33

Source: Calculated from http://dataweb.usitc.gov data (accessed 19 March 2007)
a Unit prices calculated for top 10 products in 2004 for each AGOA country's exports products in 2004 for each AGOA country's exports

The challenge to industrialise development are increasing

In the above section, we discussed four sets of factors that have supported the conventional wisdom of resources pessimism, in general, and the destructive links between resource specialisation and industrial development, in particular. These are declining terms of trade and the volatility of commodity prices, the Resource Curse and Dutch Disease, the inherent enclave nature of the resource sector producing hard (mineral and ores) and energy (oil and gas) commodities, and the demonstration effect in which industrialisation and knowledge intensive services are associated with high per capita incomes.

Much of this agenda remains relevant to policy formulation in the 21st century industrial development. Although China's command over much of low cost manufacturing had reduced the association between industrial development and high per capita incomes, it remains the case that most of the high-income economies continue to specialise in value added manufacturing and have increasingly developed knowledge intensive service sectors. The demonstration effect case for industrial development thus remains, although it is qualified by the need to position the economy in particular niches of industry and services. The volatility of commodity prices remains a problem, indeed a problem of increasing intensity over the past decade following the financialisation of most commodity markets since the mid-1990s (Farooki and Kaplinsky, 2012). Further, both the extraction of hard and energy commodities are capital intensive in nature and create few direct employment activities, whereas manufacturing and services are generally much more labour intensive in nature. Related to this, some commodities are easily 'stolen' and it remains the case that, particularly in low-income economies, commodity extraction is often accompanied by kleptocracy, dictatorships and violence. All of these factors reinforce the need for resource rich economies to diversify their industrial sectors.

However, one argument, which has been used to promote a shift out of commodities, is now subject to change. This is the historical trend towards declining commodities-manufactures terms of trade. As we saw in earlier discussion, there has been a long-term trend, stretching back well beyond a century and only occasionally interrupted for very short periods, for these terms of trade to shift in favour of manufactures.

Nevertheless, this trend has now been interrupted by two sets of developments. The first has been growing competition in manufactures as global value chains have fractured and as China and other low cost (predominantly Asian) economies have developed their industrial competences. The consequence has been that after three decades in which the prices of manufactures increased after the War, they began to fall in the late 1980s as China entered the global economy (Farooki and Kaplinsky, 2012). It is striking that this price performance was largely a consequence of China's entry into the global economy as an exporter of manufactures. The impact of this competition from China was predominantly felt by low-income economy exporters of manufactures in the 1990s and low and middle-income manufacturing exporters after 2000. A disaggregated analysis of price performance in global manufactures shows that the price trajectory of different types of manufactures was closely related to the growth of China's manufactured exports.

This can be seen from Figure 1.4 which shows the pattern of price changes of products imported into the EU, Japan and the US between 1989 and 2007, based on a detailed disaggregation of global trade (at the six- and eight-digit trade levels).

In each of the three major importing regions, the price trajectory of the 300 largest Chinese exports was compared with those of the same products exported by low income, middle-income and high-income economies, distinguishing between resource sector, low tech, medium tech and high tech products. With the exception of the high tech group, the propensity of China's product prices to fall was higher than any other of the exporting regions. These results confirm an earlier study of the association between China's exports and the export prices of other economies selling into the EU between 1989 and 2001 (Kaplinsky and Santos-Paulino 2005, 2006; Fu et al., 2009). Again focusing on the percentage of sectors experiencing falling prices, the numbers were 26 per cent for low-income countries, 18 per cent for lower middle-income economies, 17 per cent for upper middle-income economies and nine per cent for high-income economies. By contrast, more than 30 per cent of the sectors in which China was a significant exporter were characterised by falling prices.

Figure 1.3 Percentage of sectors with falling prices (1989-2007)

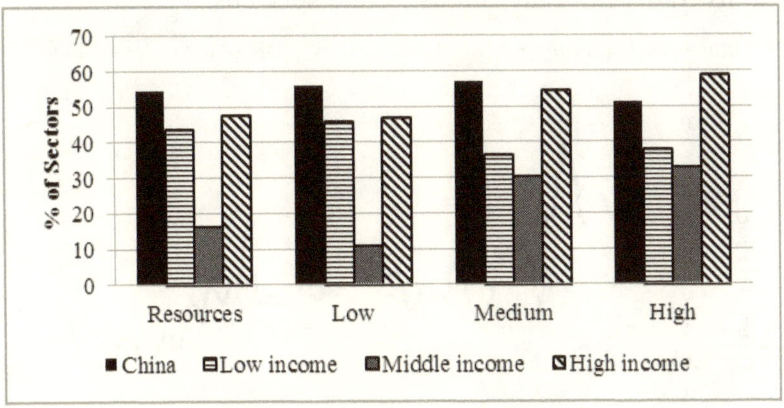

[Bar chart showing % of Sectors for Resources, Low, Medium, High categories across China, Low income, Middle income, High income groups]

Source: Kaplinsky et al. (2011)

The second factor determining the commodities-manufactures terms of trade is the price of commodities. As we saw at the outset of this chapter, after the turn of the millennium, commodity prices were on a sharply rising trend, reflected in improving terms of trade for commodities, interrupted briefly by the financial crisis of 2008, and then resuming in 2009 (Figure 1.5). The financialisation of commodity markets since the mid-1990s means that the prices of commodities are particularly turbulent and, given the renewed emergence of the global financial crisis in 2011 and the likelihood that this will endure for some years, there is every likelihood that for short-run periods the prices of commodities will collapse as they did after September 2008.

However, the long-term fundamentals are suggestive of a sustained rise in commodity prices for some years to come, based on a combination of the commodity-intensive nature of growth-paths in emerging economies, the exhaustion of easy-to-exploit hard and energy commodities, climate change which affects the supply of soft commodities, and the long gestation period involved in expanding production in many capital intensive hard and energy commodity sectors (Farooki and Kaplinsky, 2012). The implications which this terms of trade reversal has for low and middle-income resource intensive economies is that it provides a sound base for future economic growth and the resource rents which can be used to promote and fund diversification into industry and services.

Figure 1.4 The commodities-manufactures terms of trade (1949-2008)

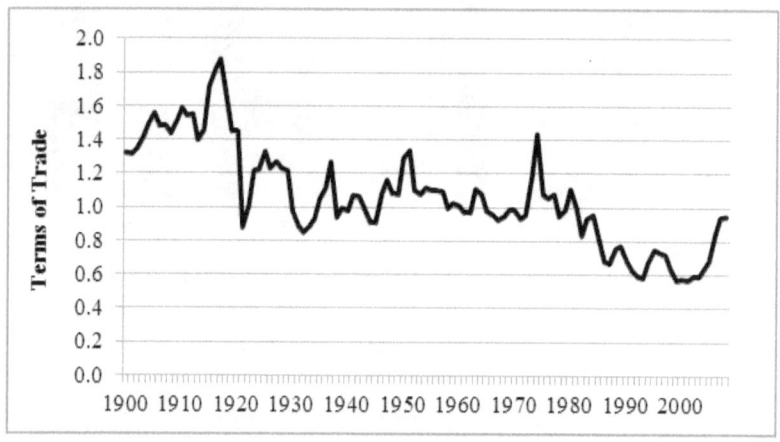

Source: Compiled from data from Pfaffenzeller et al. (2007)

The challenge for these resource-intensive economies is to determine which industrial and service sectors provide the greatest possibilities for development. The enclave thesis, which underwrote much of the resource pessimism in recent decades, would suggest that the dynamic sectors would be unrelated to the commodities sectors. However, this is a view that we will challenge in chapter 2. We will argue that the enclave thesis is based on an outdated understanding of corporate strategies and that there are fertile prospects for the industrial and service sectors to build on linkages from the resource sector. In chapters four, five and six we will focus in detail on the extent and determinants of these linkages, seeking to identify those pinch-points that lend themselves to policy intervention.

Chapter 2

'One Thing Leads to Another' – Why Local Linkages may Become the Norm Rather than the Exception

In this chapter, we will focus on the determinants of linkages into and out of the commodities sector. We will argue that the Resource Pessimism school has failed to acknowledge the extent to which linkages have developed in many low and middle-income economies and, further, that it fails to recognise new developments in corporate strategy that will lead to the deepening of linkages in the future. In later chapters we will see how these linkages have unfolded in a variety of SSA economies, distinguishing between the breadth and depth of linkages, and between backward ('upstream'), forward ('downstream') and horizontal linkages.

We begin with a discussion of taxonomy, recognising the diversity of commodities sectors and types of linkages. This is followed by a brief review of the experience of some highly industrialised northern economies that either had, or continue to have significant resource producing sectors. We then revisit Hirschman's pioneering discussion of linkage development and lastly develop a model, which we believe explains the drivers and patterns of linkage development from the commodities sector. This model will be used to explore the extent of linkage development in SSA in chapter four and the drivers of linkage development in chapter 5.

A taxonomy of commodity sectors and types of linkages

The resource sector includes a diverse set of commodities with very different production profiles. They span the range of high and low technology sectors, large and small-scale enterprises, capital and labour intensive technologies, activities which depend to varying degrees on different types of infrastructure, and commodities which have short and long shelf lives (Table 2.1) In general, soft commodities have low technological content, lend themselves to small-scale production, are labour intensive, require an heterogeneous and diffused infrastructure, and often have short shelf lives, necessitating processing soon after production. Hard commodities generally embody complex technologies and involve large-scale and capital intensive production (although small-scale artisanal mining is widespread). They tend to make intensive use of infrastructure (but this can be used by other sectors – for example, road and rail links) and produce output with a long shelf life. The energy commodities are generally very technology, scale and capital intensive and require infrastructure which has few externalities to other sectors. Although there are intra family variations, the major differences arise between the three different families of resources. Each of these differences will have important implications for linkage development.

Table 2.1 General characteristics of the three major families of commodities

Commodity	Technology	Scale	Factor intensity	Infrastructural Intensity	Shelf life
Soft	Low Medium	Low Medium	Labour intensive	Diffused and general	Often short
Hard	Medium High	High	Capital intensive	Concentrated with externalities	Long
Energy	High	High	Capital intensive	Concentrated and dedicated	Long

The primary sub-sectors of *soft commodities* are cereals (such as wheat and rice), beverages (such as tea and coffee), crops (such as cotton and timber), livestock (such as beef and pork) and fisheries. *Hard commodities* comprise precious metals (such as gold), ferrous metals (such as iron ore), non-ferrous metals (such as copper), and rare earths and minerals (such as coltan). *Energy commodities* are predominantly oil, gas and coal. Each of these commodities feeds into a series of manufacturing sectors (Table 2.2). With the exception of some industrial crops such as cotton and timber, soft commodities are predominantly used in the food sectors. Excluding precious metals, the minerals group of commodities are generally incorporated as inputs into the industrial and construction sectors. Energy commodities are used across the spectrum, both as intermediate and final consumption good inputs.

Table 2.2 Three primary commodity families and their sector of use

Commodity family	Category	Major Use	Examples
Soft	Industrial Crops	Input in manufactures	Timber, Cotton
	Fisheries	Final consumption (with limited processing)	Prawns, cod
	Cereals		Rice, Wheat
	Beverages		Tea, Coffee, Cocoa
	Livestock		Cattle, Dairy products
Hard	Precious Metals	Input in manufactures	Gold, Silver, Platinum
	Ferrous Metals	Infrastructure and Construction	Iron Ore and Steel
	Non-Ferrous Metals	Input in manufactures	Copper, Zinc, Lead, Aluminium
	Rare earths and metals	Input in manufactures	Cerium Plutonium Cobalt
Energy	Petroleum products	Fuel for industrial usage	Oil, Natural Gas, and Coal.
	Coal		
	Nuclear	Final consumption	Nuclear power
	Renewables		Renewable power

Source: Farooki and Kaplinsky (2012)

The second taxonomic distinction that we make is between different types of linkages. In his pioneering discussion of linkages, Hirschman identified three major types of linkages from the commodities sector (Hirschman, 1981). The first are fiscal linkages; the resource rents, which the government is able to harvest from the commodities sectors in the form of corporate taxes, royalties and taxes on the incomes of employees. These rents can be used to promote industrial development in sectors unrelated to commodities. The second major category of linkages is consumption linkages; the demand for the output of other sectors arising from the expenditures incurred by the commodities sector. The third form of linkages is production linkages, both forward (processing and the further transformation of commodities into manufacturing) and backward (producing inputs to be utilised in commodity production).

Our focus in this analysis of the synergies between commodities and industrial and service sector development is on production linkages. However, we go beyond Hirschman and augment his distinction between backward and forward linkages in two respects. The first is that we add a further category of production linkages, namely horizontal linkages. This is a complex set of linkages made up of suppliers and users in the chain, who develop capabilities to feed into other industrial and service chains. The second augmentation that we make is that, within forward linkages, we distinguish the processing of commodities from the beneficiation of commodities. Processing involves a deepening of value added, as a commodity is refined or processed prior to being passed on to user industries. For example, iron ore is processed into steel, copper is smelted, and cotton is carded before spinning can take place. In this sense, the 'processing' of raw materials occurs in a technologically related industry. By contrast, beneficiation describes a process of transformation in which the processed commodity is converted into an entirely different product, generally in an unrelated manufacturing activity. For example, aluminium may be transformed into engine cylinder heads or into pots and pans, and gold is used in semiconductors.

Figure 2.1 illustrates these various types of linkages through a schematic overview of the linkages in a soft commodities value chain, using the timber sector as a notional example. Feeding into the timber logging link in the chain are a series of backward 'upstream' linkages, involving tiers of suppliers. The first tier in this notional example is logging equipment, which is supported by second tier suppliers of transmissions, third tier suppliers of engines and fourth tier suppliers of components. Complementing these backward linkages are a series of forward 'downstream' linkages, also tiered into first tier processors (in this example, sawmills and woodchip producers) and second tier beneficiators (furniture and pulp and paper firms). Figure 2.1 also illustrates first and second tier horizontal linkages on the supply side (logging equipment, which is then used in sugar cane cutting which feeds into sugar production)[1]. Of course, in the real world the nature and range of linkages feeding into the timber logging sector is much more complex than the schematic picture presented in Figure 2.1. However, the essential characteristics of backward, forward, and horizontal linkages and tiers of linkages are central to all value chains, including those in the commodities sectors.

Figure 2.1 Backward, forward and horizontal linkages in the wood and timber sector

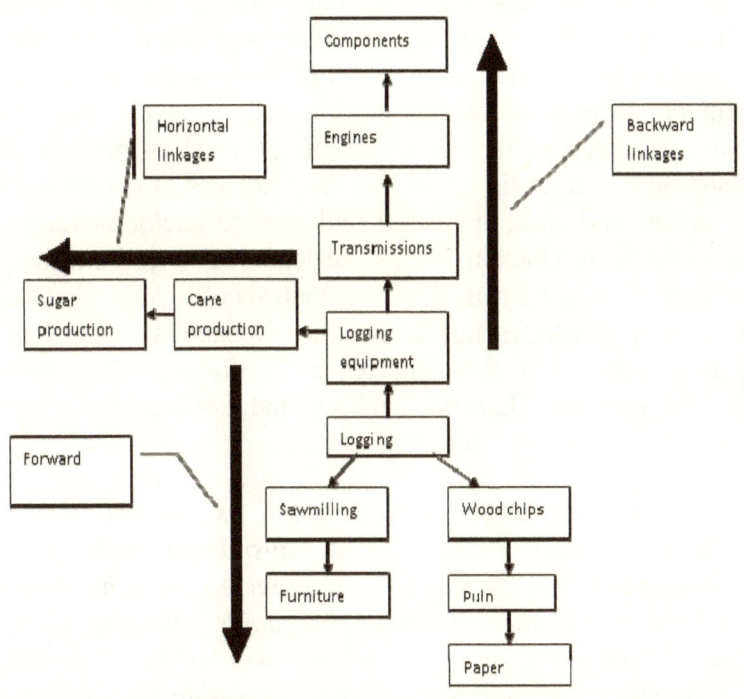

---

[1] Examples of other commodity value chains can be found in later chapters.

The third taxonomic distinction that we make is that between the breadth and depth of linkages. 'Breadth' refers to the range of inputs that feed into and emerge from resource extraction. This is reflected, for example, in the share of inputs into resource extraction, which are procured externally to the firm. However, these local supply links may merely be importers of inputs previously acquired directly by the resource extracting firm and may involve little addition of value in the supply chain. Thus, the 'depth' of linkages – the degree of value added - is a separate aspect of linkage development. An analogous picture arises with regard to the breadth and depth of forward linkages from the commodities sector. Outputs may be destined to multiple users (that is, they may be 'broad'), but the degree of value addition to these inputs may be thin. As we will see in later chapters, not only has there been much greater progress in the breadth of linkage development than in the depth of linkage development in Africa's resource value chains, but many governments fail to recognise this key distinction.

Moreover, and this is the fourth and final taxonomic distinction which we make, there is often a tendency to conflate local linkages with local ownership (i.e. the national identity of the owners). Many governments appear to 'lose the plot' in linkage development, which becomes a surrogate for the extension of local ownership in the commodities value chain rather than as a process of deepening local value added and local industrial and service sector development. Local/domestic production is thus a category distinct from the local ownership of linkage firms. A recent analysis of linkages in Ghana's gold industry illustrates this taxonomic slippage. It concludes that there have been 'very few linkages to locally owned suppliers of goods and services' (Larsen, Yankson and Fold, 2009: 259). The authors evidence this by observing that

> *A number of basic services, such as laboratory testing, cleaning, security and various consultancy tasks, are still outsourced, but to foreign companies with subsidiaries in Ghana, not to locally owned companies. Likewise, there are no significant supplies of mining machinery or equipment from local companies in Ghana: everything is imported or purchased from international dealers with established sales and service operations in the country. (ibid: 266)*

'Staples Theory' – the experience of industrialised economies with significant resource sectors

Moving beyond these core taxonomic definitions, it is instructive to recognise that many of the now industrialised economies not only have developed industrial and service sectors, but that these were built in tandem with, and on the back of, the development of the commodities sectors. This is an issue that has been extensively addressed in Staples Theory.

Staples Theory begins with an explanation of industrial development in the US between the late 17th and early 19th centuries. Callender (1909) argued that the emerging US economy had three focal points of development, each of which specialised in the production of commodities - the northwest in wheat production, the south in the production of cotton, rice and tobacco, and the northeast, which had a dual economy that included staples such as sugar and salt, and manufacturing. During this early period of development, the American economy supplied more than half of the global trade in raw materials, feeding inputs into Europe's burgeoning industrial sector. Callender argued that the production of these staples not only led to the development of local suppliers and local processors of commodities, but also spurred the development of infrastructure in America (feeding, through horizontal linkages, into other sectors).

However, Staples Theory is more widely associated with the explanation of Canada's industrial development and particularly with the divergent views of Mackintosh (1923; 1939), Fowke (1946) and Currie (1951), on the one hand, and Innis, North and Watkins on the other (Innis, 1930, 1940; North 1955; Watkins 1963). Mackintosh argued that Canada's harsh climate and small population inhibited the early development of manufacturing. The lead sectors in this early period produced staples such as fish and fur. Serving their needs in the context of weak infrastructure led to the development of backward linkages in the production of agricultural machinery and forward linkages into food processing. As late as World War I, nearly one third of Canada's industrial output was based directly upon primary production and the indirect impact of staples on the secondary and tertiary sectors (Green, 1971).

By contrast, Innis (1930; 1940; 1956) had a less rosy picture of links between commodities and industry. His viewpoint was much closer to that of Singer's enclave thesis, since he argued that whilst specialisation in cod, fur, logging, wheat, and minerals did initially contribute to the development of domestic industry in the early years of exploitation, Canada increasingly fell into a 'Staples Trap' and the linkages were primarily developed in the metropolitan economies of Europe and in the US. However, Innis did recognise that the production and export of these staples made a significant contribution to the development of Canada's infrastructure. North drew a similar conclusion in his discussion of linkages between commodities and industry in the US (North, 1955). He contrasted Europe's capitalist industrial development which emerged from feudalism, with the north American economies which were, from the outset, capitalist by nature and which, from an early stage, produced commodities for external markets (north, 1955). He concluded that the high cost of transport for imported inputs fuelled the development of local secondary and tertiary industries, as well as infrastructure and service sectors such as marketing and banking. However, like Innis and Watkins, north argued that after this initial stage of synergistic linkage development between staple crops and local industry and services, the American south fell into a 'Staples Trap' and linkages were located in other regions of the US (North, 1966). He concluded that 'the trap' was not a function of the character of the raw materials themselves but rather the institutional make-up of the society.

More recently, there has been a revival of Mackintosh-like accounts of the links between resource exploitation and industry. These recognise not just the synergistic development of industry and commodity extraction in the early industrial development of many now industrialised economies, but also in contemporary commodity producing countries such as Norway, Scotland and Australia. For example, Wright and Czelusta (2004) argue that not only did the development of the resource sector result in backward linkages to local industry in the US, but also that the capabilities developed by local suppliers fed back into the resource sector. This reduced the costs of extraction and increased the capacity to exploit profitably what were previously marginal deposits.

Similarly, it is argued that Sweden's industrialisation after the 1850s was driven by export booms in cereals and sawn wood and, later, by pulp, paper and iron ore (Blomström and Kokko, 2007).

Five key points emerge from this debate about the links between the resource and industrial sectors in now-industrialised high-income economies. First, there is widespread agreement that the early stages of resource exploitation did indeed lead to the development of local industry, both supplying inputs into the commodities sector and using the outputs of the sector. Second, the capabilities which local industry developed fed back into the resource sector, enhancing its efficiency and reducing the costs of extraction. Third, over time, there is a danger of a 'Staples Trap' emerging, that is that economies are caught in specialisation in commodities and lose their industrial capabilities. As in Singer's enclave thesis, the primary linkages are developed elsewhere. However, fourth, as Wright and Czelusta and North show, this Staples Trap is not inevitable and is subject to a number of influences, including particularly the impact of government policies and the quality of institutions. Finally, there is widespread agreement that whatever the impact of resource extraction on the development of backward and forward linkages on local suppliers and users, in almost all cases resource extraction has led to the development of infrastructure and, through this, to horizontal linkages which impact positively on the development of other sectors.

"One thing leads to another" – Hirschman's framework of linkages from the commodities sector

Albert Hirschman, a pioneer in development economics, believed that in the context of the resource intensity of many low-income economies, linkages from the commodities sector provided a path for industrial development and economic diversification. As we saw above, Hirschman identified three different sets of linkages – fiscal, consumption and production linkages - and described a process in which '…development is essentially the record of how one thing leads to another' (Hirschman, 1981:75). In other words, successful economic growth is an incremental (but not necessarily slow) unfolding of linkages between related economic activities. Hirschman argued that fiscal linkages generally tended to be limited and provide no guidance as to which sectors the commodity rents should be used to develop –

> *[the] ability to tax the enclave is hardly a sufficient condition for vigorous economic growth. For the fiscal linkage to be an effective development mechanism, the ability to tax must be combined with the ability to invest productively. [But] here lies precisely the weakness of fiscal linkages in comparison to the more direct production and consumption linkages... [since] no... guidance [on which sectors to invest] is forthcoming when a portion of the income stream earned in an enclave is siphoned off for the purpose of irrigating other areas of the economy (Hirschman, 1981: 68-69).*

Hirschman also believed that, in the context of poorly developed manufacturing sectors in many low-income economies, consumption linkages would be affected abroad as the needs of domestic consumers would be met through imports. (As we saw in chapter 1, the lowering of tariffs and the undermining of industrial policy in most low and middle-income economies means that, in the current era, consumption linkages are even more difficult to pursue than during the period in which Hirschman developed his taxonomy). For Hirschman, therefore, the direct forward and backward linkages were more likely to lead to the development of a more diversified economic structure. In other words, by relating directly to the output structure of the commodities sector, 'one thing' would indeed 'lead to another'. Although Hirschman did not explicitly address the respective roles of market forces and government in this process of linkage development, the idea that 'one thing leads to another' implicitly implies that there would be profitable, market opportunities open in the development of production linkages.

Hirschman further argued that backward linkages presented less of a technology 'strangeness' or 'alienness' than forward linkages since they involved production processes with which local economic agents were in general more familiar than they were with technologies involved in the processing of commodities

(Hirschman 1981:71-72). He also believed that these backward linkages could be 'a special push factor' for technical learning and industrial development (ibid: 63).

These two assertions of Hirschman - that 'one thing leads to another' in propelling linkage development and that there may be particular opportunities for the development of backward linkages – play an important role in the model of linkage development which we now present. However, it is worth noting that both of these assertions run against conventional wisdom. The first is countered by the widespread belief either that linkages do not exist, or that they are very limited, or that they only exist as a function of government interventions, which run against the logic of efficiency and of comparative advantage. The second assertion runs up against a policy fixation with forward linkages, in general, and beneficiation, in particular. That is, it is widely believed that diversification out of commodity dependence in low-income economies through linkages is best achieved by developing the capacity to first process and subsequently to beneficiate commodities (Girvan, 1987). For example, despite the historical evidence of the importance of backward linkages in its own industrial trajectory South Africa's current industrial policy places considerable emphasis on beneficiation, but very little on backward or horizontal linkages. In general, there has been scepticism about the scope for backward linkages.

With this backdrop of intellectual history in mind, we can now proceed to our presentation of a model, which explains the extent of linkages and the drivers of linkages from the commodities sector in nine SSA economies. In chapter 4, we will evidence the extent of these linkages and, in chapter 5, we will consider the drivers of linkages.

A model of linkage development from the resource sector

The deepening of globalisation after the 1970s led to intensified competition as firms were subject to a larger pool of competitors. One of the most important responses to this was the drive by firms to concentrate on their core competences, namely those activities in which they had distinctive competences; where there were barriers to entry and which were valuable in the market place (Hamel and Prahalad, 1994). As a consequence, there was a growing trend for non-core activities to be outsourced to low cost suppliers. Initially, these suppliers were located in the domestic economy, but increasingly in the global economy. This consequent advance of global value chains has led firms and economies to specialise in capabilities rather than wholly manufactured products (Gereffi et al., 2005; Kaplinsky and Morris, 2001).[2] As a rule, therefore, lead firms in global value chains, as well as their first and second tier suppliers and customers, increasingly search for low cost suppliers and efficient processors. This is the antithesis of the pressures for internalisation that had previously played an important role in driving foreign direct investment (Dunning, 2000; Williamson, 1985).

The global mining and oil and gas industries are relatively late entrants to this trend towards specialisation and outsourcing. Although undocumented as a general phenomenon, there is evidence that this has been occurring across a range of commodity sectors. Mines have moved away from a high-level of vertical integration towards outsourcing almost every stage in the mining process to independent firms (Urzua, 2007). This includes the provision of capital goods and intermediate inputs such as chemicals. Supplier firms responded to these opportunities to be incorporated in the chain. For example, Bell Equipment in South Africa built competences in the domestic mining sector and then became a supplier of these machines into a number of global markets, including the mining, construction, sugar and forestry sectors (Kaplinsky and Mhlongo, 1997; Walker and Jourdan, 2003). There has also been the growth of outsourcing of knowledge intensive services and this has led to the emergence of Specialised Knowledge Intensive Mining Services providers

---

[2] The share of intermediate products and services in global trade had grown sharply in many sectors (Sturgeon and Memodovic, 2010), as companies specialise in niches of global value chains. A particularly graphic example, the domestic value added in China's exports of iPhones at a unit value of US$178.96 is only US$6.50 (Xing and Detert, 2010).

(SKIMS), offering not only specialised services but also other high technology inputs. Companies, such as SRK in South Africa, which started as a service provider to Anglo American, have grown into a global mining consulting firm. Global mining companies are also actively involved in building capabilities in their suppliers. BHP Billiton, for example, has an extensive supplier development program in Chile (Barnett and Bell, 2011).

Once the lead firm has made the decision in principle to outsource non-core activities, the first task is to find the lowest cost suppliers who can produce to the required quality and meet delivery schedules reliably. Suppliers able to offer unique technological competences of their own are particularly attractive, especially in the first tier of suppliers. However, the logic is wherever possible to have these suppliers locate production and service delivery on their doorstep, rather than located abroad, or some distance from the extractive activity. An efficient proximate supplier provides the capacity for flexible and tailored responses to the needs of the commodity extractor, allows for chain inventories to be reduced, and removes uncertainties associated with extended logistics. This unfolding process of initial outsourcing ('global sourcing') to seek the lowest cost supplier which then extends in requiring the supplier to locate proximate to the factory ('follower supply') was initiated in the automobile industry (Barnes and Kaplinsky, 2000) and has spread to many other manufacturing sectors.

The same logic of unfolding outsourcing, initially to the lowest cost global supplier and then, wherever possible to low cost proximate suppliers is beginning to be observed in many of the commodities sectors, including as we shall see in SSA. This desirability of finding an efficient local supplier is particularly attractive in Africa. This is both because transport and logistics are poorly developed and goods brought in from outside may be subject to long and unpredictable delays and because government policies have often mandated the deepening of local value added.

Although the expansion of local linkages is thus in large part fostered by the growing tendency towards increased outsourcing by the core lead firms in the commodity value chain, this is not the only driver of localised production. Many inputs into the commodities sector in low-income economies were previously imported by independent suppliers and processors, for example foodstuffs for mineworkers or the cutting of timber from logs into sawn wood. When local capabilities are adequate, these activities can be undertaken domestically and, where possible, close to the point of commodity extraction to save on inventories and transport costs.

It is possible thus to construct a general model of linkage development (Figure 2.2) taking account both of the localisation of what was previously imported and the growing trend towards outsourcing by lead commodity firms. The vertical axis in Figure 2.2 represents the accretion of value added in the provision of inputs into the production of a commodity. Based on the insights drawn from the core competences framework we can distinguish on the one hand inputs which the lead commodity producers have no intrinsic interest in maintaining in-house since they do not reflect their core competences. We characterise these as win-win linkages - where lead commodity producing firms and local suppliers and customers have a potential common interest in developing efficient local linkages. On the other hand, there are a range of inputs which are central to the firm's competitiveness and which it is reluctant to see undertaken by a competitor. We consider these to be win-lose linkages – where there might be a conflict of interest between lead firms and potential suppliers and users.

We can take the diamond value chain as an example to illustrate these two categories of inputs into mining. The cutting and polishing firms may actively want auditing, office provisions and utilities to be provided by outsiders, undertaken in the best of all cases, by reliable and low cost suppliers based as close to their operations as possible. On the other hand, they are very reluctant, and have to be forced, to allow other firms to participate in the cutting and polishing of diamonds, and in the logistics, branding and marketing which guarantee their control over the profitable segments of the diamond value chain. These are their core competences (Mbayi, 2011). The horizontal axis of Figure 2.2 reflects the passage of time. The curve shows that, as a general consequence of the outsourcing of noncore competences, there is a market driven process of linkage development. Initially, the pace of outsourcing is low and is confined to very basic commodities. With the accretion of technological capacities, it then speeds up. It tails off as technological and scale requirement become very demanding and the easy hits are exhausted. Countries with weak capabilities will be located to the left of this industry curve and those with strong capabilities to the right of the curve.

There are a number of factors that determine the nature, extent and the location of these outsourced linkages. It is helpful to distinguish between intrinsic and contextual determinants of linkage development, although of course these are not watertight distinctions.

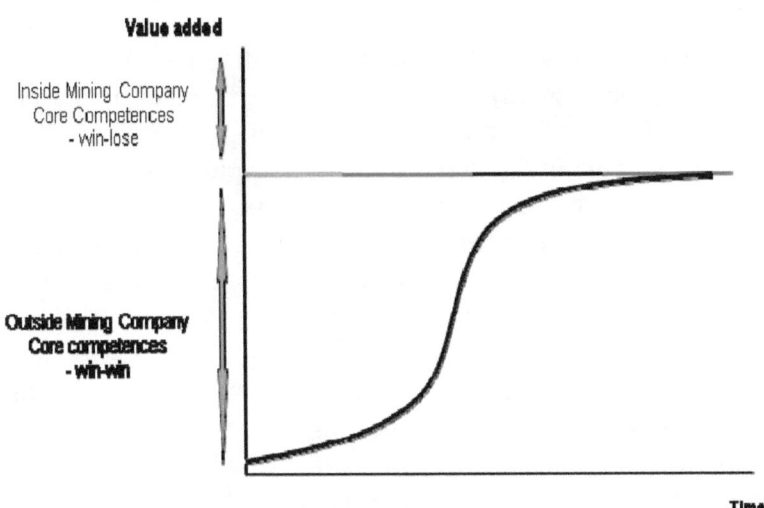

Figure 2.2 Market driven linkages over time

Intrinsic determinants of linkage development

Three primary intrinsic factors affect linkage development – the imperatives of lean production, the specificity of resource deposits, and the technological intensity of extraction and processing.

The imperatives of Lean Production

Unlike the Fordist era of mass production, modern competitiveness is increasingly a function of a complex set of Critical Success Factors (CSFs) (Womack and Jones, 1996). Clearly, cost and price are central determinants of a profitable and sustainable market presence. However, so too is the heterogeneity and quality of final products, the frequency, size and predictability of delivery, and the customisation of final output. Although these CSFs are relatively more important in the manufacturing and service sectors than in the resource sectors, they are increasingly evident across the range of soft, hard and energy commodities (Marin et al., 2009). Pioneered by Toyota and then diffusing across sectors, the introduction of lean production techniques by core producers in value chains has important implications for suppliers, summed up in the Q-C-D mantra – quality, cost and delivery. A core component of this lean production capability is the capacity of the supply chain as a whole to achieve low inventories, rapid response and flexible production.

The imperatives of lean production (both in resource extraction and in the supply chain) are important determinants of the nature and location of the outsourcing process, hence of linkage development. This is for two reasons. First, proximity of suppliers and customers is critical in some key inputs. For that reason, it is customary for most lead firms in value chains to develop long-term relationships with core first tier suppliers and to expect them to locate their supply functions close to the operations of the lead producers – a strategy of global sourcing and follower supply (Barnes and Kaplinsky, 2000). On the output side, particularly in the soft commodities sectors, processing necessarily occurs near extraction, as in the case of sugar refining; unless cane is crushed within 12 hours of harvesting, the sucrose content falls. The second is that, in order to achieve lean supply chains, lead firms are required to develop sophisticated programmes of supply chain management (Bessant, Kaplinsky and Lamming, 2003). These two linked phenomena are promoting *near* sourcing (that is, domestic linkages) as a particular subset of outsourcing, subject of course to the imperatives of cost, quality and delivery. They also promote the closer proximity of processing to commodity extraction.

Resource specificity and linkages

A key characteristic of virtually every mining or energy resource is that it is location specific. No two deposits will be identical. The technology and the accompanying knowledge and skill inputs required for efficient identification and exploitation of the resource therefore are of necessity to be applied locally on site. The need to adapt to the specificities of a commodity resource provides the possibility of drawing on local skills and knowledge, and in the process also producing local technological spill-overs as a result of the development of horizontal linkages. This need to cater for the specificity of local deposits often leads to the localisation of input provision, even in relatively poor economies with generally weak backward linkages such as Tanzania's gold mining industry as we will see in chapter 4. In the South African coal industry, the presence of poor quality coal deposits with many impurities led to the development of advanced technological capabilities in the washing of coal. Arising from the development of capabilities by supplier firms to meet this challenge, horizontal linkages developed enabling the supplier firms to penetrate new and different markets, for example washing spirals for utilisation in the Canadian tar sands. In each of these cases, the knowledge is location specific and provides the potential for local supply. Thereafter, applications of this knowledge can be used in the production of products and services that can be adapted to different markets, at home and abroad. Paradoxically, as the experience of the US shows, the local specificity of the commodity can result in deeper local linkages where deposits are of poor quality.

Technological intensity – the economies of scale and scope

As we saw above, Singer (1950) argued that the mining industry was inherently enclave in nature. His view was that mining was capital and scale intensive so that in the absence of a developed industrial base, linkages in low-income countries would be generated abroad. Where there were limited local linkages, these were predominantly low in technological intensity and there would consequently be few learning spill-overs in the domestic economy.

In general, technological barriers to entry are less evident in the soft commodities sectors, where technological complexity and learning spill-overs are less limited than in the hard and energy commodities sectors. However, even in the scale and technology intensive hard and energy commodity sectors there are multiple inputs that are relatively low in technological content and with few barriers to entry. At the most basic level, this includes the provision of food and accommodation for the workforce, transport and logistics, security, some utilities, and simple maintenance and repair. How feasible low cost and flexible local supply is, will of course reflect not only the intrinsic technological complexity of the resource sector in question, but also the extent of capabilities in the local economy. Here, too, the conventional wisdom of enclave development often overstates the shortfall in local capabilities in low-income economies.

Compared to the era in which Singer and the enclave theory was advanced, there has been a significant accretion of capabilities in very many low-income economies, often to a surprising degree. (In 1970, the height of the enclave agenda, only around two per cent of global R&D occurred in low-income countries; in 2009, this had risen to 22 per cent – Singer et al., 1970; Hollander and Soete, 2010). As a consequence, there is evidence of growing linkages even in high technology products and services in low-income economies in often surprising circumstances (as we evidence in chapter 4) in Information Technology (IT) services in Nigeria's oil industry, umbilicals in Angola's offshore oil industry and knowledge intensive service in Ghana's gold industry. In other cases, such as South Africa and Australia where domestic capabilities are much more developed, linkages extend into high technology inputs.

With regard to scale barriers to entry, where there are multiple points of production in a single country (that is, a number of different and independently owned commodity producers) particular possibilities are opened for the development of specialised suppliers who benefit from economies of scope and are able to meet the needs of a variety of customers. By contrast, where production is concentrated in a single or a limited number of producers, the specificity and scale of resources will result in economies of scale that will favour in-house production as opposed to procurement from outside suppliers.

Contextual determinants of linkage development

Beyond the above mentioned factors that are intrinsic to resource sectors across operating environments, we hypothesise a series of factors that reflect the particular context of operation. Our analysis of the drivers of linkages in SSA's commodities sectors in chapter five explores the influence of four contextual factors. Although particularly relevant to the SSA operating environment, we believe that they also have wider relevance. These are ownership, infrastructure, capabilities and policy.

Ownership

The firm is a heterogeneous entity and although each firm is individual with particular competences and business strategies, there are important structural features that influence the behaviour of firms, in general, and with regard to linkage development, in particular. Here we can distinguish three different ownership attributes.

The first is the origin of ownership and place of incorporation of the lead commodity-exploiting firm. The widely held view is that locally owned and/or locally incorporated lead firms are more deeply embedded in the local economy, have greater familiarity with local suppliers and customers, know their way around the institutional infrastructure and, crucially, that they are more committed to local development than footloose, foreign owned firms. Each of these characteristics has a potential effect on domestic linkages, with the likely outcome that locally owned and incorporated firms are more prone to participate in linkage intensive chains. Beyond the ownership and incorporation attributes of lead commodity firms is the ownership of their suppliers and customers. Their horizons too may be affected by their origins and their embeddedness in the local economy.

Second, the nationality of foreign ownership may have implications for linkage development. For example, the nature of equity markets in the home countries may predispose firms to operate with particular time horizons and attitudes to risk. Firms which are affected by shareholder value structures or which raise their funds on short term markets may have little patience with long-term local supplier or customer development. By contrast, firms with greater access to patient capital, with higher internal savings rates and which are supported and 'guided' by their governments, are more likely to be involved in long-term and risky resource extraction than are their northern competitors (Farooki and Kaplinsky, 2012) and may also have more patience with local linkage development.

Patient capital is widely argued to be characteristic of Chinese firms in the resource and infrastructure sectors. On the other hand, at least in this early stage of China's involvement in SSA, Chinese firms are reported as importing a disproportionate share of their inputs from China, or where they use locally sourced inputs, they bring their suppliers with them, leaving little space for local supplier development (Broadman, 2007; Burke and Corkin, 2006; Corkin, 2012; Suliman and Badawi, 2010).

Another element of nationality of ownership is that northern-based firms are often subject to intense pressure from civil society organisations to implement Corporate Social Responsibility (CSR) programmes to introduce supplier development schemes to spread the benefits of commodity extraction to communities living close to resource extraction. This is often an important driver of backward linkages. Firms with their bases in low-income countries, such as China and India, face fewer pressures of this sort and consequently may be less likely to promote backward linkages as a response to CSR imperatives.

Third, and beyond the nationality of ownership, is a series of firm specific attributes. The importance of this factor was prefigured by theories of imperfect competition in the 1930s (Chamberlin, 1933), developed further by Hymer (1976), and elaborated subsequently in the widely used OLI (**O**wnership, **L**ocation and **I**nternalisation) framework in Dunning's eclectic theory of foreign direct investment (Dunning, 2000). Individual firms act in very different ways even though they may operate in the same industry and in the same environment. This individual firm behaviour will reflect a number of conditioning factors, including the firm's pioneering or follower character in the industry, the firm's particular bundle of competences and the strategic visions of firm leadership, each of which affect their propensity to develop linkages.

Infrastructure

Infrastructure can take various forms. It can be 'physical', embodied in road and rail transport, utilities and telecommunication networks. In each of these cases, the effectiveness of infrastructure development is a function of reliability, quality of provision, and the cost to the user. However, there is also a compendium of 'social' infrastructures. These reflect the efficiency and cost of the administrative and regulatory regime that supports the productive sector. These characteristics of efficient infrastructure bound all economic activity, but they are particularly important not just for exporters of commodities, but also for their local suppliers and processors. Four sets of factors are important in determining the role played by infrastructure in the development of linkages into and out of the commodities sector.

First, the nature of the commodity has a significant impact on the development of infrastructure in a number of ways. Commodities produced and exported in bulk and in great volumes (such as coal or iron ore) require large-scale transport infrastructure to move their mined outputs. This may have externalities for the local economy, including for suppliers and processors. Lead commodity firms in these sectors are often able to cover the costs of these infrastructural investments - where governments are responsible for infrastructure provision, fiscal constraints may slow these investments down.

Second, and related, the nature of the infrastructure has important implications for the development of linkages. Some infrastructure is highly specific to a particular commodity producer and has very low potential for positive spill-overs, which might facilitate the growth of backward and forward linkages (for example, oil pipelines). By contrast, the development of road and rail infrastructure, as proposed in the corridor infrastructure development programmes in East and Central Africa, have the potential to lower logistics costs for suppliers and processors.

Third, if infrastructure in a commodity-exporting developing country is primarily or solely focused on meeting the requirements of the lead commodity-exploiting firm, then it is likely to result in enclave infrastructural development, which will hamper the ability of local suppliers or processors to link with and participate effectively in the country's commodities value chains.

Domestic capabilities and systems of innovation

Effective commodity extraction and, even more so, the supply of inputs into commodity extraction requires a range of skills. Even basic commodities such as foodstuffs require some level of skills and technological knowledge. As linkages develop further - more products are supplied by local producers (breadth of linkage) and as products that are supplied locally increase in local content (depth of linkage) – so the demand for skills and for product and process development capabilities will increase. Growing skills and enhancing technological capacities of commodity producers and especially of firms supplying inputs will therefore be critical to enhancing the breadth and depth of linkages. Indeed, all of the industrialised countries that succeeded in developing out of commodity extraction activities had major programmes to support skills acquisition and research and development.

The employment of local rather than expatriate skilled and managerial labour will depend crucially on the degree of local education and training. Apart from enhancing supply, skills need to be harnessed effectively, thus organisation and managerial routines are additional core requirements. Further, since technologies are changing rapidly, firms also require the capacity to identify, to assimilate effectively and to improve new technology. These capabilities are often a precursor to firms developing their own innovative technologies.

The development of national institutions that support and enhance technological development in supplier firms is especially important as the technological intensity of linkages increases. These supporting institutions may be very local in nature and comprise a 'regional system of innovation' (Braczyk et al., 1998). They also often have sectoral specificities (a 'sectoral system of innovation', Malerba, 2002). However, most typically they are assembled on an economy wide basis and comprise a 'national system of innovation', (Freeman 1995; Lundvall, 1992).

The policy environment

Policy is a critical factor in the development of linkages. It is important to distinguish between policies that are directly targeted at the resource sector itself and policies which are of relevance to a wider set of sectors, but which have important implications for the resource sector, including with regard to the intrinsic factors of ownership, infrastructure and capabilities discussed above.

The confluence of factors that makes a firm, a value chain, a region or a country competitive at a particular point in time, seldom endures. Competitors soon enter the fray and the only route to sustaining incomes is to endogenise the ability to learn and change. We can identify a number of factors that influence the effectiveness of policy design and implementation affecting linkages from the commodities sector. The first issue concerns the nature of the 'invention', that is, is there a Vision for the promotion of linkages from commodities? From this follows a series of 'management of innovation' type concerns – is the vision translated into policies, and are these policies consistent and coherent?

Are the policies backed by incentives that ensure that they are implemented effectively? Do policy makers have the capacity, and the will, to implement these policies? Does policy making involve processes of reflexivity, that is, do the various stakeholders who relate to the management of linkage policy interact and do they, as a collectivity, display the capacity to adjust policies dynamically? Finally, governments are only one actor in the policy chain. They are often also not the most important actor in the development of linkages into and out of the resource sector. Successful policy development and implementation therefore requires these capabilities in both the public and private sectors. It also requires an alignment of visions and capabilities between the state and the private sector and in some cases (since linkage development often reflects pressures for CSR) also, with civil society organisations, often operating in adjacent local communities.

Speeding up and slowing down linkage development

In the preceding discussion, and following Hirschman, we postulate that contrary to much received wisdom, linkage development in the resource sector occurs as a natural outcome of market forces. But, in Hirschman's words, 'linkage effects need time to unfold' (Hirschman, 1981: 63) – the older and more established a particular resource sector, the more likely that local linkages will have developed, Further, as we saw above in the discussion of the intrinsic determinants of linkage development, the unfolding of linkages will vary by sector, with the soft commodities at the one extreme and deep sea oil energy commodities at the other.

However, this process of unfolding is not immutable. It can be speeded up or slowed down by the context in which the resource sector operates. And, as we observed above, it is also important to recognise that linkage development is both a matter of the *breadth* of linkages (the proportion of inputs sourced locally or outputs processed locally) and the *depth* of linkages (how 'thick' the linkages are, that is, their domestic value added).

Thus, on the basis of these intrinsic and contextual determinants, we can observe different trajectories of linkage development. Where the constellation of contextual factors is appropriate, this may result in the speeding up and deepening of linkages beyond, which would occur had they just evolved through the operation of market forces. Conversely, where contextual factors are less favourable, they may impede or lead to a shallowing of this market led process of linkage development (Figure 2.3)

Figure 2.3 Different trajectories of linkage development

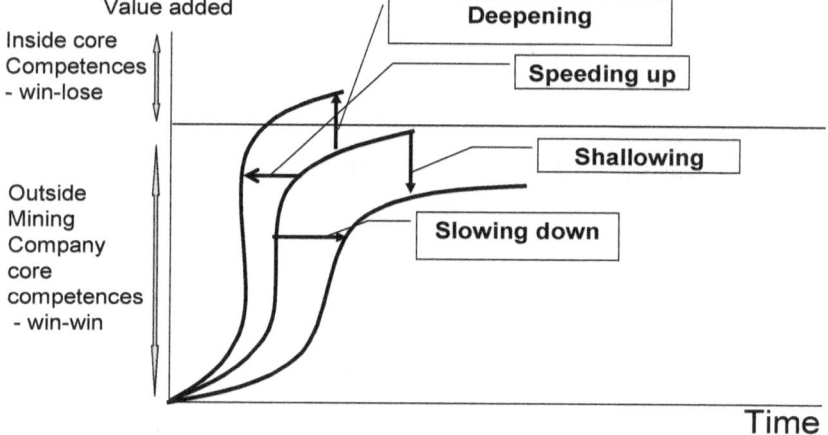

In conclusion

In chapter 1, we observed that the rise in commodity prices since 2002 is likely to be sustained for some years to come. Although these sustained resource rents remove some of the urgency for diversification out of the resource sector, it remains the case that the development of the industrial and knowledge intensive service sectors is essential for sustainable growth and for spreading the fruits of economic growth. The challenge that low and middle-income countries face is that the routes to industrial growth followed by the already industrialised northern economies and the rapidly growing emerging economies of Asia are now more problematic. Import substituting industrial policies are less attractive and are constrained by the rules of global governance. Export oriented industrialisation is made more difficult by the very success of China and other Asian exporters of manufactures.

In considering the challenge of diversification into industry and knowledge intensive services, the enclave thesis that underwrote much of the resource pessimism in recent decades suggests that the dynamic sectors will be unrelated to the commodities sectors. However, we have argued in this chapter that the commodity enclave thesis is based on an outdated understanding of corporate strategies. We have concluded from this revisiting of the arguments for and against the enclave thesis that there are fertile prospects for the industrial and service sectors to build on linkages from the resource sector, moderated of course by factors intrinsic to particular sectors and a series of contextual factors.

It is now time to turn our attention away from the abstract world of theory to the concrete world of reality. The context is that of SSA and its experience with linkage development in a number of different commodity sectors. Two sets of questions arise. First, what has been the extent of linkages that have developed in a range of sectors and economies, both in terms of the breadth and depth of linkages? On the basis of our detailed research, we report our findings in chapter 4. The second major set of questions addresses the role played by the four contextual drivers of linkages that we discussed in this chapter – ownership, infrastructure, capabilities and policy. Our findings on these contextual drivers are reported in chapter 5. However, before we report on these findings in chapter 3, we provide a short description of the methodology that we utilised to reach these conclusions.

Chapter 3
Data and Methodology

In this book, we seek to document the breadth and depth of linkages into and out of the commodities sector in a number of SSA economies and to identify the drivers that either accelerate or impede these linkages. In an ideal world, we would have engaged with a representative sample of lead commodity firms, their various levels of tiered suppliers, the users of their output, and suppliers and users feeding into other related sectors. In reality, as in the case of much social science research, particularly in the African context, our achievements have been more limited. Our research endeavour has been constrained by poor macro data on the population of firms, the inability to access many firms, poor in-house data collection within firms and limited secondary studies to act as a foundation for research. Nevertheless, we have been able to engage with a sufficient number of relevant firms in each of our research environments to provide what we believe is a representative snapshot of the extent of linkages and of their determinants. Moreover, given the paucity of scientific information on these trends in SSA and the low level of much of the secondary literature, we are confident that our research results make a significant original contribution to the corpus of knowledge on SSA in respect of the factors influencing the breadth and depth of linkages to the commodity sectors.

Much of our evidence is of a qualitative rather than a quantitative nature. In most instances, this ruled out the rigorous testing of hypotheses, including through the use of statistical analysis. Moreover, given the exigencies in particular research environments, our evidencing is uneven, hindering systematic comparison across countries and sectors. We are not unique in encountering obstacles on generating detailed quantitative data on linkages from the resource sector, particularly in the African context.

Turning in detail to our research methods, we begin with the description of our core research questions, then discuss our sampling procedures and follow this with a description of the types of data that we have been able to collect.

Core research questions

Based on a reading of related literatures discussed in chapters one and two (on the commodities sector, on linkages, on core competences, on global value chains and on supply chain development) three sets of questions and sub-questions guided our research.

1. What is the breadth and depth of linkages into and out of the commodities sectors
   - from the lead commodity firm to suppliers and users
   - from first tier suppliers and users up and down their value chains
2. Can sizeable horizontal linkages be identified in which linkages generated in the commodities sector act to enhance the efficiency of producers in other sectors?
3. To what extent is the breadth and depth of linkages a function of:
   - The intrinsic features of the sector, namely the passage of time over which the commodities sector has developed; logistics, flexibility and costs; the specificities of commodity deposits; and technological complexity and scale
   - The contextual determinants of linkages, namely ownership; infrastructure; capabilities and institutions; and the policy environment.

This terrain of enquiry constitutes a series of research questions rather than formal hypotheses. Formal hypotheses are able to be systematically verified by comprehensive data and contrasted with a series of null hypotheses. As we will see below, the data, which was collected through our intensive research process, did not allow us to rigorously interrogate hypotheses in this manner. However, as in most investigation within the social sciences, the richness of the qualitative and quantitative data did allow us to provide reasonably suggestive evidencing of the factors accelerating and impeding the breadth and depth of linkages into and out of the commodities sector.

Sectoral coverage and resource dependence in the sample economies

In choosing a sample of sectors and countries in which to examine the determinants of linkages between the commodities and industrial sectors, we were guided by the need to work with a sample of observations, which provided the capacity to generalise our research results. In so doing, we took eight factors into account in identifying our research sample.

First, there are substantial differences between soft industrial commodities on the one hand and hard and energy commodities on the other. For this reason and in order to cover the range of commodity families, we included a study of the timber industry, two studies on the oil sector and four on hard commodities (copper, diamond and two studies on gold).

Second, our *a priori* reasoning suggested that there were reasons why there might be differences in the potential between backward and forward linkages. We therefore ensured the inclusion of sectors primarily involving backward linkages (six studies) and those in which forward linkages are prominent (three studies).

Third, in chapter two we argued that there are important contextual determinants of linkages. Moreover, we also argued that the elapsed time of commodity exploitation is also an important factor in linkage development. Therefore, we researched the same sector in two economies with different vintages of large-scale mining (gold in Ghana and Tanzania).

Fourth, as we saw in chapter 1, sustainable economic growth is no longer a natural outcome of industrialisation (since competition in some industrial sectors is punishing). Moreover, the fracturing of value chains has also meant that knowledge intensive services may provide meaningful opportunities for sustainable growth. Hence, our sample includes sectors in which we had foreknowledge of links between the commodities sector and knowledge intensive services, such as IT services in Nigeria and engineering services in South Africa and Zambia.

Fifth, we also believed that regional factors mighty also determine the breadth and depth of linkages, and our research focused on southern (Botswana and South Africa), Central (Angola and Zambia), Eastern (Tanzania) and Western (Ghana, Gabon and Nigeria) Africa.

Sixth, China's resource hunger is potentially a game changer in the SSA commodities sector and, for this reason, we researched the role played by Chinese firms in Angola's infrastructure sector, in Zambia's copper sector, and in Gabon's timber sector. In addition, the Gabon timber industry research also enabled us to assess the impact of changes in final export markets on linkages in the commodities sector.

Seventh, given the critical role of infrastructure in the commodities sector, we not only considered this issue in each of the individual sector studies, but also infrastructure programmes in Africa, namely the Central Development Corridor; stretching from Tanzania to the Great Lakes region, as well as the Mozambique Zambezi Valley. This corridor is explicitly designed to promote linkages between the commodities and the agricultural, industrial and service sectors.

Finally, many of the key decisions on local sourcing reflect the way in which lead commodity producers organise the exploration, construction and management of their operations in the commodities sector. For this reason, we included a study of the different modalities of firm sourcing policy in the hard commodities sector. These various considerations and their relevance to individual sectors and countries are summarised in Table 3.1, which also identifies the links to the relevant detailed research reports.

Table 3.1 Core characteristics of case studies

Country	Subject	Establishment Period of the Commodity Sector	Linkage type	Commodity type	Emerging economy relevance	MMCP Discussion Paper*
Angola	Offshore-oil	Mid 1990s	Backward	Energy	China	No. 11
Botswana	Diamonds	1960s	Forward	Hard	---	No. 6
Gabon	Timber	Early 1960s	Forward	Soft	China, Malaysia	No. 10
Ghana	Gold	Late 19th century	Backward	Hard	---	No. 1
Nigeria	Oil	1950s	Backward	Energy	---	No. 8
South Africa	Mining capital equipment and specialist services	1880s	Backward	Hard	---	No. 5
Tanzania	Gold	1998	Backward	Hard	---	No. 7
Zambia	Copper	Early 20thC	Backward	Hard	China, India	No. 3
Angola	Infrastructure	>2004	---	---	China	No. 2
East Africa	Infrastructure	>2005	---	---	---	No. 9

http://commodities.open.ac.uk/discussionpapers and www.cssr.uct.ac.za/prism/publications

In each of these studies, sample selection was designed to promote the generalisability of research findings. In some cases, there were only a limited number of firms operating in a given activity and sample selection was easy – 'target the whole population'. In other cases, however, there was virtually no available information on the population of existing input providers and processing and beneficiating firms, and it was more difficult to ensure a representative selection of sample firms. In these cases, samples were selected through a variety of methods (random, purposeful, stratified and snowball sampling methods) designed to reflect our perspectives on the intrinsic and contextual factors which we believe to play an important role in linkage development.

We are confident that, overall, the samples are representative of the total populations in each of our country studies. In Angola, the sample covered 100 per cent of control lines contractors, 82 per cent of flow lines contractors, and 57 per cent of oil operators. The Botswana study interviewed 63 per cent of the population of cutting and polishing firms. The logging/processing companies interviewed for the Gabon study covered between 50 per cent and 70 per cent of the total concession area. The sample of Zambian mining companies represented 70 per cent of copper volume production, while the sample of suppliers covered 53 per cent of firms based in the major mining regions of Kitwe and Ndola and in the capital city Lusaka. In Nigeria, the sample represented one third of the population of oil producing firms and 50 per cent of local suppliers in the sub-sector of research enquiry. The analysis of the South African mining services sector was based on 10 in depth firm interviews plus interviews with business organisations supplemented by firm level survey data. The Central Development Corridor (Tanzania and Mozambique) drew on secondary material and supplemented this with extensive interviews with key industry informants. Table 3.2 provides a summary of the research population and its representativeness of the sector population in the core sectoral studies.

Table 3.2 Summary of sample size and composition for sectoral studies

	Lead commodity producers	Suppliers/ Processors/ Beneficiators	Public/private institutions, key informants
Angola infrastructure	9 SOEs	44 private firms (suppliers/contractors)	108 institutions
Angola/oil	8 oil firms	13 oil services companies (suppliers) 28 large-scale and SME suppliers	9 institutions
Botswana		6 suppliers, 12 cutting & polishing firms	14 institutions
Gabon	20 logging/processing firms	8 suppliers	9 institutions
Nigeria	15 oil firms	115 suppliers	Unspecified
Ghana	5 mining companies	6 suppliers	8 institutions
South Africa		12 supplier firms	7 institutions
Tanzania	3 mines, 3 exploration firms	8 suppliers	9 institutions
Zambia	8 mining companies	50 suppliers	17 institutions

In each case, data was collected though semi-structured interviews. These interviews were conducted on the basis of a questionnaire which included both open ended and closed ended questions seeking a combination of quantitative and qualitative data. All the studies also made large use of secondary data, including company reports, reports and publications by independent consultancies, sectoral organisations, international organisations, macroeconomic and trade databases, journal articles, conference papers and industry publications.

However, despite our attempts to utilise a rigorous, common and structured methodology, without exception, all of our studies (although to varying degrees) encountered substantial problems in accessing the data required to document what was being observed. Research access was very uneven between countries. In Angola, Botswana and Nigeria the majority of firms who were approached agreed to participate in the study. By contrast, in Tanzania the barriers to research access were formidable, largely because the government was revising its policy towards the mining sector and the lead mining firms were concentrating on keeping a very low profile.

More damagingly, although we set ourselves ambitious targets in collecting numerate data that would allow for rigorous and structured comparisons across sectors, these data were in general not forthcoming. There were a variety of reasons for this. To our surprise, we found that many companies – including large Trans-National Corporations (TNCs) with a global reach – did not collect the information that even they required to assess the extent of linkages from their activities and the performance of their first tier suppliers and users. Even those who did collect much of the desired data did so on a partial basis, with large gaps and invariably for a single point in time rather than over a period. Many of the international datasets made available by the UN family and the World Bank provide information of questionable value. For example, the official Figures on employment in Botswana's mining industry, which are used in the International Labour Organisation (ILO) and United Nations Industrial Development Organisation (UNIDO) databases to facilitate international comparison, show a doubling of the labour force between 2008 and 2009 from 84 to 173 workers. That is, despite the fact that Botswana not only produces more than one quarter of global diamond output, its mining sector also produces nickel, cobalt, copper, coal, soda ash, salt and gold!

Thus, despite our best intentions we largely failed to collect a combination of comparative quantitative and qualitative data that would allow us to test clearly defined hypotheses across countries and sectors. What we were able to achieve was a series of largely qualitative case studies, backed by selective numerate data, of the extent and drivers of linkages into and out of the commodities sector. We believe that in most cases we were able to capture these developments and to produce an accurate picture of these trends.

A source of bitter comfort is that we are not unique in our failure to capture structured comparative material. For example, even the International Council of Mining and Metals (ICMM) - an industry body comprising more than 20 of the world's largest mining houses and more than 30 additional related institutions – has made very slow progress recording the extent of linkages in

SSA's commodities sectors and has only recently published a Toolkit which sets out a wish list of relevant data (ICMM, 2011). To draw on a worn (and sexist) metaphor, 'in the land of the blind, the one eyed man is king'. We are confident that however imprecise the data which we present in chapters 4 and 5, these are a major contribution to knowledge in documenting the extent and drivers of linkages from the commodities sector.

In conclusion, we draw five conclusions from this review of methodology. First, the scale of our ambitions that guided our endeavours is much greater than our capacity to evidence them in a detailed, comprehensive and rigorous manner. We thus identified three sets of research questions rather than formal structured hypotheses to guide our research. Second, however imperfect our evidencing may be, it is an improvement by a considerable margin on what is known about linkages from the commodities sector in any of the countries in which our research was conducted. Third, despite the difficulties we encountered in our research, we believe that we are able to draw an accurate general picture of the reality of the breadth and depth of linkages into and out of the commodities sectors that we have researched, and to throw light on the contextual factors that determine these linkages. Fourth, despite this we are unable to provide structured comparisons spanning countries and sectors and documenting changes over time. Finally, as we note in chapter 6, whilst this general picture provides insights into the development of policies in both the public and private sectors and in the promotion of a dialogue between these sectors (and civil society organisations), the development of appropriate and effective specific policies in each country will require a more specific investigation of the dynamics of linkage development.

Chapter 4
The Breadth and Depth of Linkages

Determining the extent of linkages into and out of the commodities sector requires a focus on five sets of factors. The first is the *breadth* of linkages. On the input side, this refers to the share of the inputs of the commodity producer that is acquired locally. On the output side, this refers to the proportion of commodity production that is processed by local firms. The second factor is what we refer to as the *depth* of linkage, that is, the extent of domestic value, which is added to locally acquired inputs or locally processed/beneficiated outputs. Third, there is the need to reflect *linkages in the whole value chain*, that is, how far up and down the chain the analysis goes. Fourth is the question of depth and breadth of *horizontal linkages*, that is, the extent to which, as a direct consequence of linkages from the commodity sector, domestic value is added into inputs for or outputs of other related sectors. Fifth, and finally, production occurs in the context of value chains, so domestic value added needs to be seen in the context of value added in the whole chain rather than in a particular link under enquiry.

    Evidencing the breadth and depth of linkages thus requires a daunting degree of detailed evidence, a combination of quantitative and qualitative data, and time series data. Indeed, even with complete access to the books of firms involved in the chain (assuming that all firms keep books, that they only keep one set of books and that these records are accurate!), it would be an extremely time consuming task. The imperfect world encountered by our researchers' means that our evidence is a long way from this ideal type. As we shall see, it is only partial and, despite our best attempts to collect data on the same indicators in all of the sectoral studies, this proved to be an insuperable task. Therefore, our recounting of the depth (the accretion of local value added) and breadth (the percentage of spend which is local) of linkages in each of our case study countries is partial and uneven. Moreover, given the paucity of quantitative, much of the evidencing is of a qualitative nature.

With the above caveats in mind, we can now consider the evidence on the breadth and depth of linkages in eight country case studies – equipment provided to the offshore oil industry in Angola; the cutting and polishing of diamonds in Botswana; inputs into copper mining in Zambia; inputs into the gold mining sector in Tanzania and Ghana; the processing of timber in Gabon; the sourcing of fabrication and construction; well construction and completion; and control systems and equipment and IT services inputs into the Nigerian oil industry; and mining equipment in South Africa. In this chapter, we confine ourselves to a reporting of the results of our research. In chapter 6, we draw them together into an integrated story of linkage development across sectors and countries.

Backward linkages into offshore oil production in Angola

Angola achieved independence from Portugal in 1975, but rapidly descended into civil war. This war continued until 2002 and was a source of major social, political and economic disruption. What had been a relatively diversified economy during the colonial period, with a spread of economic activity in a variety of agricultural and mining sectors, collapsed into a bifurcated economy, with the cash economy being centred on the capital city, Luanda, and the interior of the country retreating into semi-subsistence production. Economic decline was particularly marked during the height of the war between 1988 and 1994, and despite growth reviving in the mid-1990s, it was only after the end of the civil war in 2002 that the current rapid trajectory of economic growth was established (Figure 4.1). Until recently, Angola's growth rate was below the average for SSA but after the commodities boom in 2003-2004, Angola's growth rate decisively exceeded that across the continent.

The key to the revival of Angola's growth over the past two decades has been the discovery of offshore oil. Exploration of these deposits took off in earnest in the mid-1990s and the first major offshore well began production in 1999. Angola possesses the 15th largest oil reserve in the world and the second largest reserves in Africa after Nigeria. By 2010, it had become the 15th largest oil producer in the world. As a consequence of the growth of the oil sector and the collapse in economic activity in other sectors, the Angolan economy has become increasingly dominated by oil. The oil sector not only accounts for more than half of GDP (Figure 4.2), but also accounts for more than 60 per cent of total government revenue.

The Petroleum Activity Law (Law 13/76 of 1976) assigned sole ownership of Angola's hydrocarbon resources and mining rights to the Angolan state. The latter manages the sector through Sonangol - the concessionaire of the country's oil industry and the sole owner of concession rights. Other investors can only participate in the oil extraction sector in partnership with Sonangol. However, Sonangol's ambitions go beyond merely holding property rights over oil deposits. It also sees itself as an active investor both in oil extraction and in forward processing of oil, and models itself on other National Oil Companies such as Petrobas in Brazil. In addition, as will be shown below, Sonangol is also involved in, and responsible for, driving backward linkages from the oil sector and, in particular, increasing the presence of locally owned firms.

National ownership of resources and concession rights gives the state (through Sonangol) significant bargaining power across the oil and gas value chain. Amongst other things, the government has used this leverage to advance what it sees as national interests (in this case, not just the localisation of value added, but also the localisation of ownership) in the oil sector through local content policy.

The decrees of 1982 and 2003 and the Petroleum Activity Law of 2004 instituted two main drivers of local content. The first was a series of requirements to ensure the employment of Angolan nationals in the oil industry and in the linkages, which feed into and out of the oil extracting sector. Inter alia this policy mandates (i) preferential employment of Angolans unless a lack of competent Angolan labour can be proved (ii) at the renewal of every contract and on annual basis, companies must submit a plan to recruit and train Angolan workers to meet the employment targets set by the government, and (iii) companies are required to pay a levy toward the development of Angolan human resources.

Figure 4.1 Angola annual GDP growth rate percentage (1986-2010)

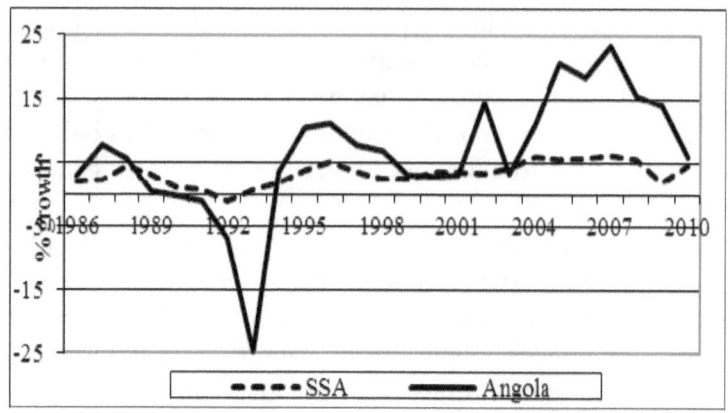

Source: World Development Indicators data online.
<http://data.worldbank.org/data-catalog/world-development-indicators>
(accessed July 2011)

Figure 4.2 Angola sectoral composition of GDP percentage (2003-2008)

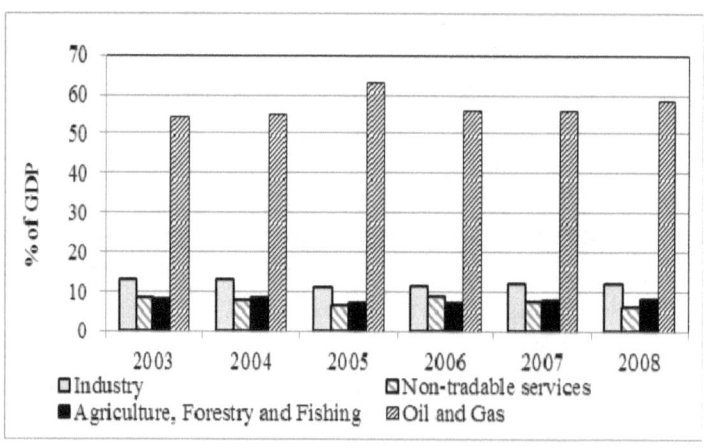

Source: Teka (2011)

Oilfield producers must contribute 15 US cents of a dollar per barrel produced per year, associate operators (oil companies without operator status) must contribute $200,000 per year, and oil service companies must contribute amounts agreed bilaterally with the Ministry of Petroleum. Table 4.1 below shows the targets set out by the government for the Angolanisation of the oil sector's labour force.

Table 4.1 Angolanisation targets

Levels (Grades)	1985	1987	1990
Up to Grade VI (Unskilled/Semi-Skilled)	100%	100%	100%
Grades VII-XI (Mid-Level Technicians)	50%	60%	70%
Grades XII-XIII (Higher Level Personnel)	--	50%	80%

Source: Teka (2011)

The second factor driving Angola's local content programme is the preferential treatment of national firms in the supply of goods and services. National firms are defined as firms having more than 51 per cent of share capital owned by Angolan citizens. The key rule is that of exclusivity, which requires that all goods and services not requiring high capital value (the decree does not specify this in detail) and lacking in-depth and specialised know-how (again, this is left unspecified) must be sourced from national firms, unless the price of these local inputs is more than 10 per cent higher than the price of imports.

Between 2004 and 2010, total investment in the Angolan oil industry was $69 billion, with a further $15 billion invested in supportive infrastructure and $1.2 billion in the marketing link in the value chain. $52 billion of this investment was directed to the construction and support of the offshore oil industry, all of which in principle could have resulted in local linkages (Teka, 2011). In reality the only linkages of significance (that is, where there was some semblance of domestic value added) was in two components of the SURF (sub-sea umbilicals, risers and flow lines) sub-sector.

Sub-sea umbilicals are cables that enable communication between sub-sea production systems (exploiting subs-sea wells) and rigs (production systems) and control centres on the shore. Flow lines (whose main components are risers and manifolds) enable a two-way flow of crude from sub-sea to surface and lubricants from surface to sub-sea production systems. This sub-sector (SURF) accounted for one fifth of total investment over the period (Table 4.2).

Table 4.2 Value and percentage share of investment in the offshore oil production sector (2004-2010)

Oilfield segments	Capital Expenditure ($ billion)	Share (%)	Local links
Engineering	4	8	Services
Procurement, construction & installation	4	8	Systems construction
Systems, equipment, piping & valves	2	4	Systems sale & construction
Sub-sea umbilicals, risers and flow lines (SURF)	11	21	Manufacture, sale & services
Sub-sea production systems	6	11	Systems sale & installation
Sub-sea services	1	2	Construction & services
Rigs & drilling	12	23	Drilling services
Drilling systems	3	6	Contracting & services
Down-hole & well	8	16	Equipment sale & services
Decommissioning	1	2	Services
Total	52	100	

Source: Teka (2011)

Table 4.3 shows the composition of cost structures in the domestic manufacture of flow lines and control lines. The bulk of costs – almost two thirds of the total - were made-up of intermediate products and raw materials. Next in importance was expenditure on labour. Together these two inputs accounted for 84 per cent of total costs. Only 6.2 per cent of expenditure was on machinery. This breakdown of expenditure reflects the fact that in both of these sub-sectors, the primary activity is assembly (although control lines production does also involve a degree of design and transformation of raw materials through the use of carousels).

Turning to the last column of Table 4.3, it is evident that the only items procured locally by the umbilicals producers were consumer goods i.e. basic goods and services (accommodation, catering, cleaning, human relations management, stationery, etc) and labour. However, much of the value of these products that were procured locally was in fact largely made up of imports. For example, basic goods and services include computers, paper and furniture, none of which are produced domestically.

Table 4.3 Percentage share of local content in domestic manufacture of flow lines, control lines

Types of inputs	Share of operating expenditure	Description	Source Import	Local
Production Machinery (Amortisation cost)	6.2	Carousels, reelers, pipe pincers, loaders, rollers, stalk racks, cranes, etc.		✓
Intermediate materials	64.2	Carbon & stainless steel, brass, Inconel., monel., polyethylene, services, etc.		✓
Raw-materials		Metal, steel, copper		✓
Labour (skilled/unskilled)	20.0	Engineers, managers, welders, etc.		
Basic General Services	5.4	Lease (rental cost of buildings/facilities)	✓	
Basic General Services	2.5	HSE, catering, cleaning, security, civil construction, labour recruitment, lease	✓	
Basic General Goods	1.4	PPE, IT & electronic equipment, office furniture, stationary, etc.		✓

Source: Teka (2011)

Focusing on the labour component of domestic value added – which accounts for one fifth of the total expenditure in domestic manufacturing – it is evident that between 2003 and 2009, there was a significant increase in the Angolanisation of the labour force (Table 4.4.). Although most of the local labour employed is unskilled and semi-skilled, the significant shift has been a marked increase in the percentage of Angolan citizens in skilled operations. There are ambitious targets for the Angolanisation of this skilled cadre of labour by 2014.

Table 4.4 Local labour content in manufacture in Angola (2003/4-2014)

Period	Control lines (%)		Flow lines (%)	
	Basic/mid-skilled	Higher-skilled (Engineers)	Basic/mid-skilled	Higher-skilled (Engineers)
2003/4	80	0	70	5
2009	90	17	72	20
2014	90	52	85	35

Source: Teka (2011)

Forward linkages in the diamond sector in Botswana

Botswana is a geographically large country roughly the size of France or Texas with a small population of 1.9 million. Over two thirds of the drought-prone country is desert, semi-desert or scrub and does not lend itself to settled agriculture. It does however have a large pastoral sector and exports beef to the EU, but unlike the more verdant New Zealand, this sector alone would not support a high standard of living. Yet in 2010, Botswana's per capita income ($8,180) ranked it as a middle-income country. This relatively high per capita income was a result of four decades of sustained economic growth (Figure 4.3) and for much of this period Botswana ranked, with China, Korea and Singapore, as one of the world's most rapidly growing economies.[3]

---

[3] Botswana was one of 13 countries identified in the World Bank Growth Commission (Spence Report) as having sustained growth of over 7% for more than 25 years.

Figure 4.3 Botswana annual percentage GDP growth (1971-2009)

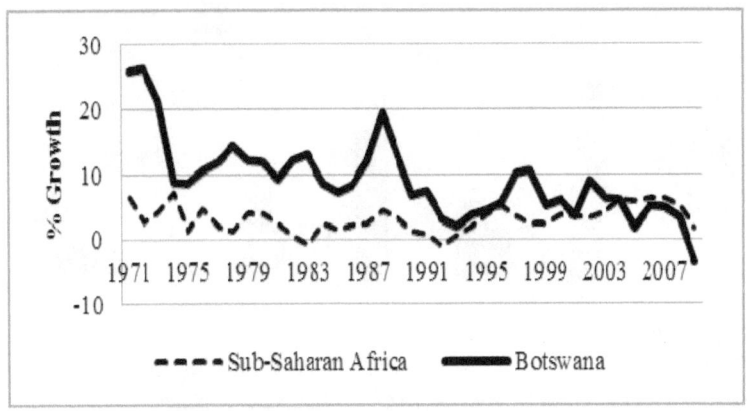

Source: World Development Indicators data online.
<http://data.worldbank.org/data-catalog/world-development-indicators>
(accessed July 2011)

The driver of this rapid economic growth and the resulting high-level of per capita income in Botswana has been the production of diamonds, a precious stone yielding large resource rents, particularly to countries such as Botswana with easily accessible surface deposits of high quality stones. Diamonds were first discovered in Botswana shortly after independence in 1966 and large-scale production began in 1971. Currently Botswana accounts for more than one quarter (by value) of global diamond production. In the context of a virtually non-existent manufacturing sector and a poorly endowed agricultural sector, the contribution of diamonds to Botswana's GDP (Figure 4.4) and to government revenues (Figure 4.5) has been very significant. Currently the sector contributes more than 40 per cent of GDP and more than half of all government revenue.

Figure 4.4 Botswana sectoral contribution to GDP (2000-2009)

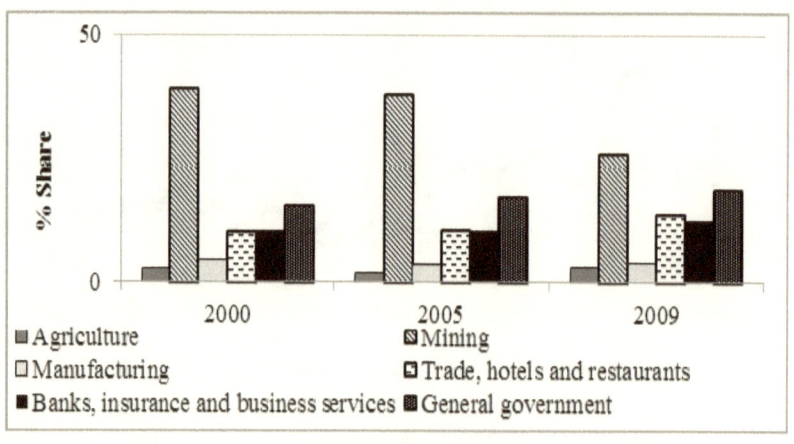

Source: Mbayi (2011)

Figure 4.5 Botswana composition of government revenue (2000-2009)

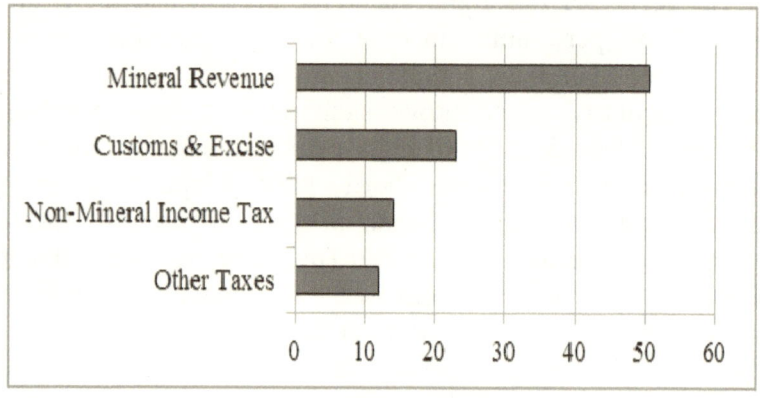

* Diamonds account for more than 90 per cent of mineral revenues

Source: Mbayi (2011)

However, the contribution of this bounty of nature to the economy is not without its problems. For one thing, the sector employs only a small proportion of the labour force and the capacity of the population to share in the resource rents depends largely on the continuation of a relatively incorrupt and efficient government. However, more problematically, the low cost surface diamonds that have hitherto sustained the industry will be exhausted. Unless new deposits can be found within two decades,

Botswana faces a major squeeze on incomes. For these reasons, the government has committed itself to a programme of diversification, based on the extension of forward production linkages from the diamond sector.

The long-recognised need to diversify out of the heavy dependence on mining had previously led the government to promote the development of a cutting and polishing industry in the early 1980s, mainly as a way of increasing employment. At the time De Beers, the global mining company that dominated production in Botswana and the sale and marketing of diamonds in the global economy argued that cutting and polishing activities were not economically viable in Botswana. Mild pressure from the government on De Beers led to the establishment of three cutting and polishing factories in the 1980s. However, none of these factories ever reported a profit. Some observers believed that these losses were artificially achieved through transfer pricing by De Beers in order to avoid pressures for further processing, but this is an untested assertion. Whatever the reality of the reasons limiting this truncated programme of forward linkages during the 1980s, Botswana's opportunity to ratchet up the pressure for forward linkages came in 2005 when De Beers' 25 year mining license was due for renewal. The government had a great deal of bargaining power due to De Beers' reliance on production from its 50-50 joint venture with Debswana which supplied around 60 per cent of De Beers' global supply of rough diamonds. Moreover, Botswana produces high quality larger diamonds, which have higher profit margins. The government insisted that this concession would only be renewed (for another 25 years) if De Beers agreed to facilitate and promote forward linkages, beginning with cutting and polishing.

After the new contract was signed, the government invited the world's leading cutting and polishing companies to establish factories in Botswana and in the process to transfer cutting and polishing skills to local citizens. Sixteen companies were selected and licensed to operate in Botswana. De Beers and the government then established the Diamond Trading Company (DTC) in 2008, which, like Debswana, is a 50-50 joint venture. DTC Botswana is responsible for the sorting and valuing of

Debswana's production. It also controls the supply of diamonds to the 16 cutting and polishing companies and is responsible for supporting the development of the cutting and polishing industry. The new agreement required DTC Botswana to release diamond to the local manufacturing industry to a value of at least $500 million a year and to develop targets for this to grow over time. It was also tasked with the creation of at least 3,000 jobs in the cutting and polishing industry. The agreement includes a penalty clause for non-performance, so in marked contrast to the previous attempt to promote beneficiation, De Beers has a vested (and financial) interest in making the programme a success. The 16 cutting and polishing companies, known as Sightholders, are only assured rough diamond allocations on condition that they hire and train locals with cutting and polishing skills.

The government has established a Diamond Office to support its primary objective of beneficiation in Botswana diamond industry. This office focuses on building strategic alliances, developing infrastructure and providing a favourable fiscal regime. The government's vision for diamond beneficiation is supported by a multi-faceted strategy aiming to create downstream competencies in the value chain in the cutting and polishing industry, jewellery manufacturing industry, diamond trading industry and ancillary businesses (Figure 4.6).

Figure 4.6 Botswana's downstream diamond value chain

[Figure: Flowchart showing Botswana's downstream diamond value chain. Main vertical flow: Exploration → Mining → Sorting & Valuing → Distribution → Cutting and Polishing (1. Planning & Marking, 2. Cutting or Sawing, 3. Bruting, 4. Polishing) → Export. Side connections: Aggregation, DTC London, DTC Botswana. Supporting elements: Buildings, Services (Consultants, Insurance, Finance, Catering, Cleaning, Security, Transport), Brokers, Capital Goods & Maintenance, Labour, Institutions (Diamond Office, Diamond Hub), Consumables, Utilities (Water & Electricity, Communications), Customs.]

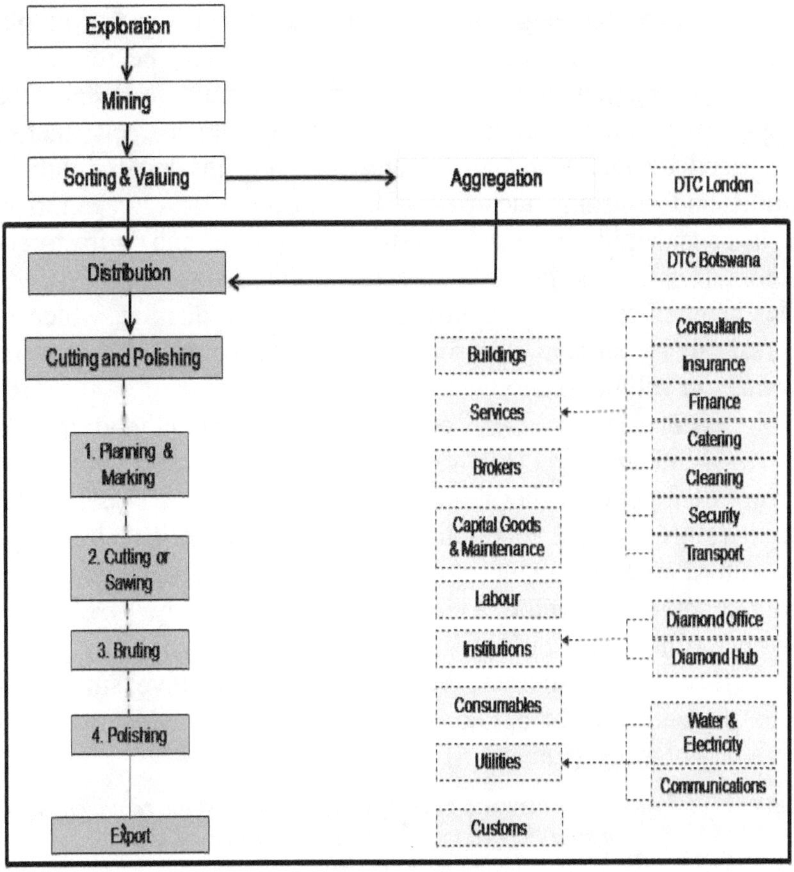

Source: Mbayi (2011)

The first part of the beneficiation strategy, and the only one to be systematically addressed by 2010, was the creation of a viable cutting and polishing industry. Policies designed to enhance competences further down the chain (for example, in jewellery manufacture[4] and trading) are still under development.

The 2005 agreement between the government and De Beers envisaged that the development of forward linkages would, over time,

---

[4] To date two of the sight-holders have started jewelry manufacturing factories in Botswana in 2011

move beyond cutting and polishing and set out a process whereby Botswana would also become a locale for sales and distribution. It was agreed that the aggregation of diamonds - which had taken place in London for over a century - would increasingly be relocated to Botswana. (Aggregation involves the mixing of all De Beers' global supply of diamond, regardless of origin, into parcels that are purchased by De Beers' customers, including the local sightholder cutting and polishing factories). The relocation of aggregation will have considerable externalities to the service and infrastructure sectors. In addition, the 2005 agreement provided for an independent sales channel for 10 per cent of Debswana's production, which will increase to 15 per cent over five years, whilst the rest of Debswana's production will be sold to De Beers/DTC London.

Hence, there is clear evidence of substantial and dynamic forward linkages in Botswana's diamond industry, driven by government policy rather than by market forces. The issues at stake are therefore whether this will be a globally competitive industry in the future and the extent to which these forward linkages will embody domestic value added. It is yet too early to determine whether Botswana's cutting and polishing industry will be globally competitive. At first glance, the answer seems negative, since labour costs per carat of cut diamond in Botswana are higher than either India or Botswana (Table 4.5).

Table 4.5 Industry and Botswana government estimates on the range of cost per carat in Botswana relative to some centres ($)

Country	Industry	Government
Botswana	45 – 120	35 – 90
India	35	10
China	20 – 25	17
Namibia	45 – 100	-

Source: Mbayi (2011)

However, there are three reasons to suspend judgement on this count. First, whilst Botswana's labour costs are indeed higher than China and India, they are much lower than those in Belgium and Israel, both of which have long established cutting and polishing industries. These high cost centres manage to maintain their presence by focusing on larger and more valuable stones, and leaving the low wage economies (India and China) to produce cheaper stones. Botswana is targeting a mid-level quality of cutting and polishing, above the small stones produced in China and India, and below the highly specialised stones produced in Europe. Second, it is dangerous to make static cost judgements, particularly in a skill intensive sector. The question is not so much whether Botswana's current production costs are high, but whether they will remain high in the future. Heavy investments in training by the government, and the need for firms to invest in skills (since, to some extent, they have no alternative but to cut and polish in Botswana), suggests that wage costs in Botswana may be a moving frontier as domestic skills improve. Third, new technologies are being introduced which substitute for the long accumulated tacit skills, which have historically dominated this industry. As in the introduction of computer-numerical-controlled machine tools in global metal industries in the 1990s, these technological innovations in lasers and computer numerically controlled cutting and polishing technologies offer the possibility of newcomers circumventing skills barriers that had historically excluded them from competitive production.

Focusing on the accretion of value in the diamond value chain, most value is added post mining, and particularly in marketing and retail (Table 4.6). Value added in the sorting, valuing, cutting and polishing stages, which Botswana aims to command in the short to medium term is substantial accounting for around 10 per cent of final product value and around one third of the value of diamond mining. If the projected development of marketing capabilities – as proposed in the 2011 legislation and included in the 'marketing and retail' category in Table 4.6 - bears fruit, the degree of domestic value added may increase significantly within the next decade.

Table 4.6 Value addition in the diamond pipeline

Stage of Global Value Chain	% of original value
Producer Selling Value	100
Sorting and Valuing	115
Cutting and Polishing	127
Polished Dealing	133
Jewellery Manufacturing	166
Marketing and Retail	320

Source: Even-Zohar (2007)

Sixteen cutting and polishing firms were producing in Botswana in 2011. (An additional two firms were expected to locate in Botswana after the 2011 Agreement with De Beers). They employ more than 3,000 people, most of whom are citizens (Table 4.7) an important outcome given the high rate of unemployment in the economy (estimated at 30 per cent of the labour force). The monthly salaries are in the range of $150 to $600 ($2=Pula 12), which is above the minimum wage for the manufacturing industry ($80 per month). Most of these firms own their premises, suggesting a long- term commitment to Botswana and continuous investment in local procurement.

Table 4.7 Ownership and employment patterns in twelve cutting and polishing firms

Origin of Parent Company	Est.	% Local Employ.	Salary Range*	Own or Rent Premises
Belgium	1982	90	-	Own
	1990s	97	P1300 – P3000	-
	2007	95	P1000	Rent
	2004	95	P1000	Own
Israel	1990	95	P1500	Own
	2007	80	-	Rent
	2007	95	P900 – P3000	Own
	2007	n/a	n/a	Own
India	2007	80	-	Rent
	2007	85	P1000 - P4000	-
South Africa	2007	83	-	Own

Source: Mbayi (2011)

The direct employment of around 3,000 people in the cutting and polishing firms results in an annual wage bill of over $135 million (Table 4.8). The portion of the wage bill accruing to the 210 expatriates employed in the industry is almost double the proportion of the wage bill going to the 2,730 local citizens. In addition to these 3,000 employees in cutting and polishing, employment is also created in second tier supplier industries.

Table 4.8 Direct employment, and wages and salaries in Botswana diamond cutting and polishing sector (2010)

	Employees % of Total employment	Employees No.	Average Monthly Wage ($)	Annual Wage Bill ($)
Total employment	100	3000	...	22,628,064
Factory	91	2730	...	7,268,160
Middle Management	7	210	...	7,799,904
Top Management	2	60	...	7,560,000
Total Locals Employed	93	2790	...	7,928,064
Factory	96	2678	200	6,428,160
Middle Management	4	107	1,167	1,499,904
Top Management	0	0	...	0
Total Expatriates Employed	7	210	...	14,700,000
Factory	20	42	1,667	840,000
Middle Management	50	105	5,000	6,300,000
Top Management	30	63	10,000	7,560,000
Gross Salaries and wages as % of total costs (excluding rough diamonds)	...	...	...	15 - 45 %

Source: Mbayi (2011)

Forward linkages into the timber sector in Gabon

Based on a ubiquitously grown soft commodity (wood) and feeding into a range of both basic and income elastic goods (furniture and construction), the timber value chain is well-developed in a wide range of countries. In recent decades, the chain has become more integrated into the global economy. A key development was the introduction of flat-pack furniture during the 1990s, an innovation that reduced the cost penalties involved in shipping bulky and relatively low value products. This transition in timber processing was intensified as many wood products are labour intensive in production and often involve noxious environmental emissions, making the industry less attractive to producers in the large northern consuming markets. Further, government policies in many low-income countries specifically fostered the timber processing industry as an entry point into industrialisation since this is a sector with relatively few technological or scale barriers to entry.

Tropical timber fills a specialised niche in this global industry. Its timber takes a long time to grow, has a distinctive appearance, is 'hard', and is in short supply. It therefore tends to sell at a premium, particularly for species such as mahogany and ebony where there are pressures to halt the depletion of global stocks and to limit supplies to renewable plantations. Tropical timber accounts for around 15 per cent of global output, with the largest five producers accounting for 70 per cent of the total. Of this, Brazil accounts for 20 per cent, Indonesia for 16 per cent, Malaysia for 16 per cent, India for 15 per cent, and Nigeria for five per cent. Although Gabon only accounts for three per cent of global tropical timber production, it consumes very little of this output domestically and is the seventh largest tropical log exporter. It possesses 23 million hectares of forests, which cover nearly 85 per cent of its total land mass, making it the second most heavily forested African country.

Situated on the African West Coast between the Congo and Cameroon, Gabon is sparsely peopled, with a total population of 1.9 million. Although it has a relatively high per capita income for the region ($7,240 in 2008), much of the population lives in poverty. GDP of $14.4 billion in 2008 was dominated by highly concentrated income streams from oil production. In 2008, around 80 per cent of total export earnings and 65 per cent of government revenue were derived from the oil industry. However, these resource rents are very unevenly distributed. In addition to oil, Gabon possesses valuable deposits of manganese, copper and precious stones. Logs, the third largest export after oil and manganese, accounted for 6.2 per cent of total exports in 2008 (OECD, 2009) and for around three per cent of GDP. It is, however, the second largest employer after the state, absorbing an estimated 28-30 per cent of the active labour force (much of this is part-time employment).

Extraction and exportation of tropical timber on an industrial scale began around 1900. Until the late 1990s, timber was predominantly exported to France and other EU markets. Since then, exports to China have grown rapidly and (in round wood equivalent volume) now exceed exports those to the EU. In 2001, the government introduced legislation designed to provide a sustainable timber industry and to encourage forward linkages. The Forestry Code (*Loi N° 016/01 Portant Code Forestier*) of 2001 included four major features. The first was the termination of the state owned company's (SNBG, *Société Nationale des Bois du Gabon*) monopoly over the commercialisation of the dominant species, Okoumé and Ozigo. The second was the introduction of a sustainable forest management system and the third saw the introduction of a higher degree of transparency to combat corruption and illegal logging. The final component of the Forestry Code was designed to promote the domestic processing of logs. It established a target of domestic processing, specifying a target of 75 per cent by January 2012. Since progress in meeting this target was slow, at the beginning of 2010 the government announced a log export ban.

Two key factors led to the introduction of the Forestry Code. First, Gabon's oil reserves are finite and oil production peaked in 1996/7. This led the government to target economic diversification, in general, and the adding of value to raw materials, in particular. The second factor was pressure from external agencies, including the IMF and the World Bank (Gabon's largest creditors), European governments, and European buyers of tropical timber and wood products. The fact that the historically dominant buyers from Europe were happy to see primary processing occurring at the site of logging removed a potential obstacle to this policy-induced promotion of forward linkages. Even though progress in meeting the January 2012 target was slow, the timber value chain in Gabon has seen a deepening of forward linkages (Figure 4.7).

Figure 4.7 Gabon's tropical timber value chain

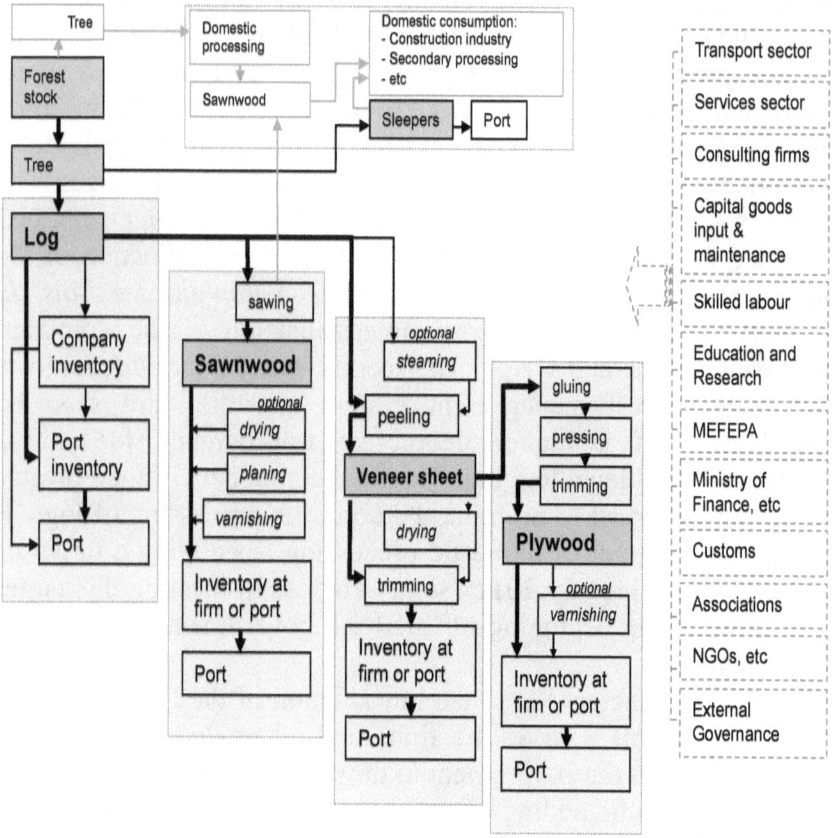

Note: Dashed lines text boxes give examples of actors external to the value chain

Source: Terheggen (2011)

After the introduction of the Forestry Code in 2001, exports of processed timber products grew rapidly, exceeding 450,000 cubic metres in 2005. Despite this growth, exports of processed timber were only 33 per cent of total timber exports in 2007 (Figure 4.8). However, there are important differences between market destinations. European buyers have imported a growing proportion of processed timber products, whereas Chinese buyers almost exclusively buy unprocessed logs.

Figure 4.8 Gabon export volumes of wood products in cubic meters (1961-2007)

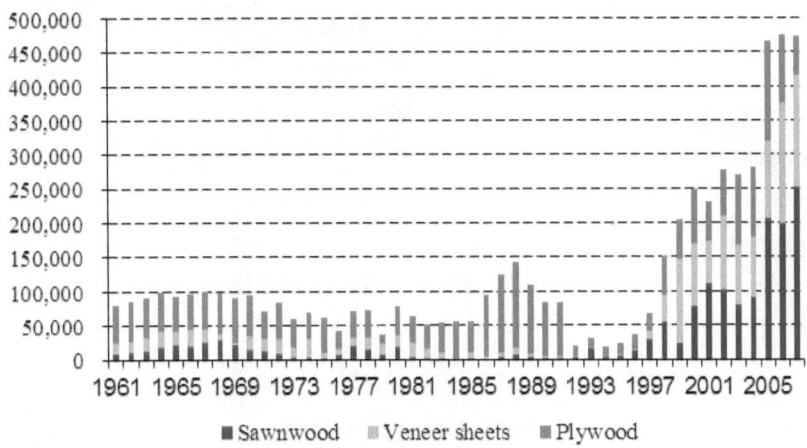

Source: ForesSTAT data online http://faostat.fao.org (accessed January 2011)

Aside from the timber, local content in the Gabonese timber industry and in the processing sector is largely confined to labour. Wage costs account for around one quarter of total production costs in a vertically integrated logging processing company. Other major cost items are capital goods (20 per cent), transportation (14 per cent), customs (22 per cent), and taxes (10 taxes). Virtually all machinery and transport equipment is directly imported by firms in the timber value chain. However, even this overstates the domestic value added component of costs, since Gabon has an acute shortage of skilled labour, and unskilled labour willing to work at the industry's wage rate. As one company observed, 'We would like to fill our senior positions with Gabonese, but... we cannot find skilled labour in Gabon'. Consequently, a high proportion of the skilled labour force and 16 per cent of unskilled labour was made up of migrants, many of whom repatriate their salaries abroad (Table 4.9). Senior management is most often sourced from Europe and/or Asia (depending on the ownership of production), whereas foreign labour in administrative positions, in transport, and in production/processing (labourers) is mostly made up of migrant labour from other Central African countries.

Table 4.9 Gabon distribution, origin and cost of labour (%, Euro)

	Distribution (per cent)	Origin (per cent) Gabon	Origin (per cent) Foreign	Cost (euro)
Management	7	24	75	5,700
Technicians	4	59	41	1,600
Administration	6	87	13	700
Labourers	74	84	16	300
Transport	6	70	31	800
Environment & Social	2	74	26	600

Source: Terheggen (2011)

An index of the value of logs and processed wood products after their respective points of production (ex-forest or ex-factory) as well as the point of exportation (at port, fob), provides an overview of the accretion of value added throughout Gabon's tropical timber industry (Figure 4.9). In the case of exported logs, the value chain starts at the forest level where the standing value of a tree is assigned an index value of 100 points. Value added in felling trees, clearing branches and transporting the log to the log collection point in the concession area adds a further 13 per cent to the value of the tree. Transporting the log to the port results in an index point value of the same log of 220 points. In the case of sawn wood, more elaborate cutting and transporting involves an in-factory price index of 163 and an ex-factory sawn-wood price index of 285.

The accretion of costs in veneer sheet manufacture (ex-factory price index of 310) and plywood (ex-factory price index of 390) involves deeper degrees of 'domestic value added'. However, since most inputs are imported into these stages of processing, including as we have seen both skilled and unskilled labour, the real extent of domestic value added is some way below the indices shown in Figure 4.9.

Figure 4.9 Gabon intra-chain value-added distributions

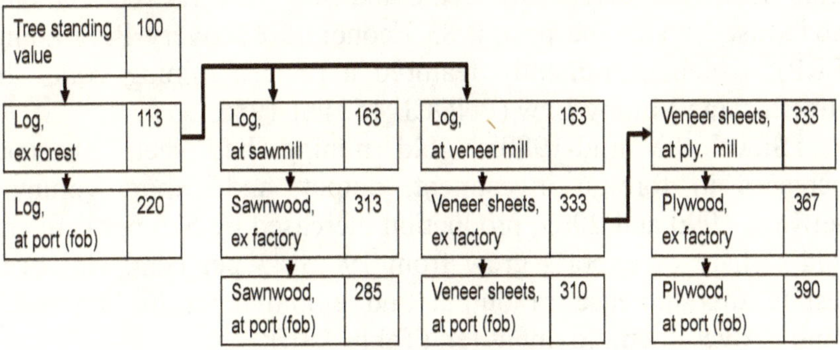

Tree standing value	100							
Log, ex forest	113	Log, at sawmill	163	Log, at veneer mill	163	Veneer sheets, at ply. mill	333
Log, at port (fob)	220	Sawnwood, ex factory	313	Veneer sheets, ex factory	333	Plywood, ex factory	367
		Sawnwood, at port (fob)	285	Veneer sheets, at port (fob)	310	Plywood, at port (fob)	390

Source: Terheggen (2011)

To some extent, the slow progress in meeting the Forestry Code objectives is a function of processing inefficiency. Exported as logs, Gabonese producers are able to command the highest share of resource rents, since Gabon is a privileged supplier of many tropical species, particularly Okoumé[5], which is prized because of the ease with which the bark can be peeled. However, to the extent that processing is inefficient by global standards, some of these resource rents are dissipated. Processing may increase domestic value added, but will lead to lower levels of profits. Insofar as these resource rents are invested productively and the returns to this investment stay in Gabon, it may be that the social interest is best met without the beneficiation of Gabon's timber wealth.

Backward linkages into the gold sector in Ghana

Gold has been produced for over 1,000 years in the territory of the Ancient Kingdom of Ghana, the Gold Coast Colony and post-independence Ghana. Large-scale industrial gold mining in Ghana dates back to the last quarter of the 19th century. After a period of

---

[5] Okoumé grows in 70-80% of Gabon's forest and in much smaller volumes in neighbouring countries. There are no perfect substitutes although Meranti (an Asian species) is a second-best option.

decline under government control in the nationalist era in the 20 years from the early 1960s, the industry was restructured and modernised under the post 1983 Economic Recovery Programme (ERP), which prominently featured a revised mining code, the Minerals and Mining Law (PNDCL 153) of 1986.

Since the mid-1980s, gold mining has seen sustained increases in foreign investment, output, and export volumes. Between 1990 and 2009, production increased by 575 per cent and gold's share of exports grew from 19 to 43 per cent. However, despite this increase in output and employment in large-scale mining, overall employment fell (Table 4.10).

Table 4.10 Ghana gold mining production (1990 – 2009)

Year	1990	1995	2000	2005	2009
Production (oz.)	541,147	1,715,867	2,457,152	2,138,944	3,119,823
Contribution to GDP (%)	4.8	5.6	5.6	5.0	5.8
Export value ($ million)	304	647	702	946	--
Share total exports (%)	19	44	36	34	43
Employment total	N.A.	19,557	15,120	13,766	17,332
Mining leases granted	3	4	2	2	6
Prospecting licenses granted	37	23	4	22	72
Reconnaissance licenses granted	1	42	1	31	21
Small-scale gold licences granted	0	0	9	21	66

Source: Ghana Minerals Commission

After a brief interruption during a period of gold price weakness at the turn of the century, production expansion resumed. Facilitated by a further revised mining code that was consolidated in the Minerals and Mining Act 703 in 2006, $3 billion was invested in the industry between 2006 and 2009. Mining's contribution to GDP, of which gold still represents some 95 per cent, was 5.8 per cent in 2009, up only a percentage point from 1990, but still higher than Ghana's other main export commodities, cocoa (3.9 per cent) and forestry (3.2 per cent). Given the rapidly escalating price of gold in the context of the post 2002 commodity boom and global economic uncertainties, investment in the mining sector has grown significantly in recent years and looks likely to continue growing in the future.

By 2009, Ghana had become the world's ninth largest gold producer and the second largest producer in Africa, accounting for 3.8 per cent of global production, up from 2.6 per cent five years earlier. The Birimian and Tarkwaian gold belts which characterise the western half of Ghana and which contain both hard rock and placer (alluvial) gold deposits extend northwards and westwards into the broader West African region. Ghana is thus simultaneously at the forefront of an expanding regional industry, as production increased significantly in the neighbouring countries of Mali, Burkina Faso, Guinea, Mauritania and Cote d'Ivoire.

Ghana has eight large mines, all of which are owned and managed by five international producers. It also possesses a small number of far smaller producers; and a significant contribution of semi-formal, small-scale producers which generate around 10 per cent of national output (triple the level of 20 years ago). In addition, there is substantial, albeit unmeasured, production from the unregistered, informal and technically illegal small-scale artisanal miners known as *galamsey*, whose activities spread through gold mining areas and are estimated to employ 50,000 to 200,000 people.

The Minerals and Mining Law of 1986 is the core legislation which frames the operations of the industry. A key component of the Economic Recovery Plan, it constituted the first ever Ghanaian legislation that was specific to mining. This law was amended with the Minerals and Mining Amendment Act of 1994 (Act 475) after the re-establishment of civilian democratic rule in 1992. Act 475 was subsequently amended by the Minerals and Mining Act of 2006 (Act 703). Act 703 is a comprehensive law that covers virtually all aspects of mining, namely, ownership of minerals and the cadastral system; mineral rights; royalties, rentals and fees; dispute resolution; reconnaissance licenses; prospecting licenses and mining leases. Other areas include surrender, suspension and cancellation of mineral rights; surface rights and compensation; industrial minerals; small-scale mining; and administration and miscellaneous provisions.

Act 703 seeks to promote a localisation policy and to facilitate production linkages to maximise the benefits of mining. In this regard, it provides for the following measures:

- A 10 per cent government stake in all large-scale gold mining companies without any financial contribution;
- The reservation of small-scale mining for Ghanaian citizens;
- Gold mining companies are to give preference to 'made in Ghana' products, to public corporations and service agencies located in the country, and to employment of Ghanaians;
- Gold mining companies are required to submit detailed programmes for the recruitment and training of Ghanaian personnel;
- Clause 50(3) of Act 703 specifically calls for eventual 'localisation' of mining staff. It defines 'localisation' to mean a training programme designed towards the eventual replacement of expatriate personnel by Ghanaian personnel

Besides restructuring the law governing the operations of the mining sector, the Minerals and Mine Law of 1986 sought to strengthen mining support institutions under the Mining Support Program. The main aims of this program were to develop the capacity of mining support institutions to enable them to promote investment in the sector and to develop mechanisms to enhance productivity and financial viability.

As a consequence of the very long history of gold mining in Ghana, and particularly following the rapid expansion of the industry after the mid-1980s, there has been a gradual development of a supplier industry. Ghana's leading Business Directory, the Surf Yellow Pages Ghana (2010 edition), indicates a large population of companies involved in supporting the mining sector, the vast majority of which are concerned with gold mining. Some 300 companies are listed under the three categories of mining companies, mining equipment, and mining services. The first tier suppliers include global mine construction companies such as

Lycopodium, and a strong showing by a number of well known, international OEM companies (Atlas Copco, Boart Longyear, Sandvik, Liebherr, Mantrac/Caterpillar), input suppliers (Carmeuse Lime Products, Castrol, Maxam, African Explosives) and agents and distributors (Barbex Technical Services, Riepco).

Locally owned firms feature more prominently amongst the smaller first tier and second tier suppliers. These are primarily in the metals and metalworking (Tema Steel), chemicals and plastics (Riepco, Interplast), civil engineering (Engineers and Planners), business services (KEK Insurance Brokers) and logistics (Allship Logistics) fields. While not presently members of the Ghana Chamber of Mines, a number of other locally owned companies (such as Western Forgings, Tropical Cable and Conductor, and Wire Weaving Industries) also provide inputs to the mines.

The major gold mines claim a large number of local suppliers. For example, Golden Star Resources lists several hundred suppliers, of which 60 are 'active suppliers' (defined as 12 or more orders a year). Gold Fields, Anglo Gold Ashanti, Chirano, and Newmont list a total of 521 suppliers. These claims are supported by Chamber of Mines data on the distribution of mining revenues (Table 4.11).

Table 4.11 Local linkages in Ghanaian gold mining: distribution of funds in Ghana chamber of mines producing members (2008)

Classification	Amount ($ million)	%
Employees	175	8
Capital Expenditure	669	29
Direct payments to Govt.	146	6
Mining Host Communities	12	1
Local Purchases (excluding Fuel/Power)	467	20
Local Purchases (Fuel/Power)	428	18
Loans	52	2
Imported Consumables	376	16
TOTAL	2,325	100

Source: Bloch and Owusu 2011

This demonstrates a large aggregate spend by producing companies. Of their total spend of $2.325 billion in 2008, 20 per cent ($467 million) was directed to local purchases (excluding fuel and power), with a further $428 million (18 per cent) on fuel and power. Imported consumables comprised 16 per cent of the total. The largest item of expenditure ($669 million, 29 per cent) was invested in capital expenditure (largely in capacity expansion), the majority of which is imported plant and equipment (Table 4.11).

A striking feature of the supplier base is that, apart from the relatively recent Act 703, it has largely been a market driven process of outsourcing and specialisation. More than 80 per cent of these suppliers are located in Greater Accra, in Accra itself or in the adjacent port/industrial city of Tema. The only other metropolitan area with a substantial number of suppliers is Takoradi in the Western Region. Kumasi, the large metropolitan commercial and political capital of Ashanti Region, is seemingly under represented as a locale for mining supply. This suggests that the industry benefits from location-specific externalities which are widely observed in the global development of industrial districts (Best, 1990).

The Chamber of Mines Supply Manager's sub-committee has identified 27 product categories which are either already being manufactured in Ghana, or should be assessed for 'import substitution potential' (Table 4.12). Annual spend on these Ghanaian owned suppliers is estimated at $120 million and the aim is to increase this to $200 million in the longer term. The Chamber is seeking to move from a sourcing policy based on percentage value of procurement spend to one based on targeting products (services are not included) which are being made, or feasibly could be made in Ghana.

Table 4.12 Ghanaian feasible products for future near term backward linkages

1	Activated Carbon	15	Conveyor Rollers, Idlers & Pulleys
2	Yelomine Pipe	16	Steel Products, including fabrication
3	Rock bolts and Split sets	17	Tyre re-treading
4	Caustic Soda	18	Heavy Duty Electric Cables
5	Explosives Manufacturing, including Ammonium Nitrate	19	Metal or PVC Core Trays
6	Ventilation Ducting	20	Chain Link Fencing, Wire Netting, Barbed Wire, Welded Mesh, Expanded Mesh, Concrete Mesh, Razor wire and Panel Mesh
7	Ammonium Sulphate	21	Motor Rewinding
8	Mill Liners	22	Plastic Sample Bags
9	Grinding Media	23	Calico Bags
10	General/Specialty Lubricants	24	Bullion Boxes
11	HDPE & PVC Pipes	25	Reversed Engineered Specialty Products
12	Overalls & Work Clothes	26	Cupels & Crucibles
13	Cement and Cement products	27	Wood Products
14	Quicklime and Hydrated Lime		

Source: Information provided by Chamber of Mines, 2011.

In 2002, the Ghana Minerals Commission mandated all mining companies to assist their host communities to develop local linkages. In response, all the large mining companies in Ghana have set up departments to promote local procurement. A case in point is Gold Field Ghana Limited's (GFG) Foundation, which was established in 2004 to promote and fund community development projects within the Tarkwa and Damang catchment area of the company's operations, under an initiative entitled the Sustainable Community Empowerment and Economic Development (SEED) programme.

The main objective of the GFG Foundation is to promote the development of the company's primary stakeholder communities. The Foundation's work is funded by a contribution of one US dollar for every ounce of gold sold by the company, as well as a deduction of 0.5 per cent of pre-tax profits. Based on this funding contribution, increases in the price of gold and in company profitability imply that there will be growing funds for community development projects. In addition, other companies providing mining support services to Gold Fields Ghana are also encouraged to contribute, in either cash or kind, to the Foundation's activities. Table 4.13 shows the contributions made by the GFG Foundation to various sectors in its primary catchment area.

Newmont has a foundation for local development, funded by a contribution of $1 for every ounce of gold sold by the company as well as a deduction of one per cent of pre-tax profits. Golden Star Mining Company has established the Golden Star Development Foundation (GSDF) to promote and fund development projects in its operational areas. Projects funded by GSDF in 2008 included the establishment of an educational scholarship scheme; provision of educational infrastructure (school building); health infrastructure (including medical supplies) and a community electrification project.

Table 4.13 GFG Foundation expenditure (%) on sectors and total contribution ($) on community development projects (2002-2009)

Sector	Financial Year								Total (%)	Total ($'000)
	2002	2003	2004	2005	2006	2007	2008	2009		
Education	57	8	57	35	31	25	36	25	31	2808
Health	21	64	8	27	3	3	5	2	12	1060
Water & Sanitation	9	17	11	19	13	17	16	11	14	1315
Agriculture	-	-	6	1	23	45	31	33	24	2213
Others	13	11	18	18	30	10	12	29	19	1710
Total ($'000)	474	721	362	915	1380	1391	1932	1931	100	9107
Projects not funded by GFG Foundation										**1382**
Grand Total										10,489

Source: Gold Fields

Backward linkages into the oil sector in Nigeria

Nigeria has a well-established oil and gas extraction industry developed after the discovery of commercial quantities of oil in 1956. However, it was not until the end of the Nigeria civil war (1970) that the oil industry began to play a prominent role in the economy. By 1982, the oil sector was providing more than 60 per cent of total government revenue and, although this share has fluctuated with volatile oil prices, it has consistently remained above 60 per cent.

The contribution of the oil industry to Nigerian GDP has been significant over the years, exceeding 20 per cent since the early 1980s, and in some years accounting for more than one third of GDP (Figure 4.10). The downturn in this share of GDP between 2004 and 2007 was interrupted by the increase in oil prices in 2009 and 2010 (although up-to-date GDP figures are not available). The likelihood that oil prices will remain high in the future ensures that the oil and gas sector will continue to play a dominant role in the economy.

In 2010, Nigeria was the 10th largest global oil producer and, until recently (when Algeria became the largest producer), the major oil exporting economy in Africa. Reserves at the end of 2007 were 36.2 billion barrels, 2.9 per cent of the global total. Nigeria's downstream oil industry is made up of four refineries with a capacity of 438,750 bbl./d. However, a series of problems - fire, sabotage, poor management, poor maintenance and corruption - have meant that the refineries often operate at less than 40 per cent of full capacity. Thus, despite being a major exporter of crude oil, Nigeria is also a significant importer of petroleum. Policy attention is focussed on increasing this downstream processing capacity.

Despite this focus on forward linkages, there has been a long history of local content policy designed to deepen backward linkages. This started with the Petroleum Act of 1969, which contained a section on the protection for indigenous Nigerian firms and a section on human capacity development. The Joint Operating Agreements (JOA) and the Production Sharing Contract (PSC), between the Nigerian government and the foreign oil companies introduced in 1991 and 1993 included measures to promote local content explicitly recognising that this might require the industry to pay more for local inputs than for imports. Policies introduced in 2005 moved beyond the tolerance of price premiums and involved the issuance of 23 directives by the Nigerian government mandating the use of selected local services and the sourcing of low-technology on shore supply of goods and services to indigenous firms.

Figure 4.10 Nigerian shares of oil in total revenue and GDP (1980-2010)

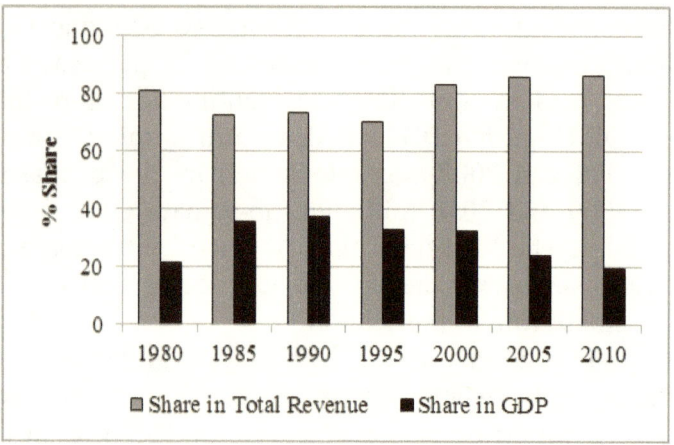

Source: Central Bank of Nigeria Statistical Bulletin (2009)

Partly as a natural working out of market forces and partly because of these local content policies, estimates of local content in the oil and gas industry has risen sharply, particularly over the past decade. Local content rose from 3-5 per cent in the 1970s to 20 per cent in 2004 (UNCTAD/CALAG, 2006). In 2005, the Nigerian Government set a local content target of 49 per cent for 2009 and 70 per cent for 2010, but these targets were not met. In 2009, local content had only reached a level of 39 per cent. Despite this failure to meet the 2010 target, Nigeria has made significant progress. Nevertheless, Nigeria's level of local sourcing is much lower than countries such as Brazil, Malaysia, Venezuela and Norway, all of which achieve local content levels of between 45 and 75 per cent (UNCTAD/CALAG, 2006). Local content levels are however much higher than in other SSA oil exporting economies such as Angola – see section above.

Nigerian policy recognises that local content – i.e. the percentage of spend procured domestically – is not the same as local value added (i.e., it is not just the breadth of local content which is important, but also its depth). Local content is defined as

> *the quantum of composite value added to, or created in the Nigerian economy through the utilization of Nigerian human and material resources and services in the exploration, development, exploitation, transportation, sale and processing of Nigerian crude oil and gas resources resulting in the development of indigenous capabilities, while encouraging foreign investment and participation, without compromising quality, health, safety and environmental standards. (NNPC, 2009)*

Most recently, the Nigerian Content Act (2010) seeks to speed up the indigenisation of the industry, privileging not just domestic supply, but domestic supply by Nigerian firms:

> *Nigerian independent operators shall be given first consideration in the award of oil blocks; oil field licenses, oil-lifting licenses and in all projects for which contract is to be awarded in the Nigerian oil and gas industry. In the bidding for any license, permit or interest and before carrying out any project in the Nigerian oil and gas industry, an operator shall submit a Nigerian content [plan] to the board demonstrating compliance with the Nigerians Content Act. Finally, the award of contract shall not solely be based on the principle of the lower bidder; where a Nigerian indigenous company has capacity to execute such job, the company shall not be disqualified exclusively on the basis that it is not the lowest financial bidder, provided the value does not exceed the lowest bid price by 10 per cent.*

The capacity to increase local content clearly follows from the quality of domestic capabilities. In 2003 a detailed study of the industry suggested that the gap between the needs of the oil and gas sector and local capabilities was smallest in seven sectors, namely in fabrication and construction; well construction and completion; modification, maintenance and operations; transportation; control systems and Information and communications technology (ICTs); design and engineering; and consultancy (Heum et al., 2003).

In the light of this assessment, our study of backward linkages into the oil and gas industry focused on three of these sub-sectors - fabrication and construction; well construction and completion; and control systems and ICTs. We chose these three sectors since they covered a range of competences and represented a discrete and researchable set of companies. We interviewed 15 of the 45 large foreign and locally owned producing firms, most of whom had Head Offices in Lagos, and 115 oil and gas industry suppliers clustered around the two oil cities of Port Harcourt and Warri (accounting for half of all known supplying firms in these regions). These cities were chosen since they were the major centres where oil prospecting, exploration, production and refining occur and local serving firms have concentrated. A multi stage sampling technique was used in the case of oil firms' suppliers. In the first instance, the population was stratified into the two regions (Port Harcourt and Warri) and each of the cities was further stratified into wards. Using the raffle variant of simple random sampling, 50 per cent of suppliers firms were selected in each ward.

What is the evidence on local sourcing which emerges from this focus on the three sub-sectors feeding into the oil industry? Beginning with data derived from the oil sector companies, nine of the 12 interviewed firms estimated that they purchased more than half of all their goods and services from local suppliers (Table 4.14). This considerable commitment to local purchasing exists despite the fact that procurement decisions (including of consumables) are largely taken by the Head Office (which is generally outside of Nigeria).

Table 4.14 Share of inputs from local suppliers/outputs sold to local processors

	Frequency	Percentage
Backward linkages:		
<u>Goods</u>: Up to 50%	3	25
51%-75%	5	41.7
Above 75%	4	33.3
<u>Services</u>: Up to 50%	3	25
51%-75%	9	75
Forward linkages		
Up to 50%	5	41.7
51%-75%	4	33.3
Above 75%	3	25
Locus of decision making		
Who is in charge of supply management?		
Local office	0	0
Head office	12	100
Does this include consumables?		
Yes	10	83.3
No	2	16.7

Source: Oyejide and Adewuyi (2011)

Despite this high-level of local sourcing, much of this occurs on an arm's length basis, suggesting that there is considerable leeway for the promotion of better links between the oil firms and their suppliers. Figure 4.11 shows the result of asking the same question of both the oil firms and their suppliers about the nature of their interchanges on a range of factors that are important in achieving systemic value chain efficiency. On a scale of 1 ('not at all') to 3 ('constantly') each of the parties were asked to score the quality and frequency of their contacts. It is clear that as a rule, the oil firms tend to rate their linkage with their servicing firms higher than the suppliers for all of these modes of interaction. The gap in perceptions was greater with regard to payment negotiations and delivery reliability and delivery frequency. However, it is interesting that with regard to quality – a critical success factor in the oil industry – there was a close alignment in the perceptions of the oil firms and their suppliers.

Figure 4.11 Alignment of perceptions on the frequency and quality of interchanges between lead oil firms and first tier suppliers in Nigeria

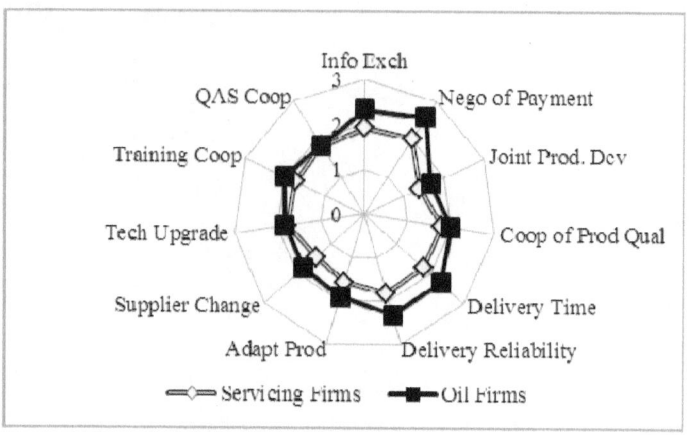

1=no cooperation, 3=continuous cooperation

Source: Oyejide and Adewuyi (2011)

This misalignment in perceptions between the oil firms and their suppliers exists despite the fact that most of the large oil firms have active supplier development programmes (Table 4.15). It is clear, however, that the International Finance Corporation (IFC) supplier development programme does not appear to be seen as useful by the oil companies. Further, although the oil companies believe that they have reasonably close relationships with their first tier own suppliers, this does not extend down the supply chain. Only one of the 12 lead commodity producers said that it provided support to second tier suppliers.

The lack of contact between lead commodity producers and second and third tier suppliers raises the associated question on the depth of local content provision. In other words, are local sources merely a front for the importation of goods and services? Table 4.16 provides data on the local purchasing by 80 first tier suppliers to the oil industry in the three sub-sectors. They reported substantial levels of local content in their own purchases. Taken as a whole, 55.1 per cent of 80 first tier supplying firms purchased more than half of their services from local second tier suppliers. This level of local sourcing was highest in the fabrication and construction sub-sector and in the well construction and completion sub-sector. In these two sub-sectors 45.5 per cent and 41.1 per cent respectively source more than 75 per cent of their inputs locally. The significance of this data is that it suggests a considerable depth to backward linkages in the Nigerian oil and gas industry. That is, unlike the experience of 'local supply' in many of SSA's commodity sectors, where 'local' represents merely the localisation of the importation function, in the Nigerian oil and gas industry a large measure of 'local supply' does indeed reflect local value added

Table 4.15 Responses to supply chain development programmes

	%
Provide assistance to suppliers in meeting up with standards	
Yes	75
No	25
Have a strategy for supply development for local business	
Yes	75
No	25
Participate in IFC suppliers development programme	
Yes	8.3
No	91.7
Keep relationship with firms that provide input to suppliers	
Yes	8.3
No	91.7

Source: Oyejide and Adewuyi (2011)

Table 4.16 Percentage share of local content in purchases by first tier suppliers to the oil and gas industry

Sector	0-25%	26-50%	51-75%	76-100%
Control system & ICT	31.6	21.1	21.1	26.3
Fabrication & construction	13.6	22.7	18.2	45.5
Well construction & completion	20.6	20.6	17.6	41.1
Others	40	40	20	-
Total	22.5	22.5	18.8	36.3

Source: Oyejide and Adewuyi (2011)

Backward linkages into mining equipment and services in South Africa

The large-scale exploitation of minerals in South Africa dates back more than 150 years to the discovery of diamonds and subsequently during the 1870s to the discovery and exploitation of deep deposits of gold ore. South Africa not only possesses the most developed mining and mining supply industry in SSA, but in some important respects also stands out as a world-leading producer of individual minerals such as platinum. It also possesses extensive forward linkages from the commodities sectors, not just in the processing of many ores, but also especially in the processing of soft industrial commodities. In some cases, as in the incorporation of platinum in catalytic exhausts for automobiles (where it is the world's largest producer), forward linkages have moved beyond processing to the beneficiation of minerals. South Africa possesses a well-developed industrial sector, the origin of which rests principally in mineral extraction and the development of extensive linkages to this sector. South Africa thus provides a cogent challenge to two of the central tenets of the Resource Curse theory, that is, that the commodities sector acts as an enclave industry and that resource exploitation undermines industrial activity.

In recent years, mining has seen a decline in its share of GDP (from 8.8 per cent in 2000 to 6.3 per cent in 2010). Its share of exports (41 per cent in 2010) remained roughly stable over the decade, but fell and then rose in tandem with global commodity prices (Table 4.17).

Table 4.17 South African percentage share of mining and quarrying in GDP and exports (2000-2010)

Year	Value Added In GDP	Exports
2000	8.8	39
2001	8.5	39
2002	8.3	37
2003	8.4	33
2004	8.1	32
2005	7.8	32
2006	7.3	33
2007	6.9	32
2008	6.3	33
2009	6.1	39
2010	6.3	41

Source: Value Added GDP values from South Africa Statistical Yearbook (2011).

Exports values from http://apps.thedti.gov.za/econdb/rapportt/rapstruc.html

In the early years, economic policies with regard to mining had two main thrusts. The first was to provide a favourable environment for mining investors. This, in turn, entailed keeping costs down, notably the wage costs of African miners. At the same time, a second thrust entailed a number of policies that sought to advance backward linkages. Prominent in the past were policies of tariff protection that provided support for domestic industry. The protective regime was significantly weakened in the years prior to, and soon after, transition to democratic rule in 1994.

Currently, a major thrust of government policy with respect to mineral products is to promote downstream beneficiation. Beneficiation features strongly in the National Industrial Policy Framework and in the Industrial Policy Action Plan (IPAP). The IPAP envisages minimum beneficiation levels for 10 'selected commodities.' These commodities are not specified, but presumably involve all of the major mineral products. Thus, the IPAP Key Action Programme 12.5.1, specifies

Setting minimum beneficiation levels for key commodity chains. Nature of the intervention: The Department of Mineral Resources (DMR) to establish and define minimum levels of beneficiation for each of the 10 selected commodities. This will lay the foundations to create specific value chains, including in five instances up to the fourth level of minerals value addition.

Our natural comparative advantage in the underlying resource based industries along with additional factor endowments (especially relatively inexpensive electricity costs) provides us with an opportunity to be competitive in downstream value addition. The end game is to acquire a competitive position as far down the value chain towards finished product production as is possible.

However, this is not the only approach driving the development of industrial policy. The International Panel on Accelerated and Shared Growth Initiative for South Africa (ASGISA) argued that

... both theory and practice provide reasons to question the presumption that downstream processing is an appropriate development path. The skills and other inputs required to process raw material and market finished products could be very different from those required to mine or grow them... Moreover ... as transportation costs have declined, and global markets have become more integrated, the advantage of proximity to raw material production has diminished. (Hausmann, Klinger and Lawrence, 2008:1)

Leaving aside the current policy debate on whether to promote forward or backward linkages from the commodities sector in the future, past developments have meant that insofar as South Africa has a globally competitive industrial structure in hard commodities value chains, this is to be found in regard to backward linkages, particularly mining equipment and specialist services. This comparative advantage can be evidenced in a number of ways.

The first is with regard to innovative capabilities, in general, and patents, in particular. The quantity and quality of South African mining and related technologies were assessed utilising 1976-2006

USPTO patent data from the United States Patent and Technology Office (USPTO).[6] South Africa has a considerable number of patents. Mining related technology patents make up a much larger share of South Africa's total patenting activity than for other comparator countries that have significant mining industries and are considered to be at the technology frontier (Table 4.18).

Patent quality can be assessed by examining the number of citations received. In aggregate, South African patents received fewer citations than patents in the comparator countries. By contrast, South African mining and related patents received more citations than patents of comparator countries. By this measure, the value of South African patents is higher than for comparator countries. Randomly matching each South African patent to a similar American, Canadian, or Australian patent gives somewhat weaker results. The average number of citations for a South African mining technology patent is likely to be less than that of a similar Canadian or US patent. However, a South African mining patent is more cited than that of a comparable Australian patent.

Table 4.18 All patents and mining technology patents at the USPTO; South Africa and comparator countries (1976-2006)

	All Patents	Mining Tech. Patents	Share (%)
South Africa	3151	142	4.51
United States	1,587,915	7,882	0.50
Australia	16,283	311	1.90
Canada	65,580	853	1.30
Global total/average	3,189,941	17,098	0.54

Note: A patent belongs to the 'Mining Related Technologies' cluster if it belongs to one of the following 3-digit USPC classes: 299 - Mining or In Situ Disintegration of Hard Material, 051 - Abrasive Tool Making Process, Material, and Composition, 023 - Chemistry: Physical Processes, 037 – Excavating, 075 - Specialized Metallurgical Processes, 172 - Earth Working

Source: United States Patent Office database

---

[6] The data and analysis on South African patents were provided by Professor Lee Bransetter to a World Bank Study entitled 'Closing the Skills and Technology Gaps in South Africa.'

A second indicator of the development of globally competitive backward linkages from South Africa's hard commodities sector is the share of this sector in external trade. The level, and particularly the growth, of exports of mining equipment and specialist services is one clear manifestation of global competitiveness. This is particularly the case in light of the fact that these exports have not benefited from any specially designated state support. Exports can be divided into two broad categories. The first category is exports related to new projects – new mines or mineral processing activities. The second category is the aftermarket – to existing mines or mineral processing activities. The competitive edge to supply to the aftermarket is often secured through firms being engaged in projects from the outset.

The determination of specifically mining exports is a complex issue. Since trade data is categorized by product rather than by customer, it is very difficult to determine precisely what is destined for mining as opposed to other markets. The South African Capital Equipment Council (SACEC) has assessed, (for South Africa) at an eight digit HS level, which capital equipment products are destined for the mining sector. SACEC categorisation has been used in the data below. Currently exports of mining capital equipment are running at approximately $4 billion. Exports have been growing rapidly – in nominal terms quadrupling since 2000.[7]

For all capital equipment, South African imports exceed exports by a large margin – in 2008 and 2009, imports were three times larger than exports. In respect of mining equipment, however South Africa is a net exporter. This overall positive trade balance reflects a negative trade balance with the rest of the world, but a strong positive trade balance with Sub-Saharan Africa (Table 4.19). The dense network of mining production and services companies result in a high local value added for this sector – estimated at approximately 90% (Kaplan, 2011).

---

[7] Prior to 2000, there were a number of changes in the definition of products that make it difficult to construct a clear time series.

Table 4.19 South African mining equipment exports and imports $'000 (2005-2009)

	2005	2006	2007	2008	2009
		Trade with World			
Exports	3,292,256	4,721,750	6,200,709	6,742,700	4,130,184
Imports	3,173,526	4,285,689	5,987,691	6,174,743	3,668,875
Trade Balance	118,730	436,061	213,081	567,957	461,309
		Trade with SSA			
Exports	786,793	1,025,801	1,494,146	1,935,971	1,542,666
Imports	10,972	13,423	15,317	24,485	32,232
Share of Total Exports	24%	22%	24%	29%	37%

Source: Calculated from COMTRADE database accessed through WITS online <https://wits.worldbank.org/WITS/WITS/Restricted/Login.aspx> (accessed February 2011)

Much of these exports result from the global expansion of South African mining houses, which then utilise their existing supplier base in South Africa. African countries – notably in the southern Africa region – are the major markets for South African exports of capital goods. Eight of the top 10 destination countries are Africa and all except Nigeria are located in the sub-region. Unfortunately, the services export data do not allow for mining services to be isolated. However, net export earnings are likely to be substantial and significantly positive.

Beyond this aggregate data, more specific enquiry supports the conclusion that the South African supplier industry has developed globally competitive capabilities on the basis of its experience in serving the domestic mining industry. South Africa is a world leader in a host of mining equipment products. These include spirals for washing coal; pumping up water from deep levels; hydropower; tracked mining; underground locomotives; ventilation; shaft sinking; turnkey new mine design and operation; and many others. The area where South African expertise is particularly advanced and is at the global frontier is in deep level mining and associated competencies. South Africa is much weaker in the so called 'yellow metal' areas – such as mining vehicles – where scale economies are critical and where large TNCs dominate. There are also examples of horizontal linkages, where competences were built in other sectors and then applied to mining, for example, in transport and haulage equipment where South Africa has leading global products (Morris et al., 2011a). Similarly, as in the case of hydraulic equipment, there are also cases where the mining sector provided the initial source of demand and successful domestic firms then branched out to serve the needs of other sectors.

Focusing on the depth and breadth of backward linkages in South Africa it is possible to draw six conclusions. First, South African mining activities have, from a very early stage, required the utilisation of advanced technologies and systems. This has in large part been a consequence of the geological specificity of mining deposits in South Africa, particularly the need to mine gold at great depths. Second, the local deployment of such technologies and systems combined with a particular structure of the South African mining industry and state directed policies, allowed for the early development of considerable local technological expertise. State policies have been critical in the past. Government provided not only tariff support but also financial and technological support to local industry. Linkages with the National System of Innovation (NSI) have been important for the mining sector and for local industry. Third, the technological content of mining and mining related activities everywhere has increased significantly over the last two decades as a result of a number of factors – including increased globalisation, market segmentation, the changing role of TNCs and the engagement of generic technologies, particularly Information Technology. Fourth, the significantly enhanced technological content of mining related activities coincided with two critical changes in South Africa: the decline of mining output for some minerals, notably gold, and the end of apartheid in 1994. As a result, South African mining firms have engaged in substantial expansion abroad. This, in turn, has created significant opportunities for exports of mining related equipment and services. Fifth, South Africa has a significant cluster of firms in mining equipment and related services, which are at the global technological frontier. This is evident in respect of exports, intellectual property and leading products and companies. Indeed, this cluster is the only significant area of industrial activity where South Africa is located at the global technological frontier. Sixth, the constrained supply of high-level skills and limited institutional and policy supports in relation to research and product development are curtailing development in the higher 'end' of new product development, while the constrained supply of middle level skills, such as artisans, and relatively high wage costs are constraining growth at the 'lower' manufacturing end (Kaplan, 2011).

Backward linkages into the gold sector in Tanzania

Historically gold production has been dominated by a few large producers. For many years, South Africa accounted for more than 60 per cent of total global production. Recent decline in its production and the rise in production in other countries have meant hat in 2010, the world's largest gold producer was China, followed by the US and then South Africa. Beyond a group of eight large gold producers (together accounting for almost one half of the global total in 2010), are a clutch of around 90 smaller producers. Tanzania, with production capacity of 50 tonnes in 2009 fits into the second tier of producing countries, along with Argentina, Bolivia, Brazil, Chile, Colombia, Ghana Kazakhstan, Zimbabwe, Mali, Morocco, Mexico, Papua, and the Philippines

Since Independence in 1961, Tanzania has had a stuttering growth experience. For much of the 1980s and 1990s, economic growth was slow. Average annual growth between 1988 and 1993 was 1.1 per cent (less than the rate of population growth), which compared poorly with that for SSA as a whole (2.7 per cent). However, since the late 1990s, economic growth has revived. Between 2000 and 2010, the Tanzanian economy grew at an annual rate of 6.8 per cent, above the average for SSA as a whole (4.6 per cent).

One major factor underlying this revival in growth was the development and expansion of Tanzania's gold mining industry. Following the onset of large-scale production in 1998, there are now six active gold mines in Tanzania and gold has emerged as the country's leading foreign exchange earner. Gold exports more than trebled between 2000 and 2010, reaching nearly $2 billion in 2011 and accounting for more than 20 per cent of total exports (Figure 4.12). However, the low tax regime introduced to foster the gold industry meant that the contribution of the gold sector to total government revenue was only $46.5 million in 2004-5 (the most recent year for which data is available), contributing only 1.4 per cent of total government revenue.

Figure 4.12 Tanzanian value of gold exports and percentage share of total exports (2000-2011)

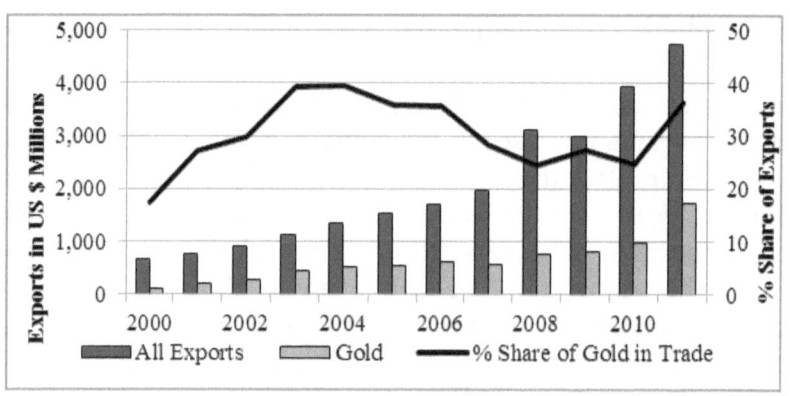

Source: Calculated from COMTRADE database accessed through WITS online <https://wits.worldbank.org/WITS/WITS/Restricted/Login.aspx> (accessed April 2012)

The legislation affecting access to the country's mineral resources, has been formulated most recently in the Mining Act of 1998, was in a process of revision in 2010[8]. This 1998 legislation represented a radical departure from the 1979 Act, which had previously restricted access to mineral deposits to the

---

[8] This research was carried out before the Tanzanian Parliament legislated a new Mineral Act in April 2010.

state. The 1998 policy opened the mining sector to local and foreign private sector investors. It reserved two sets of activities for firms wholly owned by Tanzanian citizens - Primary Prospecting Licences (PPL) and Primary Mining Licences (PML). However, local firms could sell these rights to foreign firms at a later stage, if they entered into joint ventures with local partners. Whilst licences for other activities which are issued to foreign firms require proof of both technical and financial capacity and capabilities, these requirements are not specified for wholly locally owned firms.

Section 10 of the 1998 Mining Act has provisions that allow the Minister of Minerals and Energy to negotiate and grant tax exemptions and environmental impact assessment exemptions with individual investors, without being restricted by other legal requirements. The Mining Development Agreements (MDA) is designed to provide large investors with the assurance of stability in long-term mining projects. A MDA is negotiated and granted in addition to other incentives provided to all investors, such as depreciation allowances of 100 per cent, repatriation of capital and profit directly related to mining, exemption of import duty and (VAT) on equipment and essential materials.

Government policy recognises the need to develop linkages into and out of the gold mining sector. However, other than the exclusive primary prospecting and mining rights granted to local citizens, there are no other elements of the legislation which specifically target local content or which restrict the capacity of the mining firms to import their inputs.

The structure of the gold mining value chain in Tanzania is shown in Figure 4.13. It consists of three primary sets of activities – exploration, the development and construction of the mine, and the operation of the mine. Our analysis of backward linkages focuses on linkages into the exploration and production sub-chains.

Figure 4.13 Tanzanian gold mining value chain

[Figure: Flowchart showing the Tanzanian gold mining value chain. Exploration phase: Early Exploration → Early Exploration Evaluation → Late Exploration → Exploration Evaluation. Development phase: Mine Design → Mine Construction. Production phase: Drill and Blast (Mine) → Haulage → Processing, with Transport and Rehabilitate branches.]

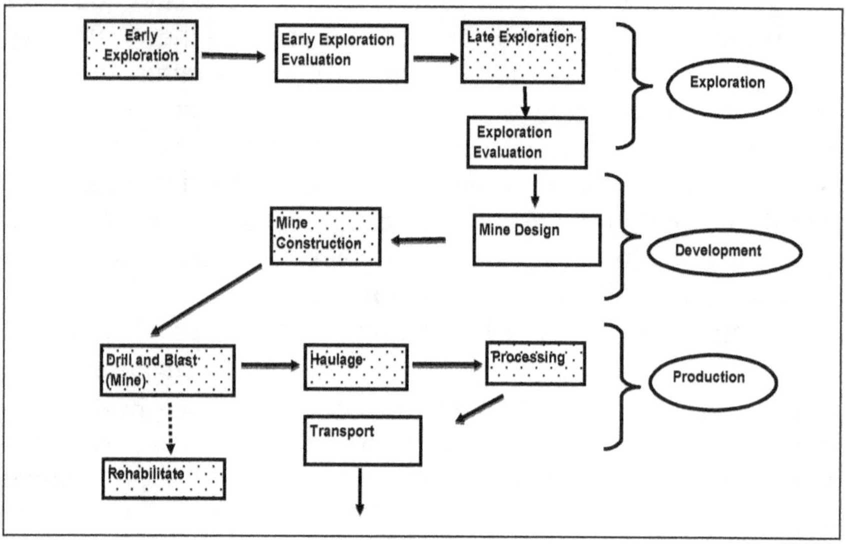

Source: Mjimba (2011)

Linkages to local provision of inputs into both these subchains are weak. In the exploration link of the chain, the three large-scale mining firms active in Tanzania have their own inhouse greenfield exploration departments. AngloGold Ashanti (AGA) has an exploration branch with head offices in Johannesburg, South Africa and its exploration team in Tanzania comprises both Tanzanian citizens and expatriate staff. A similar pattern exists for Resolute and Africa Barrick. Nevertheless, each of the large mining houses also out sources part of their exploration activities (Table 4.20). Consequently, there is a range of exploration firms operating locally. However, with two exceptions, all of these are foreign owned and draw their inputs from abroad (Table 4.21).

Table 4.20 Outsourced and in-house activities in exploration sub-chain

Service/Process	In-house	Outsourced
Target generation	Y	N
Area selection	Y	N
Geophysical work	N	Y
Laboratory work	N	Y
Quality assurance and quality control	Y	N
Drawing up contracts	Y	N
Reserve estimation	Y	N
Logistics	N	Y
Data capture and processing	Y	N
Drilling	N	Y

Source: Mjimba (2011)

Table 4.21 Gold exploration firms active in Tanzania

Firm	Head quarters	Ownership structure (shares)		Service scope	Works location in Tanzania
Canaco Resources	Canada	0	100	Junior explorer	Magambazi
Zari Exploration	Tanzania	Majority	Minority	Junior explorer	Imweru and Lupa
Curries Rose Resources	Canada	0	100	Junior gold explorer	SusiRiver and Mabele Hills
Shanta Gold	Guernsey	0	100	Gold exploration and development	Lupa gold field, Mgusu and Singida
Kibo Mining plc	Republic of Ireland	0	100	Gold and Nickel deposit exploration and development	Itetemia, Luhala and Morogoro
Helio Resources Corporation	Canada	0	100	Junior gold explorer	Saza and Makongolisi
Sub-Saharan Resources N.L.	Australia	0	100	Mineral exploration and development	Nyanzaga
Macquarie Harbour Mining Limited	Australia	0	100	Mineral exploration	Miyabi and Igurubi
African Eagle Resources Corp	United Kingdom	0	100	Mineral exploration and development	Miyabi
Peak Resources	Australia	0	100	Mineral exploration and development	Imweru
MDN Exploration	Canada	0	100	Gold and base metal Exploration and development	Ikungu, Isambara, Mnekezi, Vinyoza and Msasa projects
Tan-Zoz Exploration	Tanzania	Majority	Minority	Junior explorer	Not indicated
Gold Finders	Tanzania	100	0	Junior explorer	Not indicated
Tanzimex	Tanzania	100	0	Junior explorer	Kinyambwiga

Source: Mjimba (2011)

There are a limited number of local linkages from these first-tier exploration firms to second-tier suppliers. The linkages are limited to relatively simple geophysical and geochemical exploration works such as ground based magnetic surveys and exploration, drilling; and general services such exploration logistic services.

The structure of suppliers providing geochemical services – that is the collection and analysis of rock samples – is somewhat different in that three sets of activities are also provided by state owned Tanzanian firms (Table 4.22). These are the Geological Survey of Tanzania (GST) (which engages in geological mapping, surveys and analysis), and STAMICO and SEAMIC (both providing drilling services). These three locally owned providers have been operating for many years and reflect the pre 1997 environment in which the state had exclusive control over the gold mining industry.

Table 4.22 Exploration geochemical works goods/services providers in Tanzania

Firm	Head Office	Service scope	Ownership structure (shares)		
			Local	Foreign	Public
GST	Tanzania	Geological mapping, geophysical and geophysical surveys and analysis	100	0	100
STAMICO	Tanzania	Drilling (scope and range not ascertained), mineral exploration and property consultancy and Joint Venturing	100	0	100
SEAMIC	Tanzania	Geological mapping, geochemical and geophysical surveys and analysis	100	0	100
Tan Zoz	Tanzania	Drilling (scope not ascertained)	Majority	Minority	0
Gold Finders	Tanzania	Stream sediment, soil and rock chip sampling	100	0	0
Capital Drilling	Singapore	Surface diamond core, high air capacity, reverse circular, grade control, heli-porTable diamond, deep directional core orientation, air core, geotechnical, and coal and coal-bed methane drilling services.	0	100	0
Layne Drilling Tanzania (formerly Stanley Mining Services)	Australia	Rotary air blast (RBA), kit bit, reverse circulation, diamond, directional and grade control drilling services.	0	100	0
Africa Mining Services (Owned by Ausdrill)	Australia	Reverse circulation, surface diamond, directional, RBA and air core drilling services	0	100	0
Major Drilling	Canada	Surface and underground coring, directional, reverse circulation, geotechnical coal and coal-bed methane drilling services	0	100	0
ALX Chemex	Australia	Sample preparation and analysis	0	100	0
SGS Laboratories	Italy	Sample preparation, analysis and turnkey surveys	0	100	0

Source: Mjimba (2011)

Local content in the geochemical services link in the exploration sub-chain is very low and is largely limited to local labour inputs. For example, all drilling equipment and components used in Tanzania are imported without any local value addition. The maintenance of the machinery is effectively a closed system with the drilling firms dealing directly with machinery and spare manufactures who service their global operations. Two such firms with worldwide operations supplying drilling machinery and spares are Atlas Copco and Sandvik Mining and Construction. Both have established subsidiaries in Tanzania to service equipment used in the large mines. Typically, they source specialised skills from their global labour force rather than from Tanzania. Local sourcing of manufactured inputs is only at an embryonic stage. For example, containers for rock samples (which have to be made of inert and durable materials) are imported from South Africa and Australia. In 2010, local suppliers began producing these containers in small volumes.

The exploration sub-chain also draws on geophysical services (Table 4.23). Here, too, foreign owned firms dominate and almost exclusively draw their skills from their global labour pool rather than from Tanzania. There is, however, one locally owned firm that participates in this sub-sector, providing ground based magnetometer surveys.

Table 4.23 Geophysical work service providers active in Tanzania

Firm	Head Office	Service scope	Ownership structure share	
			Local	Foreign
Fugro Airborne Survey	South Africa	Airborne geophysical surveys	0	100
Geophysics GPR	Zimbabwe	Ground based geophysical surveys	0	100
Geoimage	Australia	Satellite imagery and geo-spatial solution provider (Quick bird images)	0	100
Jigsaw Geosciences	Australia	Geological mapping	0	100
UTS Geophysics	Australia	Airborne magnetic surveys	0	100
Gold Finders	Tanzania	Ground magnetometer surveys	100	0

Source: Mjimba (2011)

A similar story of very limited local purchases emerges in the case of the production link in the gold value chain. The major local purchase is of liquid fuel required for the heavy drilling and earthmoving equipment used in gold mining. Liquid fuel is imported and reaches the mines at great cost due to the poor quality of infrastructure. A group procurement manager illustrating the point observed that

> *If you think about your Caterpillar truck,... your average fuel consumption [during typical mining operations] is about between 95 litres to 100 litres per hour and you can work it out if you have 30 trucks, 24 hours a day, 360 days a year... that excludes the loaders. (Interview, November 2009).*

The maintenance and repair of the heavy equipment, which is utilised in the mine, is generally outsourced, but to the global firms that supply this equipment for the global operations of the mining companies. Caterpillar operates as Mantrac with local branches in Dar es Salaam, Mwanza, Tanga and Moshi. The firm offers a range of comprehensive repair and maintenance contracts to the mining (and other) sectors. The Mwanza workshop services the country's gold mining sectors. Komatsu operates as Pan African Mining Services Tanzania Limited, with maintenance and repair contracts with individual mines. There were almost no changes in this sourcing structure between 2005 and 2009 for a range of goods reflecting varying degrees of technological content (Mjimba, 2011). These data are also interesting since they show the heavy presence of South African and Australian suppliers. Both countries have developed mining industries and have, over the years, seen the emergence of significant backward linkages.

Linkages into the copper sector in Zambia

Zambia has a long history of copper mining, dating back to the early 20th century. Soon after independence in 1964, the copper mines were nationalised and later consolidated into the Zambia Consolidated Copper Mines (ZCCM), majority owned by government (60 per cent of equity), with a minority share owned by Anglo American Corporation (27.3 per cent). One of the objectives pursued by nationalisation was to promote industrialisation in the form of backward and forward linkages to copper mining. In order to do this, the Zambian government combined a number of policy interventions: state-ownership of some supply firms, preferential procurement policies, import-substitution industrialisation policies, and value chain cooperation between ZCCM, the supply firms, and the education and research institutes in the National System of Innovation. Copper mining generated the bulk of government revenues in the early post-independence period. From the mid-1970s, Zambia's copper mining sector came under mounting pressures from plummeting world prices and low levels of reinvestment in ZCCM. Furthermore, lack of competition and poor supply chain management on the part of ZCCM discouraged suppliers' technological innovation and upgrading processes. Consequently, production levels fell sharply.

The Structural Adjustment Programmes (SAP) introduced in Zambia during the 1990s resulted in the gradual privatisation of the mines, a process completed by 2004. Policies towards the mines were subsumed under the general provision of the SAPs and no specific mining vision was adopted, either during the SAPs or subsequently. In the face of low copper prices in the 1990s, the Zambian government was anxious to conclude the privatisation process. Hence, the bilateral development agreement between Zambia and each mining company included very favourable provisions to the latter, especially in terms of mining taxation. Inter alia, because of the absence of a vision towards the mining sector, there are currently no provisions in any of the legislation, which explicitly target backward linkages and local content.

The bilateral development agreements entered into by the government with each mining company generally incorporated a statement of intent by the mining companies to promote local business development, but these did not contain specific targets and the commitments were not legally binding. They were largely ignored by the mining companies and the government. Government and public opinion largely focused on taxation and labour conditions, rather than local suppliers. Moreover, Zambia developmental discourse was geared towards diversification away from the mining sector.

However, as a consequence of the liberal fiscal regime accompanying privatisation, virtually none of the resource rents accruing from copper mining in Zambia has gone to the government. That is, whereas copper mining had contributed an average of 45 per cent of government revenues between 1965 and 1975, it made virtually no direct contribution to government revenues during the post 2002 price boom (Bova, 2009). The low revenue stream was due to the very generous fiscal regime included in the bilateral development agreements. Moreover alleged transfer pricing, whereby copper was sold by the mining companies to their subsidiaries at prices well below market prices, further lowered the corporate taxable basis (Al Jazeera, 18 June 2011). There is considerable breadth to both forward and backward linkages in Zambia's copper value chain (Figure 4.14).

Figure 4.14 Zambian copper value chain

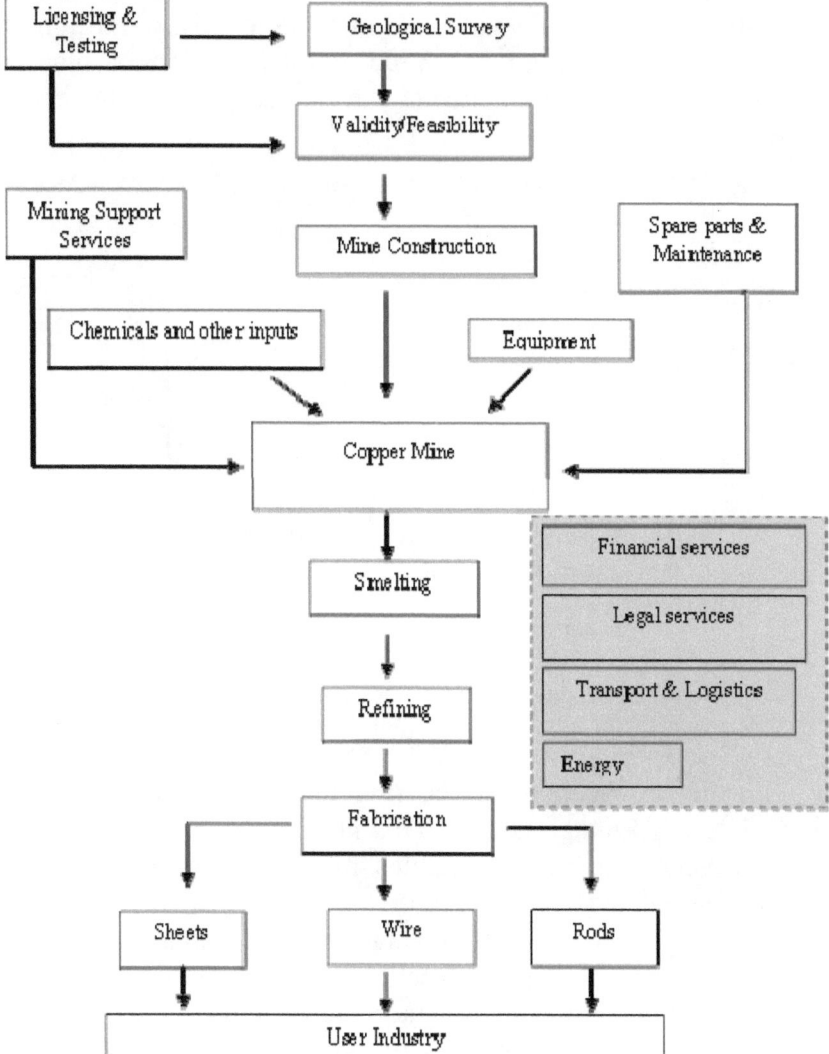

The operational phase of a mining project consisted of ore extraction, crushing, concentration, smelting and refining. Focusing on forward linkages, 95 per cent of copper is exported in refined form (as cathodes), representing a number of value added stages after mining (Figure 4.15). In recent years, there has been substantial investment to increase productive capacity in downstream processing, including the construction of two new smelters (one of $310 million by a Chinese firm, and a smaller investment in the Nchanga smelter by an Indian firm). In addition, a Swiss-Canadian firm invested $190 million to expand an existing smelter to 850,000 tons per annum, making this the largest copper smelter in Africa and the fifth largest in the world.

Figure 4.15 Zambian copper exports by composition in $ '000 (2000-2009)

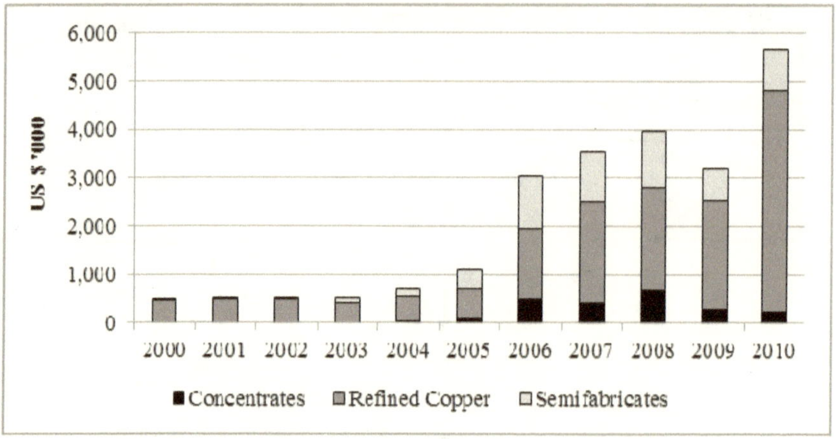

Notes: concentrates includes ores, concentrates, unrefined.

Source: Fessehaie (2011)

Further downstream processing into semi-fabricates takes place, but this linkage is thin. This is because of Zambia's low competitiveness in semi-fabricates manufacturing due to high labour cost and poor infrastructure, in particular energy. Semi-fabricates represents the first stage of processing for refined copper and feed into the construction and manufacturing sectors.

Zambian exports of semi-fabricates include copper plates, sheets and strips, and copper wire, and export values increased substantially over the years, though official figures are inconsistent.[9] Downstream processing is currently almost

---

[9] COMTRADE, which sources data from the revenue and customs authority, records exports of engineering products totalling more than $1 billion in 2008. For the same year, Zambia Development Agency data record exports of only $210.5 million. This latter (and lower) figure is almost certainly more reliable as it is directly sourced from the company.

exclusively undertaken by one company, which is a subsidiary of a large US metal processing conglomerate. However, in 2007, a Chinese SOE undertook an $800 million investment in the Chambishi China-Zambia Economic Cooperation Zone, which will deepen forward linkages by building large-scale semi-fabricates manufacturing capacity.

There have also been substantial backward linkages to the mining sector (Fessehaie, 2011). From data supplied by the Kitwe Chamber of Commerce and Industry and the mining companies it is possible to estimate the total population of suppliers to be around 150 - 200 firms. This estimate comprises established formal sector industrial suppliers. Before the late 2000s, there were also a number of informal traders, but many of these exited the industry (see below).

The breadth of linkages from the mines, particularly the larger mines, is significant. Large mines procure between 60 per cent and 86 per cent of inputs locally (the higher figure includes fuel). Small mines procure between 35 per cent and 80 per cent (Table 4.24). This procurement reflects the purchase of goods and services required for the operation of the mines, rather than for their construction. Whilst the Chinese mine internalised engineering services and foundry products manufacturing (thereby curtailing opportunities for local suppliers), they tend to procure a vast array of goods and services on a competitive basis. This opens access to their supply chain for local suppliers but also leaves them vulnerable to summary exclusion by cheaper imports. The smaller mines are less mechanised and mainly consist of small, open pit operations. Therefore their demand for specialised capital equipment such as hydraulic equipment, pumps and valves, is low but the degree of local sourcing figures is high because, rather than importing equipment and spares, small-scale mines often hire equipment from local firms.

Table 4.24 Local sourcing as percentage of total spending among selected mining companies in Zambia

Mine Size	Share of local sourcing
Large-scale mine A	82% (of capital goods only)
Large-scale mine B	86% (this includes fuel, labour and electricity)
Medium scale mine C	60%
Small-scale mine D	Equipment and spares: 10% purchased from local suppliers 90% directly imported Consumables: 60% purchased from local suppliers 40% directly imported
Small-scale mine E	Production costs are disaggregated as follows: 80% on equipment and consumables – purchased from local suppliers 10% food 10% labour
Small-scale mine F	Supply chain: 25% is directly imported (mainly spares) 75% purchased from local suppliers (but 70% are purchased from importers)
Small-scale mine G	Supply chain: 80% purchased from local suppliers 20% directly imported

Source: Fessehaie (2011)

The first tier suppliers, mostly based in the copper-belt, fall into three categories. The first are manufacturing firms producing a wide range of inputs, such as metallurgical, plastic and rubber products, engineering products, paints and foundries. In 2010, there were less than 40 of these firms operating. With the exception of one large steel foundry, they are relatively small sized. The local value added content of these suppliers tends to be substantial, but most of the firms in this category are finding it increasingly difficult to compete with imports from South Africa and China. In 2010, for example, two engineering companies and two foundries were exiting or had just exited the mining supply chain.

The second group consists of medium and large-scale services providers, predominantly subsidiaries of TNC Original Equipment Manufacturers (OEMs), large distributors and agents, and specialised service providers (such as engineering companies, drilling companies, and providers of specialised transport). Value added amongst this set of suppliers is significantly lower than among the manufacturing firms, but some of them operate in skills intensive sectors, such as specialised engineering services. Approximately 100 firms operate in this category. Some agents and distributors provide stockholding and back up services, often developing agreements with sole manufacturers abroad and slowly graduating into sole distributors. There were also low value added services providers, which imported basic products (pharmaceuticals, stationery) or provided basic services (cleaning, gardening).

In addition to these formal sector suppliers (approximately 40 local manufacturing firms and 150 TNC OEM subsidiaries) there is a third, and more numerous, category of very small-scale suppliers, with very low levels of local content. Estimates range from few hundred to 5,000 firms in this category - characterised by low entry and exit barriers – which are widely referred to as 'briefcase businessmen' because they operated 'out of a briefcase'. They engage in small-scale importation of supplies, often securing contracts in an illicit manner and with no value added in after sale services. Often secured orders were later sub-contracted to more established suppliers. After the 2008 copper price crisis, most of the copper mines restructured their supply chains, and eliminated these largely inefficient suppliers, drastically reducing their number.

Although the local acquisition of inputs represents a substantial spend by the mines, this needs some qualification. First, in some cases, the level of outsourcing is illusory, since as in the case of the 'briefcase businessmen', the suppliers are merely importing intermediaries. Second, after the crisis the level of procurement has fallen. Third, the Chinese firm have internalised activities, which other mines outsource. For example, the Chinese mines developed in house engineering services and built a foundry. Fourthly, the Indian mining company, which is the most recent investor, has relatively little experience in the industry and its arms-length, market based supply chain strategy hampers the development of local suppliers.

A key factor leading to the thinning out of the Zambian supply chain was the privatisation of the mines. This dramatically changed the rules of the game. The privatisation of these state owned mines occurred in the context of tariff liberalisation and the collapse in industrial policies. It also occurred in a context of low copper prices and the need to recapitalise the mines. The privatised mines imposed high performance requirements on local suppliers. Moreover, they had previous relationships with global suppliers, hence buyers shifted from local suppliers to cheaper imports, especially from South Africa, but also from Europe, Canada and Australia.

Major changes also took place within their supply chains. Local manufacturers had to compete not only with imports, but also with foreign owned suppliers locating production, or often only distribution facilities in Zambia. Often lacking the necessary technological capabilities and economies of scale of competitors, and no longer protected by high import tariffs, they found it increasingly difficult to compete with the quality and prices of foreign suppliers. Consequently, in the early 2000s, many suppliers who had previously added value to the products they were selling to the mines, exited the mining supply chain, and were replaced by services providers, both Zambian and foreign owned.

Only a fraction of the latter engaged in value added services. Moreover, and as part of a global trend, many first tier OEM suppliers established a direct presence in the copper-belt, in order to tighten control over the quality of the goods and services provided to the mines, and to increase revenues streams from highly profitable after sale services (Table 4.25). This had two implications for local suppliers. First, it cut out local manufacturers as well as agents from the supply links for spares and components. Second, it cut out local engineering firms from maintenance and repair linkages (although demand for these remained high in general). By contrast, before privatisation, foreign exchange shortages encouraged import substitution, which in turn bolstered demand for locally produced spares and components and for repair services.

Table 4.25 Key participants in the copper mining supply chain in Zambia

During nationalisation	Post privatisation
Large number of state owned and privately owned manufacturers (providing specialised mining components, spares and consumables	Importers. A large number of briefcase businessmen (now disappearing), agents and distributors. of components, spares and consumables)
Independent agents and distributors of capital equipment (some locally owned)	OEMs subsidiaries (only distribution and after sale services)
Specialised services providers	Specialised services providers
Some OEMs with manufacturing capabilities, for capital equipment	Privately owned manufacturers, mostly Zambian owned (providing consumables and protective equipment)

Note: In term of the category of firms dominating the supply chain (in numbers)

Source: Interview data in Fessehaie (2011)

The diminishing capability of local suppliers in the context of the rising technological complexity of mining is reflected in the judgements of two sets of buyers – the 'northern/traditional' investors (including South African buyers) and the new emerging country investor from China. These different groups of buyers rate the capabilities of local suppliers differentially (Figure 4.16).

Figure 4.16 Comparative rating of supplier capabilities by northern buyers', Chinese buyers and by the supply chain itself in Zambia

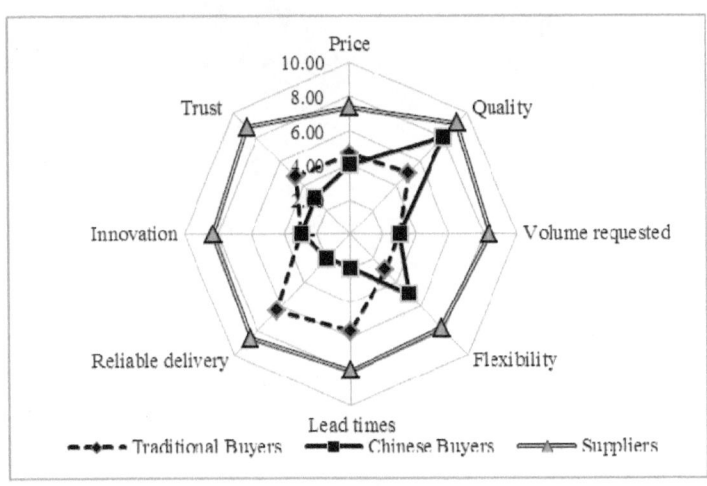

1=poor performance, 10=highest level performance

Source: Fessehaie (2011)

The 'northern' buyers have over the years established relationships with their supply chains, which have led them to identify and work with a relatively stable set of local suppliers. By contrast, the Chinese entrant tend to have more arms-length relationships with suppliers and to have less confidence in their capabilities. The Chinese, and particularly the Indian, mines tend to place more emphasis on price in their negotiations with suppliers. It is notable, and this reflects international experience in environments of immature supply chains, that the suppliers failed to recognise their weaknesses and had a much higher confidence in their capabilities and performance than did the buyers.

We have thus observed a complex pattern of linkage development across a range of countries and sectors. This includes cases where linkage development is long lived and others where linkages are a recent phenomenon. It also includes examples of very thin levels of value added in local supply of inputs and processing of commodity outputs. However, this is not always the case since we have also observed cases of relatively broad and deep linkage development. What explains these different outcomes? Are they driven by sectoral characteristics that result in an inevitable pattern of linkage unfolding or are they also a result of the specific context of development? We will now consider these issues in chapter 5.

Chapter 5
The Contextual Drivers of Linkages

In this chapter, we will focus on a series of contextual drivers that affect the development of linkages into and out of the commodities sector. As we saw in chapter 2, there are an additional series of drivers which are intrinsic to individual sectors and which also have an influence on linkage development. However, our focus in this discussion is on those determinants of linkages, which are subject to influence by the decisions of stakeholders. This is generally not the case for the intrinsic drivers of linkages. We will therefore focus on the contextual drivers:

1. The nature of ownership of lead commodity firms and their suppliers and customers
2. The nature and quality of infrastructure
3. The nature of capabilities, skills and the National System of Innovation
4. Policies and their implementation

In each case, we begin with a brief restatement of the factors (discussed in detail in chapter 2) which we anticipated would determine the impact of each of these drivers on linkage development. We follow this by presenting the results of our fieldwork that explored the impact of these drivers on linkages. As we observed in chapter 3, this evidence is predominantly qualitative in nature and is uneven between sectors and countries. As in chapter 4, unless otherwise stated, the empirical data presented below is drawn from the individual MMCP Discussion Papers, which can be downloaded from http://commodities.open.ac.uk/discussionpapers or www.cssr.uct.ac.za/prism/projects/mmcp.

Ownership as a determinant of linkage development

The firm is a heterogeneous entity and, although each firm is individual with particular competences and business strategies, there are important structural features that influence the behaviour of firms in general, and with regard to linkage development in particular. In our research, we hypothesised that a key differentiating factor in firm behaviour was ownership. In chapter 2, we identified three different ownership attributes, which might have a bearing on linkages. The first of these is whether the firm is locally or foreign owned. A widely held view is that locally owned firms are more deeply embedded in the local economy, have greater familiarity with local suppliers and customers, know their way around the institutional infrastructure and, crucially, that they are more committed to local development than footloose, foreign owned firms are. Second, a subsidiary component of the nationality of ownership is that as a reflection of their particular country of origin, foreign owned firms emanating from different national bases may behave differentially with regard to linkages. Third, beyond the nationality and origin of ownership are a series of firm specific attributes. Individual firms act in very different ways even though they operate in the same industry and the same environment.

The relative importance on linkage development of these three ownership factors – foreign/national, origin of home country and firm specific attributes – will vary with regard to their impact on four different sets of actors in the chain. The first of these are buyers. There is considerable evidence that independent buyers – that is, those that are not linked to lead commodity firms - play a crucial role in the extent and nature of outsourcing in global value chains (Gereffi, 1994; Schmitz and Knorringa, 2000; Kaplinsky and Morris, 2001). The second concerns the ownership character of the lead commodity producing firms, the companies that mine minerals, extract oil and grow the major soft industrial commodities. The third reflects the influence of ownership of suppliers to lead commodity firms and the fourth is the influence of ownership of the users of commodities. The architecture of these ownership specific factors and types of linkage firms is summarised in Figure 5.1.

Figure 5.1 A framework for assessing the impact of ownership on linkages

	Independent Buyers	Lead commodity firms	Backward linkage firms	Forward linkage firms

Local or foreign ownership
Nationality of foreign ownership
Firm specific behaviour

Buyers as a determinant of linkages

The distinctive character of Chinese presence in Africa's resource sector and its impact on linkages surfaces in part as a consequence of the nature of the Chinese final market and the preferences of Chinese buyers. By comparison with the formerly dominant northern final markets, the Chinese market comprises a set of much lower income users. This has implications for the nature of demand and affects linkage development in two important respects – the inter country division of labour and the standards involved in commodity value chains. Both of these linkage impacts are evident in the case of the timber value chain in Gabon.

As was shown in the discussion of the breadth and depth of linkages in chapter 4, Gabon's timber value chain was built on exports to the EU (and predominantly to France). Over the past two decades, French owned timber firms have made large investments in the processing of timber, including in sawmilling, veneer and plywood manufacture. These investments were partly a consequence of their longevity of operations in Gabon, partly because wage costs were higher in France than in Gabon (since timber processing is a relatively labour intensive industry), and partly because some parts of timber processing are polluting. It also reflected the drive by Gabon's Forestry Code to encourage forward linkages from the logging sector.

By 2009, exports to China were as large as those to the EU. However, whereas EU buyers had encouraged an intra-chain division of labour in which the labour intensive and environmentally polluting chain links were undertaken in Gabon (sawn-wood, veneer and plywood), the same is not true for Chinese and Malaysian firms, who are almost wholly focused on log extraction. Their forward linkages were minimal (Table 5.1). It is notable that the nationally owned firms, which were predominantly exporting to China, were similarly reluctant to invest in forward linkages. As a consequence of the speed with which forward linkages were being undermined by this shift in final markets, in early 2011 the government placed a blanket ban on log exports in order to protect timber forward linkage firms.

Table 5.1 Ownership and forward linkages in the Gabon timber sector sub-sector activities and final markets (n = 15)

Ownership / Activity	China				MY		EU			Gabon		
Logging	■	■	■	■	■	■	■	■		■	■	■
Sawn wood	■	■	■	■	■	■		■	■	■	■	■
Veneer		■	■	■		■	■	*	■	■	■	■
Plywood			■	■			■	■		■	■	■
Log export share [a]	70%				70%		38%			90%		
Log export destination [c]	C	C	C	C	C	E	C		C	C	C	C

a share of total log production exported unprocessed
b share of total log production channelled into linked processing sub-sectors
c C=China, E=Europe

Source: Terheggen (2011)

A second characteristic of relatively low per capita incomes in the Chinese final market is that Chinese consumers are far less concerned with producers meeting environmental and sustainability standards than consumers in the European market. This applies both to the standards set by buying firms themselves (reflecting the critical success factors in their final markets) and standards set by governments in the importing countries (Figure 5.2). An associated difference is that Chinese buyers are less discerning about product variety than are EU buyers.

These differences in the requirements of buyers have implications for backward linkages, since there is extensive evidence from the analysis across global value chains (www.globalvaluechains.org) that meeting global process and product standards and the requirements of buyers for particular product characteristics (in this case variety) contributes to the development of dynamic capabilities in producing firms.

It also affects the development of horizontal linkages since the service providers assisting logging and timber processing companies to meet generic standards (such as ISO-8000 and ISO-14000 standards) may potentially also assist firms in non-timber value chains. On the other hand, standards are often a barrier to entry for small-scale and informal sector producers, so that selling into less discerning markets simultaneously also enhances the prospects of linkages into the commodities by a new category of small and medium scale suppliers and users. As we will see below, these final market characteristics are also an important determinant of the behaviour of individual lead firms in a variety of other commodity value chains.

Figure 5.2 European and Chinese buyers' public and private standards in Gabon

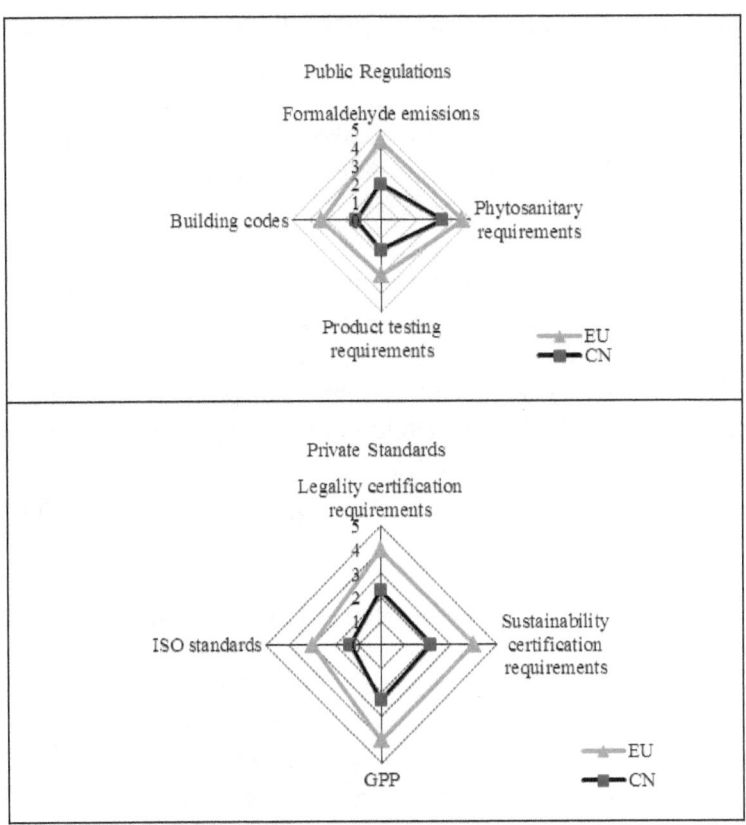

1 = not important, 5 = critically important

GPP=Green public procurement; ISO standards=ISO 14001

Source: Terheggen (2011)

A subsidiary factor arising from this shift in final markets is that there have been a number of occasions when Chinese buyers reneged on contracts or required a readjustment of prices downwards after the timber had been delivered. European buyers have by and large not operated in the same way. This has exacerbated the problems faced by Gabonese firms seeking to establish themselves in the industry.

Ownership of lead commodity firms as a determinant of linkages

With the exception of South Africa, in none of the other seven economies under investigation were there locally owned lead commodity firms with international operations. This has an important bearing on linkages, since firms operating in a global environment have invariably learned to introduce structured programmes of supply chain development as part of their purchasing function and this is an important potential factor inducing linkage development. We would therefore expect these foreign multinationals to have internalised the importance of local sourcing and supply chain development upgrading in their operations in SSA.

However, two factors undermine this policy commitment by TNCs to supply chain development. First, because of lead commodity producers committing themselves globally to long-term, trust intensive relationships with their suppliers, they have adopted a global sourcing follower supply policy (Barnes, Kaplinsky and Morris, 2004). Global sourcing reflects an arrangement whereby core suppliers meet the global needs of the lead firm in the chain. Follower-supply then involves these lead suppliers locating their supply operations in close proximity to the lead purchaser in all its global operations. This motivates local supply, but not by locally owned firms. Second, firms with global operations tend to recruit purchasing managers from abroad. Particularly when these managers are working in remote and hostile environments, they have little feel for local conditions. Typically, they will work on an eight week on, two week off rota. The first week of this involves settling down and the last week preparing for their return home, leaving only a narrow window in which they can develop relations with local suppliers. Moreover, a consequence of the large groupings of expatriates living together in remote sites, where they have little or no knowledge of the local economy, is that there is a culture of residential and recreational segregation. This often leads to an antipathy towards anything local, which translates into scepticism about the abilities of local employees and potential suppliers. Further, many purchasing officers are monitored by their ability to deliver within budget and within agreed time scales. Moving to new suppliers is a move into the unknown and there are potentially negative effects on performance.

An example drawn from the Tanzanian gold mining sector exemplifies these problems. One TNC has declared a strong global commitment to local sourcing and an equally strong commitment to this in their Tanzanian operations. However, the reality is rather different, due to the 'sociology of purchasing' rather than to duplicitous statements by senior management. Local suppliers find that the purchasing systems that are used and mandated by Head Office are too cumbersome. There is a great deal of paperwork and the timescales allocated to supply once a purchase order has been issued are unrealistic. Typically, payment of invoices takes over 60 days, which is often too large a financial exposure for local suppliers to cope with, particularly when they are small-scale firms and inflation is high. Moreover, many potential suppliers reported that they had experienced corrupt practices in the purchasing department of this mine (which, in 2011 had to close for some months due to its own staff stealing its fuel supplies!).

By contrast, the TNC oil companies in Nigeria have been operating for some time and have been subject to intense and prolonged criticism in their home countries on the lack of positive economic spill over in their Nigerian operations. Reflecting the political pressures which have built up to promote linkages, - both in the host and home countries - many of the lead foreign owned mining companies have instituted local procurement as part of their Corporate Social Responsibility (CSR) programmes. Most often, these CSR programmes promote linkages with suppliers in close proximity to their mining operations, often sourcing from community organisations rather than from formal sector commercial firms. These external pressures to promote CSR are often supported by domestic pressures.

In 2002, the Ghana Mining Council mandated all mining companies to adopt CSR programmes to assist their host communities (Tememg and Abew 2009). The resulting CSR initiatives have not only improved mining company host community relationships, but more importantly, have provided critically needed social and physical infrastructure which otherwise lay within the mandate of local and central (state) governments. CSR programmes promoting local supply have also been introduced by mining companies in Tanzania, where it is CSR rather than efficient mine operations that seem to be driving what limited local sourcing exists in supporting the on-going operations of the mines, particularly that involving near sourcing.

By contrast, in Angola, it is the national ownership of the lead oil-extracting firm, which explains the growth of backward linkages. Sonangol, the state owned company that dominates the oil sector, is explicitly tasked with promoting backward linkages. As a consequence of this commitment, it initiated, and is a 50-50 partner in, a joint venture supplying control lines to the sub-sea oil sector, an enterprise that is beginning to go beyond assembly to include the transformation of materials into the final product.

The origin of foreign ownership as a determinant of linkages

There are clear indications that the origin of foreign ownership has an important bearing on linkages, particularly in the case of the Chinese, Indian and Brazilian firms who have become recent investors in Africa's resource sectors.

The ownership structure of the Zambia mining sector is diversified and includes northern (Canadian, Australian and European), South African, Chinese and Indian mining companies. The national origins of these companies helped to shape value chain governance and, in so doing, affect the incorporation of local suppliers in these chains in three ways. First, China's policy towards outward FDI – the 'going out policy' – shaped the strategic behaviour of Chinese mining firms, which tended to be less risk averse and more countercyclical in nature than their northern counterparts (Buckley et al., 2007; Cheung and Qian, 2009; Davies, 2009; Yao et al., 2010; Ren et al., 2010). Thus, while global FDI flows fell in 2008 and 2009 and northern FDI in Zambia's mining sector stagnated, the Chinese mining companies in Zambia responded counter cyclically. Backed by soft budget constraints and strategic intent to command access to resources, not only did Chinese mining firms expand their presence in Zambia, but at the same time, and backed by Chinese aid, a large industrial park was established as a future base for suppliers into the mines. During the same period, the northern (but not the South African) owned mines sought to cut costs rather than to increase capacity and, in the process, rationalised and thinned out their supply chains.

A second indicator of home country ownership determinants was that whilst the traditional northern mining houses worked independently of government and saw supply chain development as part of their corporate agenda, Chinese buyers relied heavily on government-to-government intermediation to promote linkages. This is leading to the aforementioned Chinese aid funded $800 million industrial zone designed in part to promote supplier development to the mines.

Third, Chinese, Indian and northern mines differed in the governance of their supply chains. In general, northern and South African buyers actively sought to outsource activities outside of their core competences. By contrast, Chinese and Indian buyers were more reluctant to do so. When they did, and when local firms did not meet their expectations, instead of promoting capabilities in their suppliers, they tended to bring back and internalise these supplies. Partly as a consequence (or perhaps also as a partial cause) of this greater self-reliance, Chinese and Indian buyers were less embedded in the local business community (Table 5.2). What this meant was that whereas the entry barriers were high for suppliers participating in value chains governed by the traditional northern TNCs, once they were in these chains, contact was relatively frequent and the support provided by the buyers helped the suppliers to upgrade their capabilities. By contrast, entry barriers for local suppliers into Chinese and Indian firm governed value chains were low, but exit was frequent and minimal support was provided to suppliers. There was also a difference in the behaviour of Chinese and Indian firms, with the former more likely to promote long-term relations with suppliers and to build relations of trust. The Indian mining house was disproportionately focused on the price of its inputs rather than on quality.

Table 5.2 Selection of new entrants in the copper industry supply chain in Zambia

Supply chain	Main selection criteria	Secondary selection criteria	Entry barriers for suppliers
northern buyers	Historical relationships	Increasing reliance on auditing to cut briefcase businessmen. Selective auditing.	High entry barriers for new entrants
Chinese buyers	Extensive auditing	Trust built with considerable effort	Low entry barriers for new entrants
Indian buyers	Ensure a large suppliers' base	Increase competition between new and regular suppliers	Low entry barriers for new entrants

Source: Fessehaie (2011)

In summary, therefore, we can observe a spectrum of supplier development strategies in the Zambian copper industry. At the one end are the northern based global mining houses with relatively well established and advanced programmes developing long-term, trust intensive relationships with suppliers. At the other end of the spectrum is the Indian mining firm which focuses on short term, arms-length relationships in which price is the overwhelming single critical success factor. Somewhere between these two extremes are the Chinese investors, probably closer to the Indian firm end of the spectrum than to the northern firm end.

The distinctive nature of Chinese firms operating in Africa as procurers of local supplies is also evident in Angola. Here, too, a determining factor was the mode of entry of Chinese firms, linked closely to China's 'going out policy' and its strategic search for access to Africa's resources. Between 2004 and 2007, China's Exim Bank extended a total of $4.5 billion in oil backed credit lines to the Angolan government. In July 2010, the Angolan Minister of Finance was finalising a further $6 billion from China Exim Bank to assist with Angola's reconstruction. Most of the Chinese investors that gained access to the large-scale China Exim Bank contracts in Angola were SOEs or large 'national champion' private companies. The key determinant of their sourcing behaviour, therefore, was not private or state ownership, but whether they operated through China's Exim Bank credit line. These credit lines tied a minimum of 50 per cent of procurement of the total contract value of the project to imports from China for loans obtained outside the realm of the China-Angola agreement, and 15 per cent of Chinese procurement for loans within the terms of the agreement. In reality, the degree of imports from China was considerably higher than the minimum of 15 per cent. Local purchases of Chinese firms involved in the construction of infrastructure were limited to basic materials such as cement, bitumen, stone and sand, and occasionally paint, corrugated iron and timber. In many cases – for example, cement - many of these basic inputs were imported from China. One Chinese SOE reported that its local purchases were less than five per cent of its annual spend and these were all very basic, low value products (such as gravel and charcoal). Many of these large-scale Chinese investors also made extensive use of semi-skilled migrant labour from China.

Where there were backward linkages in Angola, these predominantly involved incoming Chinese suppliers. This happened either through vertical integration or outsourcing. Some Chinese companies established their own factories to manufacture bricks and building inputs such as wooden doorframes, windows and balustrades, in a few limited cases using locally sourced inputs such as clay and timber. Chinese brick making machinery has often replaced Angolan equipment. Locals only supplied emergency shortfalls. This also extended to basic consumables such as vegetables. Much of this outsourcing was to smaller private Chinese companies in Angola, which distributed Chinese products and services required for the construction industry. A similar story can be told with regard to Chinese investments in Sudan's oil sector, where backward linkages have been developed, but almost exclusively to incoming Chinese owned suppliers, of whom there were 97 in 2010 employing 4700 workers (Suliman and Badawi 2010).

However, not all Chinese firms act in the same manner in respect of linkage development and the operations of large SOEs and 'national champion' firms was distinctively different from small and medium sized Chinese firms. This is evidenced in the case of Angola where Chinese SOEs tended to be more risk averse than private companies and entered the Angolan market under China Exim Bank financing. They avoided pursuing other projects funded by the Angolan government or international donors. By contrast, private Chinese companies did not receive such support from their government. They ventured into Africa because of high domestic competition or because they saw market opportunities and were, as a rule, much more likely to draw on local suppliers than their large sized government backed SOE counterparts. This reflects a broader pattern of Chinese FDI in SSA in which Chinese private owned Small and Medium Enterprises (SMEs) obtained very little support from the Chinese government, from Exim bank funds or from local embassies and had much closer links with the local economy than their SOE counterparts (Gu, 2009; Kaplinsky and Morris, 2009, Mohan, 2011).

There is thus evidence across a range of countries (Angola, Gabon, Zambia and Sudan) and sectors (construction, copper. timber and oil) that China's growing presence in Africa's resource sector has considerable implications for both backward and forward linkages. Chinese firms – particularly, but not exclusively the large SOEs operating under the aegis of Exim Bank 'aid' (the so called 'Angola mode') – seem to operate with a higher degree of internalisation than do the northern firms which have historically dominated the commodities sector in Africa. On the forward linkage side, the similarity of labour costs in China and Africa (at least by comparison between Africa and Europe) and the relative insensitivity of Chinese buyers to low environmental and ethical standards, has also meant that forward linkages have been lower than those associated with northern firms operating in Africa's resource sector.

However, it is an open question whether these differences reflect the recent vintage of Chinese investment, or are a consequence of the mode of financing of Chinese firms and the nature of the Chinese final market. To the extent that the sourcing behaviour of Chinese firms reflects their lack of experience rather than factors intrinsic to Chinese political economy, then there might be expectations that the behaviour of Chinese firms with regard to both forward and backward linkages will become increasingly similar to that of their northern competitors. There is evidence that some degree of convergence is indeed occurring. In Zambia, the Chinese supply chain was becoming more quality driven for critical supply inputs. In this, it was becoming more similar to the northern and South African supply chains. A Chinese copper mining company also announced in 2010 that a suppliers development programme would be launched for a newly acquired mine. In Angola, private Chinese companies are increasingly sourcing inputs and labour locally. Private firms are driven by profit maximisation and, as the cost of importing labour and goods from China has increased, they have responded by broadening their supply base to local labour and firms. It is however too early to conclude that the reality of operating in Africa's resource sector will lead to a closer degree of convergence between Chinese and northern firms. Many of the factors driving these differences – the mode of firm financing, nature of final markets, the differences in wage costs, sensitivity to environmental standards and to calls for CSR programmes – will continue to play a role in the determination of both backward and forward linkages for some years to come.

Firm specific attributes and their impact on linkages

When individual firms shape whole industries or are major participants in an industry, they may play a disproportionate role in the development of linkages. The capacity of a firm to shape an industry is evident in the case of diamonds, where De Beers has for many decades coordinated a cartel limiting the supplies of diamonds onto the market. For much of this period, De Beers acted as a playmaker in the global diamond value chain, controlling upstream linkages through its command over the downstream segments of the chain. This gave it the capacity to shape the final demand for diamonds and, in so doing, to determine the capabilities required by the cutting and polishing firms beneficiating diamonds and thereby to determine the location of forward linkage firms.

The irony of De Beers command over the global diamond industry is that it has now itself become the tool of another party controlling access to diamonds. Now it is the Botswana government rather than De Beers, which actively controls the major source of high quality and low cost global diamond supply. It has used this power to force a joint venture on De Beers

(Debswana) and to use this to begin a process of broadening and deepening of forward linkages in Botswana.

Although not all industries are dominated by a single firm as is the case of diamonds, there are other cases where individual firms have distinctive strategies which shape the structure of value chains, hence the degree of linkages, in particular contexts. An example of this is the gold industry in Tanzania and the DRC. In earlier discussion, we showed how a verbal commitment by a large mining firm in Tanzania to increase backward linkages had little content in reality. By contrast, a Canadian firm, BANRO, which is building the first of four planned mines in neighbouring DRC, appears to have taken a much more thorough and proactive approach towards increasing backward linkages. Before mining operations start, BANRO is assessing and enhancing the capacity of local and regional suppliers to provide inputs into the mine. Their procurement officers are engaging with local suppliers and have, for example, travelled to each of the regional urban areas to determine the availability and quality of products that they will require during the operational cycle of the mining operation. Thus 100 per cent of the fresh produce used to feed its mine staff will be obtained from local producers in south Kivu Province, which is not the case in the adjacent Tanzanian gold mines despite their decade long operating history. There are additional regional linkage outcomes to this firm specific behaviour in the DRC. During the construction phase, the main contractor was a South African firm and therefore there have been significant regional linkage spillovers. In Tanzania, the major contractors were outside of Africa and most of the linkages were strengthened in Australia, Europe and North America.

Firm specific differences on sourcing are also evident within the Tanzanian gold mining industry. The Golden Pride Mine contracts the drilling, blasting, loading and hauling function to a third party, Caspian (Tanzania) Limited. The decision to contract out the drilling, blasting, loading and hauling services was driven by the need to reduce the perceived 'burden' of heavy investments in earth moving equipment. In contracting out these functions to a third party the mine has however retained the core function of determining the drilling sites and drilling techniques and patterns as dictated by ore geology. By contrast a second mining firm retained the bulk of drilling and blasting in-house, arguing that there is little capacity in the Tanzanian economy to draw on, despite Golden Pride's demonstrable success in this regard. A third mining firm adopted a case-by-case approach to its drilling, blasting, loading and hauling operations, as it does routinely in its global mining ventures.

In Angola's offshore oil sector, oil-producing companies tend to source from global suppliers through Engineering, Procurement, Construction and Installation (EPCI) turnkey contracts. By outsourcing the entire supply to sub-sea production systems contractors, oil companies reduce transaction costs and the risks associated with investing in asset specific technologies. As a consequence, it is customary for flow lines and control lines to be subcontracted to global sub-sea production systems contractors. This has limited market access for independent and domestically based flow lines and control lines manufacturers. With Angolan local content policy assigning preference for joint venture companies, a manufacturer of control lines, which in the past had been locked out of the Angolan market, grasped the opportunity and entered into a joint venture with Sonangol, the Angolan State National Oil Company. As one of its senior management observed

> *Local content for us is a legal motivation. Why [is this firm in a] joint venture with Sonangol? Without it, it was hard to have contracts. That is why we chose to do joint venture and enter the umbilical cable [control lines] manufacturing in Angola... [Previous to this joint venture], [w]e had the experience of bidding for tenders but not winning not because we lacked in any technical requirement but because we did not have the local content advantage... (Teka 2011: 39)*

In Ghana, Newmont appointed dedicated staff within the Ahafo mine procurement department with the task of maximising local sourcing of goods and services. It entered into an agreement with the community setting targets for local employment over an agreed timescale (Prescott, 2009). Newmont staff identified capacity gaps in local suppliers and these are addressed within the joint Newmont–IFC Ahafo Linkages Program (ALP). In 2009, 50 local companies received over $4 million worth of contracts, representing a 200 per cent increase between 2006 and 2007, and more than 200 businesses were registered for the mentoring program. Newmont also developed local capabilities to control erosion during mine rehabilitation. Rather than importing non-biodegradable plastic sheeting from China, Newmont assisted local women's cooperatives to produce jute mats. This resulted in a reduction in long-term costs of supply, creating sustainable income generating activities and improved environmental management (as the bark used for the mats was a pest for local farmers and the materials used are biodegradable).

In Nigeria, a survey of the lead oil-producing firms showed significant commitment to local sourcing and supply chain development. 42 per cent of the oil firms claim that between 50-75 per cent of their share of local procurement of goods and services is sourced from local firms, whilst one third claims that three quarters of their share is sourced locally. In terms of assisting these firms in their supply chain, 75 per cent of the oil firms indicated that they have internalised supply development strategies for local firms in their supply chains. The same 75 per cent also claim to provide assistance to suppliers in meeting up with standards. However, what are the ownership specific characteristics of these locally based suppliers?

Almost 80 per cent of the suppliers in the Nigerian oil services sector are nationally owned, a further six per cent were joint ventures with foreign firms and only 16 per cent were foreign owned (Table 5.3). Two sub-sectors - fabrication and construction, and well construction and completion - had the highest degrees of national ownership, mostly established before the 1990s. Control systems and ICT showed the largest presence of multinationals. Very few of the national suppliers were listed – in general, they were small - and almost all the major owners had university degrees. Hence, even though the Nigerian legislation on local content does not specify local ownership, *de facto* most of the suppliers in these sub-sectors are owned by local entrepreneurs.

Table 5.3 Ownership characteristics of oil service suppliers in Nigeria

Characteristics	Control system & ICT	Fabrication & construction	Well construction & completion	Other sector	Total
Ownership Status					
nationals only	84.2	86.4	70.6	100	78.8
multinational	21.1	9.1	17.6	-	15
joint ventures	-	4.5	11.8	-	6.3
Year Of Registration					
	-	4.5	17.6	-	8.80
1970 - 1980	21.1	31.8	14.7	40	22.5
1981 - 1990	5.8	18.2	8.8	20	13.8
1991 - 2000	36.8	18.2	26.5	20	26.3
2001 till date	26.3	27.3	32.4	20	28.8
not indicated					
Company Listed					
yes	21.1	13.6	17.6	-	16.3
No	78.9	86.4	82.4	100	83.8
Educational Status of Major Owner					
none	-	-	-	-	-
secondary (O/A levels)	-	9.1	-	-	2.5
Diploma	15.8	9.1	5.9	-	8.75
Degrees	84.2	81.8	94.1	100	88.8

Source: Oyejide and Adewuyi (2011)

Infrastructure as a determinant of linkage development

Infrastructure can take various forms. It can be 'hard', as in road and rail transport, utilities (energy and water) and telecommunication networks. In each of these cases, the effectiveness of infrastructure development is a function of availability, reliability, quality of provision and the cost to the user. However, there is also a compendium of 'soft' infrastructure. This reflects the efficiency and cost of the administrative and regulatory regime which supports the productive sector and which has a determining impact on chain logistics, speeding up and reducing the costs of transactions between lead firms and their tiers of suppliers and customers in both the domestic and external economy. The efficiency of infrastructure bounds all economic activity, including the capacity of domestic suppliers and users to link effectively with lead commodity producers.

As we saw in chapter 2, two important sets of factors determine the role played by infrastructure in the development of linkages into and out of the commodities sector. First, the nature of the commodity has a significant impact on the development of infrastructure. Some infrastructure is specific to a particular commodity and has very low potential for positive spill-overs, which might facilitate the growth of backward, forward or horizontal linkages. This is, for example, the case with regard to oil pipelines, which are used in the export of oil and which cannot be used by other links in the chain. By contrast, commodities produced and exported in bulk and in great volumes (such as coal, copper or iron ore) require large-scale transport infrastructure to move their mined outputs. For example the TanZam railway line between Zambia's landlocked copper-belt and the port of Dar es Salaam in Tanzania which was built in the 1970s and the new rail corridor under construction to link the coal producing areas of the Mozambique Zambezi Valley to the coast, have the potential to meet the needs of multiple users outside of the mining sector.

Second, by its nature, infrastructure is a public good. For example, a road can be utilised by many different consumers. This makes it difficult – although not always impossible – for investors in infrastructure to appropriate the fruits of their investments. Another public good characteristic of infrastructure is that there are network effects. That is, to be delivered at low unit cost, infrastructure requires many users to spread the costs of network construction.

Finally, in many cases infrastructure requires large sums of investment, putting such investments beyond the reach of an individual investor, or even often groups of investors. For all of these reasons, it is common for infrastructure to be provided by governments rather than by individual investors. A complicating factor is that when infrastructure spans national boundaries, this requires a decision making and distributive arrangement involving at least two - and often more than two - national governments and in many cases also, a number of foreign donors.

In discussing the role played by infrastructure on linkage development, we will begin by considering the oil sector

(Angola and Nigeria). This is a sector that is often seen as a quintessential enclave activity, wholly dedicated to commodity exports and with few externalities to the surrounding economy. Also, by holding the commodity constant, it serves to explore the importance of country specific factors and the age of the commodity sector. We follow this with a discussion of the role played by infrastructure in Zambia, Mozambique and Gabon where in each case high volume commodity exports have spurred the development of infrastructure with high externalities for other sectors. We conclude with a discussion of diamonds in Botswana and gold in Ghana and Tanzania. In these instances, there are asymmetrical infrastructure needs between inputs (large and often bulky volumes of imports, but which can also meet the needs of other sectors) and outputs (low volume and high value exports with few spill-overs to other sectors). In addition, holding the commodity constant between two economies (gold in Ghana and Tanzania) provides further insights on country and time specific determinants of linkage development.

Oil: enclave infrastructure with different linkage outcomes

The oil industries in Angola and Nigeria are classic cases of enclave infrastructural development but with very different linkage outcomes. In both countries the oil firms' required the construction of purpose built terminals to bulk load and export oil from offshore production wells. This reflects the commodity specific needs of their operations. However, the oil operators also require a range of infrastructural inputs, which are generic to many of their domestic suppliers and customers, such as power, water and communications technologies. How has this second set of infrastructures affected linkage development in these two economies? In both countries the poor development of national infrastructure - which in other contexts (such as oil development in the north Sea) oil producers could assume reliable local supply – has led the lead oil firms to create insulated oil terminals in which they invested directly in the supply of key infrastructural inputs, including transport, power and water. However, there are major differences between the two countries in infrastructure provision in the wider economy and this has had an important bearing on linkage development.

Angola's post-independence infrastructural inheritance was severely debilitated by three decades of conflict. Eighty per cent of Angola's transport infrastructure was not operational in 2009 (Business Monitor International, 2009:6). The World Bank, in its 2010 Logistics Performance Index ranked Angola as 142nd out of 155 countries (Arvis et al, 2010). Customs, Infrastructure and Logistics Quality and Competence were the worst three performing indicators. Business Monitor International (2009) placed Angola at the bottom of its ranking of infrastructure in SSA. Only 10.4 per cent of Angola's roads are paved although rapid on-going road construction by Chinese firms will result in a much higher proportion (24 per cent) in the near future (MOFCOM, 2010).

Given this parlous state of hard infrastructure, the firms involved in the supply of control lines and flow lines in Angola leased premises in one of the eight major oil terminals within an industrial park located along the Kwanza Basin in Lobito where the country's major offshore blocks are located. In contrast, local second and third tier SMEs outside the terminal had to face the challenges posed by poor and unstable electricity and water supply, inefficient customs services and very limited access to financial and ICT services. This severely hampered their ability to develop supply linkages to the oil companies. For similar reasons, in the Angolan construction industry the large Chinese companies provided their own water and electricity, whereas the smaller Chinese and national construction firms suffered from lack of access to reliable and low costs access to these key inputs.

In Nigeria, although the general state of infrastructure was poor by comparison to North Sea producers and suppliers, the lead oil companies in the oil enclaves found infrastructure generally adequate to their needs (Table 5.4). Telecoms and water utilities were rated as adequate or very adequate and transportation received a mean score from respondents of 4.5 (on a scale of 1 to 5). By comparison with Angola, this reduced the need for these lead firms to invest directly in the supply of non-oil-line-infrastructure. The exception was power and internet functioning which remained inadequate even for the lead oil producers.

However, their supplier firms operating outside the oil terminals were much less satisfied with the quality and cost of infrastructure provision, particularly in regard to transport, energy and internet services (Table 5.5). They considered that public supply of energy was the largest inhibiting factor, with 84 per cent of suppliers indicating that provision was either inadequate or very inadequate. Outside of the oil terminals, the provision of electricity is so poor and unreliable in Nigeria that most industrial firms provide their own power to run operations through petrol fed generators. This is a major cost constraint on their ability to be competitive, since the unit cost of private power is roughly 10 times that of the cost of public electricity. Further, suppliers also considered that there had been a deterioration in public power and water supplies. On the other hand, they reported that telephone/communication, internet services and transportation were improving.

Table 5.4 Infrastructure performance assessment by oil firms in Nigeria

	Very adequate	Adequate	Can't say	Inadequate	Very inadequate	Mean
Public power supply/electricity	8.3	16.7	-	58.3	16.7	2.42
Water supply	16.7	58.3	-	8.3	16.7	3.41
Telephone and communication	16.7	75	-	-	8.3	3.92
Internet services	16.7	33.3	-	50	-	3.17
Transportation	58.3	33.3	8.3	-	-	4.50

Note: Very inadequate =1, inadequate = 2, can't say = 3, adequate = 4, very adequate = 5.

Source: Oyejide and Adewuyi (2011)

142 One Thing Leads to Another

Table 5.5 Infrastructure performance assessment by suppliers to oil industry in Nigeria

	Very adequate	Adequate	Can't say	Inadequate	Very inadequate	Mean
Public power supply/electricity	1.3	5	10	41.3	42.5	1.81
Water supply	10	40	8.8	18.8	22.5	2.96
Telephone and communication	10	57.5	8.8	13.8	10	3.44
Internet services	8.8	55	6.3	21.3	8.8	3.34
Transportation	8.8	46.3	11.3	25	8.8	3.21

Note: Very inadequate =1, inadequate = 2, can't say = 3, adequate = 4, very adequate = 5.

Source: Oyejide and Adewuyi (2011)

This differential Nigerian experience between lead commodity producers and their suppliers is reflected in the views of oil firms and suppliers on their satisfaction with infrastructure provision. The former are systematically less negative about the quality and cost of infrastructure, with the exception of access to the internet (Figure 5.3).

Figure 5.3 Perception of Infrastructure performance in Nigeria

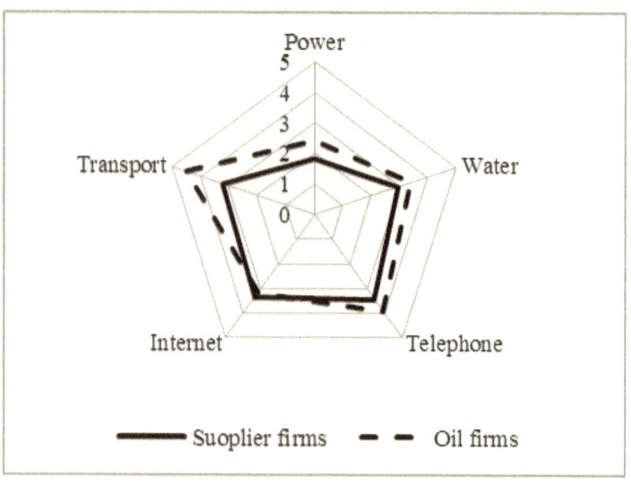

1= very inadequate, 5 = very adequate

Source: Oyejide and Adewuyi (2011)

Corridor infrastructure in Zambia, Mozambique and Gabon

In Zambia, Mozambique and Gabon, the need to transport high volumes of bulky commodities led to the development of roads and rail, in the first two countries, and water based transportation, in the latter. Whilst in Gabon infrastructure is poor and seriously inadequate in supporting linkage development, in Zambia relatively well-developed transport infrastructure has led to a level of industrial agglomeration facilitating near sourcing by lead copper firms. Mozambique represents a different case of prospective infrastructural development. It is implementing an integrated plan to coordinate mining investment, infrastructural development and promotion of businesses and agricultural activities in northern Mozambique through the Zambezi Valley corridor. In each of these cases, meeting the needs of the lead commodity producing firms also provides infrastructure for firms and farmers in other sectors.

Policy and public provision have been crucial in the development of infrastructure in Zambia. This public provision has a long history. Historically, copper mining in Zambia spurred the development of a rail line from South Africa through Zimbabwe to the copper-belt and through to the Congo and to Lobito Bay in Angola. In the 1970s, China funded the construction of the TanZam railway linking the copper-belt to Dar es Salaam. At that time, and for many years after, this was China's largest external aid project. Further, to meet the demand of the mining industry for low cost electrical power and energy, the Kariba Dam and the hydroelectric power stations on the Zambezi and Kafue Rivers were developed. However, the decline of the mining sector between the early 1980s and 2005 negatively affected the maintenance and expansion of infrastructure. This has now become a comparatively high cost inputs for producers. Transport prices for the route from Lusaka to Durban in South Africa were $6 per tonne/km in 2007, against $5 in China and $3.50 in Brazil (World Bank, 2009). Three factors help to explain these high transport costs. First, there are problems with the soft infrastructural component of transport links, with particularly long border crossing delays on the Chirundu Border with Zimbabwe. It was estimated that a 20 per cent reduction in border crossing time would reduce transport prices to the importers by 10-15 per cent. Second, fuel prices are high - almost 80 per cent of the fuel prices in Zambia were constituted by taxes and levies, which meant that 40 per cent of total transport costs were linked to taxation (World Bank, 2009). Third, the quality of physical infrastructure was poor due to lack of investment. This is particularly evident on the TanZam railway, which provides a highly erratic and costly route to the East Coast shipping route.

This poor infrastructure presents a major problem not just to the lead copper producing firms but also to their suppliers and customers. To address this issue, the Zambia government, together with other neighbouring countries, launched the North-South Corridor Programme in April 2009. This ambitious programme seeks to reduce transport costs on two main routes, from the copper-belt to Dar es Salaam, and from the copper-belt to Durban. This is to be achieved by rehabilitating both hard physical infrastructure and soft infrastructure (reducing cross border clearing procedures, harmonising transit and transport regulations, and simplifying administrative requirements). The programme aims to involve the expanding extractive industries in Zambia and the DRC as key drivers (North-South Corridor International Financing Conference, 2009) and as a way of spreading the heavy costs of investment across multiple users. The first concrete step to implement the programme took place in 2009, when Zambia adopted the One Stop Border Post Act, the legal foundation for the joint administration of the Zambia-Zimbabwe border post.

In terms of corridor development policy, Mozambique is far ahead of any other country in the region. Based on its positive experience with the Mozal gas facility, Mozambique sees the coal mining operations in and around Tete in north-west Mozambique as an opportunity to combine a complementary set of resources – minerals and inexpensive power - into a range of possible industrial development projects. Mozambique wants to avoid 'enclave' development of coal mining operations, and maximise backward, forward and horizontal linkages, by promoting 'feeder' infrastructure servicing the agricultural, forestry and agro-processing sectors. Three originally distinct but currently integrated development corridor initiatives are being pursued: the

Beira, Nacala and Sena-Zambezi Spatial Development Initiatives (SDIs).

In light of these objectives, the Mozambique government is actively pursuing efficient transport solutions, which explicitly aim to meet the needs not only of the lead commodity firms, but also those of their suppliers and users, and of other sectors. This investment programme is taking place in partnership with the private sector. The key investor in the Moatize coal concession, the Brazilian firm CVRD (Vale), has been increasingly involved in the development and management of the railway required for the transport of bulk volumes of coal. (Vale is not only the world's largest mining company, but has extensive presence in the infrastructure sector). In order to facilitate this partnership, the government has reformed its regulatory framework, terminated an unsatisfactory railway concession, made resources available for co-funding, and facilitated coordination between mining companies. This decisive approach is unusual in SSA and reflects a high-level of political commitment.

In the timber sector, there are three ways (road, rail, water) of transporting logs and wood products, each with different unit costs. Gabon has the poorest road network density of the Central African region (around 30 metre per square kilometre). Road infrastructure is not only limited in length but is also of poor quality and poorly maintained. The Trans-Gabonese railway is limited, consisting of a single track running from Franceville (in the southeast of Gabon) to the industrial centre Owendo in Libreville (the capital located in the northwest of the country). The river is the cheapest mode for the plantation owners but provides a limited alternative, since it is only suitable for the transport of a limited variety of species, notably Okoumé logs; other hardwood do not float well. Moreover, capacity in the harbour is constrained. As a consequence, of all of these deficiencies, the costs for domestic transportation of logs and wood products made up a substantial part of total production costs varying between 14 per cent and 25 per cent. However, this water borne transport infrastructure is not only unsuitable for non-Okoumé logs, but is also of little use to linkage firms.

The Gabonese government is not geared to counter these infrastructural obstacles to commodity exploitation and (especially) for linkages from the commodities sector. The ministries responsible for infrastructure have mandates which are restricted to meeting the needs of lead commodity firms alone, such as SEPBG (Société des Parcs à Bois du Gabon) which handles log and wood product transportation at the port, and COMILOG (a mining company), which acquired the rights to manage the Trans-Gabon railway. Moreover, most of these state bodies are inefficient and notoriously corrupt. Despite the termination of state owned monopolies in the utilities sector, the new privately owned monopolies such as the energy and water company SEEG, do not appear to operate with much greater levels of efficiency than the public monopolies which they replaced.

Gold and diamonds

Tanzania and Ghana are countries where gold extraction is associated with very different outcomes on linkages and patterns of infrastructural development. In Ghana, backward linkages are relatively well-developed and public provision of infrastructure is generally good. By contrast, in Tanzania, linkages are weak and the quality of infrastructure is poor. However, this is not a simple story of government commitment to infrastructure since gold production in Tanzania is barely a decade old by comparison with almost a century's large-scale gold production in Ghana.

In Ghana, resource rich areas such as gold mining areas have continued to receive government investments to develop their infrastructure. The success of the mining sector in recent decades is widely attributed in part to the huge investments in infrastructure in mining areas made by government with support from the World Bank/IMF and other international donors (Owusu 2001; Aryeetey et al. 2009). The enhanced infrastructure in gold mining areas, particularly that of the road network and ICT, also broadened and deepened consumption (final demand) linkages, and has supported the physical connectivity that allow backward linkages to operate. Due to improved infrastructure, notably air transport, roads, and power supplies, many gold mining support companies have now located their headquarters in Accra and many of the mining companies and lead OEMs have located regional offices in Ghana. The benefits, such a situation produces in terms of job creation, demand for services/goods and other benefits to the national economy and a region such as Accra where no gold is mined, is apparent.

In Tanzania, the gold mines are located in remote areas with very weak infrastructure. This places a particular burden on the input side, where machinery and equipment is often both costly and bulky and where extensive supplies of energy are required to operate equipment. By contrast, gold is a high value low volume product and is easily transported by air to South Africa (flown directly from the mine sites) for beneficiation. The very poor quality and high cost of the transport infrastructure to the mines severely constrains the operations of the lead mining firms. However, this is not only a problem of hard infrastructure. In 2011 (when one of the largest mines had to close down operations for some months since much of its stored fuel had been stolen by its own staff!) mining companies also suffered severely from long delays in customs clearance, often accompanied by high levels of corruption. The weak provision and in many cases the non-provision of publicly supplied energy and other utilities has also meant that the mining houses have to provide these services themselves. This not only involves a high pecuniary cost, but also a high cost in terms of managerial attention. Mining companies consistently complained about the negative impact of inadequate, unreliable and poor infrastructure on their operating cost.

All of these factors were of compounded significance for suppliers to the mining industry. Unlike the large foreign owned lead commodity firms that had access to large supplies of capital, many of the locally owned supplying firms, and potential suppliers, lacked the resources and the scale to provide for their own infrastructure needs. There is no doubt that weak infrastructure is one of the major factors holding back backward linkages in the Tanzanian gold mining sector. Partly because of this weak infrastructure, the Tanzanian gold mining industry remains a largely enclave activity, in significant contrast to Ghana where both the breadth and depth of linkages are growing.

In response to these widely acknowledged problems of poor infrastructure in Tanzania and the wider region, the Central Development Corridor (CDC) is designed to connect the Tanzanian maritime Port of Dar es Salaam with its Great Lakes hinterland. The objective is not only to meet the needs of the minerals sectors, but also to assist agriculture, fisheries and tourism sectors. By providing transport and energy infrastructure, these sectors would help the region's growth and diversification processes. However, despite this ambitious intent, unlike Mozambique, Tanzania never mainstreamed the CDC vision into effective policies and effective policy delivery. Moreover, there have been enormous backlogs in implementation, lack of funding from the government and its donors, institutional bottlenecks and a marked failure to coordinate activities between neighbouring countries.

By contrast, with this dismal story of infrastructural development in Tanzania, the Botswana diamond beneficiation industry presents a much more heartening story. Like Tanzania, the commodity is a low volume high value product and presents relatively few transport challenges, other than with regard to security. However, whereas gold is flown out directly from the Tanzanian mines to external customers, in Botswana some of the output is also processed locally, and the remainder is flown out of the country's capital city, Gaborone. In order to guarantee the security of these high value commodity exports, a purpose built, high security and exclusive road was constructed, connecting the diamond hub with the airport.

Most of the forward linkage diamond beneficiating firms are located in the Gaborone area and are able to draw on a well-developed national transport, power and telecommunications infrastructure. Outside of Gaborone, some sets of infrastructure are less well-developed and this creates problems for some linkage firms. For example, water supply in Serowe is less reliable and this has negatively affected the diamond beneficiating firm located there. Moreover, a significant amount of Botswana's electricity – up to 40 per cent at times – has been imported from South Africa and other neighbouring countries. This has opened Botswana to insecurity of supply given the power supply shortages that South Africa's electricity utility has experienced in recent years. Since cutting and polishing equipment and technology is dependent on electricity, most firms have installed backup generators. Internet has been unreliable in Botswana and slows during peak times. However, the government is installing fibre optic cables and expects telecommunication speed and prices to improve in the short term.

Capabilities: skills and the National System of Innovation

In chapter 2, we argued as one of our central propositions that lead commodity firms have an active interest in the promotion of linkages in areas outside of their core competences, core competences being defined as capabilities, which are unique to the firm, difficult to copy and of value to customers. Moreover, given the desire to promote low cost, low inventory production, and the need to ensure the continual availability of capital intensive equipment, the lead commodity firms not only wish to outsource noncore competences, but also to near source them.

However, this does not mean that lead commodity firms will thoughtlessly outsource all noncore competencies, let alone to outsource them to proximate suppliers and customers. The extent to which they outsource will necessarily reflect a variety of competing factors including competitive cost analysis and inherited prejudices. A key component will be the capabilities of their suppliers and customers. However, capabilities need to be dynamic, continually upgraded to reflect the march of technology and competition. In the discussion of capabilities and their influence on the development of linkages, we will consider two sets of issues. The extent to which skills represent a bottleneck to capability building and the extent to which these capabilities are supported by national, regional and sectoral systems of innovation. Clearly, these are not the only components of capabilities in either the lead commodity firms or the linkage firms. But they are critical and are easier to document than the internal firm routines which characteristically translate capacity to capability (Teece, Pisano and Shuen, 1997).

Before considering the findings with regard to capabilities and linkage development in SSA's commodities sectors, it is important to keep in mind the central role that capabilities play in all economic sectors and in all countries. Capabilities are the key to sustainable incomes. The more they are exclusive to a particular firm, chain or economy, the more likely that they will support high incomes. Hence, virtually all firms face a capability gap and we should not be surprised to find their presence in SSA's commodities sectors or in the firms linking into these sectors. The point is not so much the existence of capability gaps, but the level, nature, extent and trajectory of these capabilities.

Skill as a constraint and an enabler of linkage capabilities

The pervasiveness of skill shortages

Skill shortages are pervasive across all of the sectors and countries under review, although the level of skills in which shortages are experienced varies greatly. In summary, the country-by-country picture is as follows:

In **Angola**, the government has set exacting targets for the growth of locally employed skill workers. In oilfield services providing control lines to the oil sector, there has been a steady increase in the share of citizens who in 2009 accounted for 90 per cent of total employment in the basic and mid skilled categories, 45 per cent of managers, but only 17 per cent of engineers (Table 5.6).

Table 5.6 Percentage share of Angolans in skills in backward linkages feeding into the Angolan oil sector (2004-2014)

Period	Total Workforce	Local (Angolan) workforce		
		Basic & Mid-Skilled	Managers	Engineers
Control Lines				
2004	50	80	30	0
2009	160	90	45	17
2014*	180	90	60	52
Flow Lines				
2003	-	70	-	5
2009	-	72	-	20
2014*	-	85	-	35

*: projected

Source: Teka (2011)

The manufacturers of flow-lines, which are more recent in origin than the control line manufacturer, employ a smaller share of basic and mid-level skilled locals, and a similarly low share of local engineers. Thus, in both of these backward linkage firms, the short-term need for skills is met through the use of migrant labour. A similar pattern of skills shortage was observed in the construction sector, leading most of the Chinese firms to import skills from China. The Chinese firms reported not just a shortage of skills, but also argued that Chinese labour was used to working at a higher pace and for much longer hours than the Angolan employees, and frequently also at lower wage rates. In **Botswana**, where the forward linkage into diamond cutting and polishing is made up almost entirely of labour, skills are *the* key obstacle to the deepening of linkages. In the cutting and polishing sector itself, expatriates made up only seven per cent of the total labour force, but more than half of top management and one third of middle management. In a selection of supplier firms, expatriates made up less than five per cent of the total labour force.

In **South Africa** – the country with the most highly educated population in SSA – firms supplying mining equipment and specialist services identified the shortage of skills as a significant constraint. Skills shortages exist at all levels – managerial and artisanal as well as technical levels such as engineers and machine operators. The shortage has been exacerbated in recent years – particularly at the managerial and higher skill levels – by emigration, most significantly to Australia. At the same time, South African firms complain that they are unable to import skills because they encounter difficulties in obtaining work permits. Enterprise Survey (ES) data for 2003 and 2007 provide further confirmation of the importance of the skill shortage. In 2003, firms in the capital goods sector cited skills shortage as their most significant constraint. In 2007, skills shortage was identified as the second most important constraint after crime. It is cited by firms as one of the major reasons why they are increasingly relocating the manufacture of products outside of South Africa – notably to China. However, firms also cite the skills shortage as having an impact on the location of research and development, with South African firms increasingly locating their operations in Australia, which offers both better availability of skills and strong linkages with well-endowed publicly supported research institutions in the NSI.

In **Gabon**, an absence of domestic skilled labour proved to be a major cost penalty for all companies in the timber chain. With their international connections and deeper pockets, large-scale companies found it easier to bear the 'skill cost' penalty. Smaller Gabonese owned companies were most severely affected and found it more difficult to deepen forward linkages. This shortfall in skills led to the recruitment of skills from abroad. Senior positions (management, technicians) were most often filled by labour recruited from Europe and/or Asia (depending on the ownership of production). In administration, transport and in production, skilled labour was sourced from neighbouring Central African countries where wages were approximately one third of those in Gabon. It is striking that the skill shortage is so severe in Gabon that 15 per cent of unskilled labour was migrant (Table 5.7)

Table 5.7 Percentage share within employment categories and country of origin in Gabon's timber value chain (2009)

Category	Distribution	Origin Gabon	Origin Foreign
Management	7	24	75
Technicians	4	59	41
Administration	6	87	13
Labourers	75	84	16
Transport	6	70	31
Environment & Social	2	74	26
Total	100	-	-

Source: Terheggen (2011)

In **Nigeria,** skill constraints appear to be less severe, at least seen from the perspective of backward linkage firms feeding into the oil sector. Eighty per cent of these firms were satisfied with the availability of skilled labour, although one third of firms nevertheless recruited skills from abroad. In the ICT sector where skill shortages were considered most severe, almost half of the firms recruited from abroad (Table 5.8). Reflecting the relative absence of skill constraints, 56 per cent of firms believed that the

Nigerian educational and training system met their needs adequately, although there were sub-sectoral differences with the levels of satisfaction being lower in control systems and ICT (47 per cent) and higher in the fabrication and construction sector (68 per cent).

Table 5.8 Perceptions of skill availability in firms supplying to the Nigerian oil industry (number and % of firms)

	Control systems & ICT	Fabrication & construction	Well construction & completion	Others	Total
Can find adequate skilled labour	84.2	81.8	73.5	100	80
Have to employ skilled labour educated abroad	47.4	31.8	23.5	20	31.3
Share of non-Nigeria skilled labour					
up to 10%	22.2	42.9	50	-	36
11%-20%	55.6	14.3	50	100	44
above 20%	22.2	42.9	-	-	20
Educations/training provided in Nigeria meet company's requirement	47.4	68.2	52.9	60	56.3

Source: Oyejide and Adewuyi (2011)

A similar story of skill constraints, particularly in managerial and technical skills was also evidenced in Ghana and Tanzania, both in the lead gold mining firms and in their suppliers.

The training response

In the context of these skill shortages inhibiting the competitiveness of the lead commodities firms and their suppliers and customers, both governments and firms responded with training programmes, albeit to a varying degree.

In **Angola,** the supplier firms ran intensive in-house training programmes, involving both on-the-job training and sending labour to affiliates abroad (Table 5.9). Most of the training abroad is undertaken in the US and Europe (83 per cent), but some also occurs in Brazil (25 per cent) and South Africa (10 per cent). Most of the firms (88 per cent) have funded local learning institutions, of which the bulk (54 per cent) was directed to the National Petroleum Institute (INP). Nearly half the respondents (43 per cent) have collaborated with local institutions in curriculum development. Of these, 83 per cent have collaborated with the INP.

Table 5.9 Local content and intra-firm training in Angola (% of respondents)

	Yes	No	INP	Various
Do you have in-house training programmes	100	0	--	--
Do you train employees on-the-job	100	0	--	--
Do you train employees abroad	100	0	--	--
Do you have a funding policy for local learning institutions	88	12	--	--
Which local learning institutions have you funded to date	--	--	54	46
Have you collaborated in curriculum development with any local institution	43	57	--	--
Which local institutions have you collaborated with in curriculum development	--	--	83	27

Source: Teka (2011)

Given its single minded focus on increasing participation by Angolans in the oil industry (which as we saw in chapter four reflects the Angolan government's perception of domestic content), there have been extensive developments in training in publicly funded institutions, particularly those involving secondary and professional level skills. There is some disquiet in the private sector however that the focus on these skills training programmes was decided without consultation with the private sector. Thus, many of the skills being produced do not meet the specific skills gaps, which are constraining linkages to the oil sector, especially higher-level skills. This criticism is levelled particularly at the INP and the Ministry of Industry's professional training programmes. The INP was established in 1983 to provide technical and professional training for oil industry workers and has been supported financially by oil companies and oil services companies. However, since it was established in 1983, the INP has produced a total of only 1,910 graduates, an average of 72 graduates per annum. The Agostinho Neto University, which is the largest, oldest and the only publicly funded university in the country, only produces around 30 engineers per annum. Courses in the private universities that have emerged following the legalisation of private education in 1991 are geared mostly toward social sciences (law, international relations, philosophy, etc.) and to some extent information technology. The state owned oil company, Sonangol, has established three corporate training centres, but only one of the three centres involves higher (tertiary) level skills training. The latter's annual enrolment capacity is 480. Thus, despite these different initiatives, the cumulative output of the engineering output by the different higher education institutions is well below the oil sector's needs, let alone meeting the needs of linkage firms. Oil companies have estimated that Angola needs to produce around 1,300 higher-level technicians (engineers) annually if the targeted rate of Angolanisation of human resources in the oil sector is to succeed.

Moving away from oil to the Angolan infrastructure and construction sectors, at the 2006 Forum on China Africa Co-operation (FOCAC) Summit held in Beijing, China's President Hu Jintao announced, as part of an eight point plan, that China would provide training for African professionals. Chinese small and medium enterprises operating in Angola were encouraged to invest in human resources development. In the construction sector, some of the larger SOEs sent students to China to study engineering and architecture and other relevant skills, but expected them either to work for the SOE on their return or to work in other infrastructure projects in Angola.

In **Nigeria**, almost all the major oil companies invest in training programmes and sponsored education through scholarships. A good example is Shell, which has made wide ranging commitments to training which includes:

- The Shell Intensive Training Programme, introduced in 1998 with the objective of preparing young graduates for employment in the oil industry
- University scholarship grants for about 850 university scholarships annually
- The endowment of Shell Professorial Chairs in seven universities;
- Youth Development Schemes through which they have trained youths in a range of skills such as welding,

pipefitting and carpentry, entrepreneurship and leadership development, and conflict management;
- Building of infrastructure that promotes education. For example, in 2004 Shell completed a total of 86 infrastructural projects, including classroom blocks, teachers' quarters and libraries.

However, most of sponsored training programmes are designed to meet their own needs, the needs of the oil extracting sector or wider society. None is specifically focused on enhancing skills in the industries supplying inputs to Shell or other oil companies.

The Nigerian government has made large investments in training to meet the needs of the oil industry. The Petroleum Technology Development Fund (PTDF) was established in 1973 and was given responsibility for developing, promoting and implementing petroleum technology and human resource development. This was to be achieved through a combination of research and the training of Nigerian graduates, technicians and craftsmen in the fields of petroleum and other engineering, geology, geosciences, management, economics and other relevant fields in petroleum and solid minerals industry, both locally and abroad. The PTDF endowment programme has focused on advancing petroleum technology education in six Nigerian Federal Universities, providing limited funding of between $66,000 and $400,000 (N10 million and N60 million) per university. The PTDF also carries out a number of programmes including an Engineering Design Training Programme (EDTP), a Welders Training and Certification Programme (WTCP), a Local Scholarship Scheme (LSS) and the Overseas Scholarship Scheme (OSS). Between 2001 and 2006, 450 M.Sc. and 84 Ph.D. scholars were trained in the OSS programme.

In **Tanzania**, the Mineral Policy (1997) called for the establishment of training institutions in relevant core and industry supporting skills and for foreign investors in the field to train Tanzanians. However, beyond this broad verbal commitment, the Mineral Policy concern with skill development has seen little effective action. The Act did not specify either target levels for training, or a time scale for the achievement of its (loosely specified) goals. Moreover, a provision in the act provides the space for each of the large mines to bargain for specific exemptions. Most of these Mining Development Agreements (MDA) allow for the unrestricted employment of expatriate labour, both in their own operations and in their lead suppliers. African Barrick Gold and AngloGold Ashanti, in collaboration with the Tanzanian Chamber of Minerals and Energy (TCME) and Vocational Education and Training Authority (VETA) have embarked on a technical training project, the Integrated Mining Technical Training (IMTT). The programme is specifically designed to train artisans (tradesmen) and is located at the Moshi VETA institute.

Botswana's diamond linkage policy was very effective in aligning skills demand with skills development through mandating and enforcing intensive training at the firm level. Cutting and polishing are very firm specific skills, which constitute the firms' core competitive advantage. Locals are mostly trained to specialise in a section of the manufacturing process, in order to protect the firms' competitive command over the whole process. Skills were developed by the cutting and polishing factories through a combination of on-the-job training and apprenticeships in the firm's other operations. For the companies to operate efficiently they need a low labour turnover in order to justify the investment they make when training their workers. The firms have made a tacit agreement through Botswana's Diamond Manufacturers Association to refrain from poaching each other's workers.

Despite this clear commitment to training skills relevant to the development of forward linkages, there are signs that the Botswana government has failed to grasp the longer term challenge of skill development in diamond cutting and polishing. Until recently cutting and polishing has been a heavily skilled based sector requiring many years of skill development and reflected in the tacit knowledge required to perform these tasks. This was a similar phenomenon in the global metal-working and print industries prior to the 1990s. However, the introduction of Computer Numerically Controlled (CNC) machinery in these industries allowed for the codification and automation of these skills. This did not reduce the need for skills, but changed the nature of skills demand from craft machining skills to the programming and maintenance of CNC equipment. Diamond cutting technology is on the verge of an analogous change, in this case involving not just CNC cutting and polishing machines, but also Computer Aided Design (CAD) and laser equipment. This is a training challenge of considerable importance to the Botswana forward linkage industry, but one that does not seem to have entered the radar of skill development provision.

In **South Africa**, training is fairly widespread in the industry, particularly on the part of foreign owned firms. Data from the 2003 ES showed that 76 per cent of foreign firms in the sector offered training. However, there are some indications that the number of firms offering training has declined. In the 2007 survey, only 59 per cent of foreign firms and 44 per cent of domestic firms offered training. Firms regard the Skills Education Training Authorities (SETA) training system as cumbersome and ineffective. Many firms complained about the declining number of mining engineers and the Chamber of Mines described the situation as 'dire.'

Mobility of skills

Public involvement in skill development arises from the fact that investors in most forms of training are unable to appropriate the fruits of their investment. This means that skills produced by a particular firm may be used by other firms, either by competitors or by firms in other sectors and other countries. It is for this reason that as a general global phenomenon, cutting across countries and sectors, there is systematic market failure in skill provision. But not all skill loss is a loss to the economy. The 'leakage' of skills from one firm may be a gain to another, helping to diffuse knowledge and skills through the economy. Where skills leak abroad, the loss may have few positive externalities, except in cases where 'brain drain' subsequently turns into 'brain gain' as nationals return home after gaining experience abroad.

In **Nigeria,** skills spill over from the mining companies to upstream and downstream, industries and into other sectors has been significant (Table 5.10). More than half of the supplier firms were aware of ex-employees who had developed expertise with the company and were now engaged in other sectors. However, an even larger number of firms (69 per cent) employed personnel previously employed by the oil companies. More than 90 per cent of the oil firms confirmed they were aware of ex-employees now in other sectors, whilst more than 80 per cent have employed personnel previously working for their suppliers.

Table 5.10 Skill spill-overs in backward linkages in the Nigerian oil sector (% of firms)

	Oil supply firms				
	Control system & ICT	Fabrication & construction	Well construction & completion	Others	Total
Aware of ex-employees who developed expertise with the company and are now engaged in other sectors	52.6	59.1	61.8	40	457.5
Employ personnel who were previously employed by the oil companies	68.4	72.7	64.7	80	568.8
Oil companies					
Aware of ex-employees who developed expertise with the company and are now engaged in other sectors					91.7
Employ personnel who were previously employed by supplier firms					83.3

Source: Oyejide and Adewuyi (2011)

In **Zambia**, following the retrenchment of staff, which followed the privatisation of the mines in the late 1990s, there was an outflow of ex-employees from the mines' operations departments to the supply chain. During the course of their employment in the mines, they had acquired a combination of technical, marketing, purchasing and managerial skills. Although these skills spill-overs were of benefit to suppliers, it is striking that in general suppliers did not consider these skills to be critical to their operations (Table 5.11). Around half of the suppliers had employed workers retrenched from the mines, but there was little correlation between these firms and their growth and profitability trajectories. Of the 24 supplier firms who employed personnel who used to work in the mining companies, slightly more than 50 per cent fared well, but one third did not and exited from the supply chain.

Table 5.11 Zambian suppliers employing ex-staff from the mines

	Positive performance	Static trajectory	Negative performance	Total
Employed staff from the mines	14	2	8	24
Not employed staff from the mines	9	5	7	21
Not responded	3	-	2	5
Total	26	7	17	50

Source: Fessehaie (2011)

In **Tanzania**, there were limited instances in which skills spill-overs took place. Three exploration firms were established by ex-employees of mining firms, but these were isolated cases. In the context of a pervasive skill shortage, the mining sector swept up the bulk of relevantly trained skills and offered better wages and prospects than supplier firms. Thus, in contrast to Zambia, the major skill spill-overs occurred as a consequence of mining companies poaching skills from suppliers, particularly personnel with experience (and contact) in logistics. There has however been a significant (although not systematically recorded) leakage of skills abroad and there is reports of Tanzanian mining engineers working in the DRC and other countries. (On the other hand, there are also Ghanaian mining engineers working in Tanzania).

In the **Angola** construction sector, skills migration occurred from the Chinese firms operating in the construction sector. Chinese white collar workers left Chinese SOEs to form their own companies and to operate in the Angolan market. An example is a Chinese design firm of which four of the five directors had previously worked with large SOEs in the construction sector. One director estimated that links to their previous employer accounted for around 80 per cent of their turnover.

In **South Africa,** a combination of factors is leading to the leakage of skills abroad. The skills shortage observed above has resulted in some companies moving some of their operations overseas, notably to China. For example, one of the largest South African operations now fabricates 20 per cent of needed capital equipment in China whereas previously equipment was produced exclusively in South Africa. Of more concern to the long-term future of supply of mining equipment and knowledge intensive services to the mining industry is that some of the major mining companies are locating their research and development activities abroad. The country favoured is almost invariably Australia, with the main attraction being the availability of highly skilled labour and the linkages to well-funded research centres. Moreover, based on individual decisions reflecting the transition to majority rule in South Africa, a significant number of highly skilled white workers are moving abroad, a process made easier by the global shortage of mining skills in a context of a sustained boom in commodity prices and the decline in South African mining activity.

However, the picture is not uniformly negative. The decline in local mining output, particularly in gold, has resulted in a number of highly skilled South Africans selling their consulting expertise abroad from a South African base and/or moving into mining related activities where they can engage their skills and experience. A number or the specialist mining service companies that have emerged in South Africa in recent years have been founded and developed by persons with skills and experience developed in mining and related activities.

Supportive institutions in the National Systems of Innovation

Given the underdeveloped nature of the industrial sectors in most of SSA, in most cases the role that the NSI plays in the existing pattern of linkages from the commodities sector is limited.

In **Ghana**, a number of RTOs have been established over the years. These include the National Research Council out of which emerged the Ghana Academy of Arts and Sciences and the Council for Scientific and Industrial Research (CSIR), the Noguchi Memorial Institute for Medical Research, the Ghana Atomic Energy Commission (GAEC), the Ghana Standards Board (GSB) and the Cocoa Research Institute. However, total expenditure on research and development as a percentage of GDP is less than one per cent and Ghana's NSI remains weak due not only to a lack of investment but also to an absence of strategic vision and a lack of proper management of Science and Technology. Moreover, despite the long lived nature of Ghana's mining industry and the prominence of gold mining in the economy, it is specifically weak in relation to institutions focusing on either the needs of the gold sector or its suppliers and users.

Tanzania's 1997 Mineral Policy articulates a vision of establishing 'centres of technical excellence in various fields for capacity building, and setting up mechanisms for exchange of knowledge and experience' and specifically targets linkages with universities, colleges, research institutions and industry. This sectoral policy vision resonates with the vision of the Tanzania Commission for Science and Technology. The evidence, however, is that this coalescence of visions is yet to be implemented. First, there are no centres of excellence to support the mining industry in Tanzania. The Tanzania Industrial Research and Development (TIRDO) does not include mining sector research in its portfolio, nor does it target linkages with the mining sector. Secondly, there is limited interaction between those NSI institutions that do exist and the commodities sector. Mining companies reported that their only interaction with the universities was when undergraduate students receiving training from the mines as part of the curriculum and when students conducted firm sponsored research projects as part of their final year undergraduate studies. An exploration manager with a mining firm characterised these interactions as 'minor and inadequate'.

In **Angola**, public expenditure on education has grown from five per cent of government expenditure in 2001 to 7.9 per cent (of a much larger budget) in 2009 (Table 5.12). Nevertheless, the country's output in terms of research, science and technology remains very weak. The overwhelming share of this expenditure is directed to education rather than research, reflecting in very low levels of R&D indicators such as patents and journal publications.

Table 5.12 Angolan education expenditure and research output (2001-2009)

Education budget		Research output per million population		
Year	% share of budget	Year	Scientific & technical journals	Patents granted by USPTO
2001	5.0	--	--	--
2003	6.2	--	--	--
2005	7.1	1993-1997	--	--
2006	3.8	1995	0.16	--
2007	5.6	2001-2005	--	0.01
2008	7.9	2004-2005	0.22	--
2009	7.9	2009-2010	--	--

Source: MINFIN (2010); GOA (2007/8); UNCTAD (2008)

In **Nigeria** the NSI and its interactions with the oil and gas value chain is more developed than in Angola. This arises from the relatively higher level of education in Nigeria and the depth of investments in the NSI since independence. This generalised capacity is reflected in the innovative capabilities of the industries supplying inputs into the oil sector, as well as in the source of support for these innovations (Table 5.13). More than two thirds of the firms interviewed had access to new technology. This resulted from agreements for upgrading and maintenance with their own suppliers and from technology agreements with foreign companies. A smaller proportion of firms – one third – had developed relationships with universities and local Research and Technology Organisations (RTOs) such as the Petroleum Training Institute and the Nigerian Institute of Welders. Past attempts by government in establishing a national system of innovation also include the establishment of the Petroleum Training Institute (PTI) in Delta State (in 1973), the Federal University of Petroleum Resources in Delta State, and also the National College of Petroleum Studies in Kaduna (NCPS, in 1995). The PTI functions as an educational institution and also trains lower and middle level manpower to meet the indigenous labour requirements of the oil and gas sector, while the NCPS trains high-level manpower.

Table 5.13 Nigerian innovative activities amongst suppliers and the sources of innovative support (% within sector)

	Control system & ICT	Fabrication & construction	Well construction & completion	Others	Total
Access to new technology	78.9	81.8	67.6	100	76.3
local innovation/tech agreements with foreign companies	57.9	40.9	44.1	60	47.5
agreements for upgrading & maintenance	63.2	50	58.8	80	58.8
relationship with local research centres or the university	42.1	27.3	32.4	40	33.8

Source: Oyejide and Adewuyi (2011)

Botswana's 2005 National Research, Science and Technology plan focused research into five key strategic areas - mining bi-product utilisation, downstream processing and beneficiation of mining products, research seeking to improve the efficiency of current processing technologies (including environmentally cleaner production technologies), ICT research to support process control and chemical sciences, and engineering and research into improved extraction and processing technologies. Insofar as the mining sector and its linkage firms are concerned, this largely remains a vision. None of the interviewed firms reported any linkages with the NSI.

Zambia's total budget allocated for innovation and skills creation has been low. Activity based budgets are available only for 2004 and reveal that, on average, less than one per cent of the total government budget was devoted to innovation and skills in that year. Moreover, most of the allocation was spent on recurrent expenses. This was compounded by very low private sector R&D. Linkages between public institutions in the NSI and the private sectors were almost non-existent. This meant that the research conducted in public institutions was rarely exploited commercially. The 1997 Science and Technology Act established a number of institutions, which from 2009 were endowed with a Strategic Research Fund. The latter, however, did not target specific industries. Respondents from the National Technology Business Centre (NTBC), the body responsible for working jointly with the private sector on innovation technology, reported undertaking no project with the suppliers in the copper-belt.

In **Gabon**, there is a shortage of trained scientists in domestic scientific institutions. For example, the Agricultural and Forestry Research Institute (IRAF), which is part of the National Scientific and Technological Research Centre (CENAREST), has 22 full time researchers for four departments, including only one in forestry science. The same holds true for educational institutions such as the Schools of Forestry at the University of Omar Bongo and the National Water and Forestry School (ENEF) at the University of Masuku. Graduates are reluctant to work in the logging and processing sectors. None of the logging and processing companies was familiar with what training programmes existed. Nor were they willing to invest time and financial resources into developing links with these institutions.

In **South Africa**, the competitiveness of the mining equipment industry is hampered by deteriorating mining related research capacity at the CSIR and the formerly world leading industry research body, MINTEK. MINTEK was started in 1934 as a direct consequence of the need to support the backward linkage firms who were helping mines to tailor their operations to the specific needs of South Africa's geology and to support the mining sectors' competitiveness. In recent years, skilled personnel have been lost from both the CSIR and MINTEK, and a number of programmes have been closed, particularly at the CSIR. Formerly COMRO – the research arm of the Chamber of Mines – undertook very significant research on behalf of the industry. The CSIR, which absorbed COMRO, continued to have large-scale mining research projects – principally in trackless mining and rock engineering. However, these research programmes had a limited life and the capacity at the CSIR has been depleted almost to point of extinction. It is widely stated in the industry that MINTEK has seen a significant decline in its capacities. The Council for

Geosciences is similarly said to be experiencing difficulty and losing staff.

Few of the firms interviewed in mining specialist services and equipment in South Africa had significant links with the Science Councils, which fund research. Where they did, these links were becoming more limited over time. Firms made much more use of privately funded research. There appears to have been a significant growth in local research consultancies that serve the industry that undertake research or provide specialist consultancy services. Local firms are increasingly importing knowledge inputs from publicly funded research institutions and universities abroad, particularly from Australia.

In conclusion, and drawing together lessons learned from the experience of linkage development in the case studies which we have documented as well as comparative experience in other settings, we can draw three general conclusions with respect to the role of capabilities in linkage development First, all of the countries that succeeded in developing and spreading capabilities affecting linkage development had extensive programmes for education and skill development. However, whilst the presence of a well-educated labour force allows firms to grow their capabilities, in order to use these capabilities productively, this has to be matched with in-house training schemes and managerial routines, which maximise the returns in utilising human resources.

Second, competencies required in commodity production and in the beneficiation of mineral and energy commodities are largely technical in nature. This requires major commitments to the development of often very specific technical and engineering skills in the tertiary educational system and in the support provided by the NSI to the commodities sector.

Third, there are particular opportunities in the provision of basic engineering and repair services. These are critical to the efficient production on the part of commodity producers - especially mining companies. Currently most of these services are provided by 'foreigners' who fly in on a regular basis or when special needs arise incurring significant expense and with considerable delays. Commodity producers accordingly have a strong interest in securing these services locally. These technical/engineering capabilities have potential applications in a wide range of other sectors that require machine adaptation, repair and maintenance.

Policy development, management and implementation

In chapter 2, we observed that important lessons on the role played by policy in linkage development could be learned from the discussion of innovation management in business science and innovation studies. The key insights are that implementation may be less intellectually taxing than the process of knowledge discovery, but it is often in practice much the harder stage in the innovation cycle. Moreover, successful innovation management involves close interaction between the producers and users of innovations and requires various parts of the innovation cycle to be undertaken in parallel rather than in sequence.

Our analysis of the role that policies play in the promotion of linkages with the commodities sector draws on these insights from innovation management. We begin by asking the question about the nature of the 'invention' in the policy cycle, that is, do governments and firms have a Vision for the promotion of linkages from commodities? From this follow a series of 'management of innovation' type concerns – is the vision translated into policies, and are these policies consistent and coherent? Are these policies backed by incentives that ensure that they are implemented effectively? Do the government and the corporate sector have the capacity and the will to implement these policies? Finally, there is the issue of reflexivity – do the various stakeholders involved in the management of linkage policy interact and, do they as a collectivity, display the capacity to adjust policies dynamically? As in the previous discussion, we report our findings on a country-by-country basis.

Angola

The primary focus on local content on backward linkages in Angola has been on the Angolanisation of the labour force. To all intents and purposes, the Angolan government has conflated 'local value' with local ownership. This is as much an agenda of national identity as one of promoting the development of the local economy through the development of linkages from the oil sector. Targets were set on the proportion of Angolan labour in both the extractive and supply industries, which aimed at 100 per cent Angolan labour at basic skills level, 80 per cent at mid-skills level and 70 per cent at higher-skills level. However, an industry wide assessment carried out in 2004 indicated that while the targets for basic and mid skills levels were exceeded, the target for higher skills level remained below target.

The focus on national ownership as a prime objective of linkage development is reflected in the strategic approach towards the development of backward linkages. As we saw in the discussion of the breadth and depth of linkages (in chapter 4), a three tier system was established for Angolan content in the supply industry (supply of goods and services). Goods and services of low capital and knowledge intensity have to be purchased from national companies. Goods and services with average levels of capital and expertise have to be supplied by joint venture companies between national and foreign companies. Lastly, no preferential treatment is applied to highly technological and capital intensive goods and services.

Local content policy does not identify these products in detail and these are settled by bilateral negotiation between government and the oil industry, providing much scope for discretionary decisions (and bribery) by individual government offices. However, preferential treatment applies only to inputs supplied at a premium of less than 10 per cent over the cost of imports. These provisions apply to all contracts above $150,000. National suppliers are defined as firms in which at least 51 per cent of share capital is owned by Angolan citizens or the state. It is notable that there appear to be no provisions targeting the degree of local content in these domestically sourced inputs, hence in most cases local content has only minimal local value added.

This policy environment suggests a broad, but poorly specified vision on linkages. That is, government knows what it wants (skills development, more local employment, and ownership), but this is weakly translated into policies designed to promote any depth in backward linkages. Sonangol has responsibility for implementation, together with the Ministry of Petroleum, but there is a limited institutional and support base to realise these targets.

There is a range of problems in the implementation of the local content policy. The allocation of inputs in the three tiers of technological complexity (Table 5.14) appear to have been arbitrarily determined and, given the state of local capabilities, underestimates the technology and capital content of most of the products the policy designates to be of average technology and capital levels.

Table 5.14 Angolan categories of preferential products since 2003

Exclusive to local firms	Exclusive to joint venture firms
Food stuffs & Catering,	Purchase/processing of geographical data;
Transportation of equipment & materials,	Vertical, directional, horizontal drilling of wells & completion;
Supply of technical materials (IT & electric equipment, etc.),	Geological control of drilling (mud logging);
General Cleaning & Gardening	Production tests;
General maintenance of equipment & vehicles,	Operation & maintenance of oil production installation;
Operation and management of supply points (service stations),	Operators & managers of terminals;
Retailers of lighting oil, gas & lubricants, and	Manufacture of plastic/synthetic fibres for the oil industry;
Transport of goods from terminals to supply points	Drilling, production material, etc.

Source: Teka (2011)

Moreover, as we saw above in the discussion of capabilities, the national training institutes focused disproportionately on mid-level technical skills. Finally, there is a lack of coordination and integration between industrial policy and policy directed to the oil sector. Industrial policy is the responsibility of the Ministry of Industry, whilst policy towards the oil sector (including with regard to backward linkages) is the responsibility of the Ministry of Petroleum and Sonangol. There are no joint working arrangements in policy design and implementation between the Ministry of Industry and Sonangol and the Ministry of Petroleum. Consequently, there is a lack of policy coordination between industrialisation policy (as far as incentives and capability development programmes are concerned) and oil sector policies.

For example, Business Development Service Centres (BDS) are a public-private business capacity development initiative intended for local SME development in the different sectors of the economy. It is an initiative between the Angolan government, the United Nations Development Programme (UNDP) and Chevron (American oil producing company and the oldest operator in the Angolan oil market). This initiative is implemented by Chevron in collaboration with other oil operators and Sonangol without any involvement from the National Private Investment Agency (ANIP) or the Ministry of Industry. Moreover, Sonangol (as the public sector partner) does not support the initiative with any incentives comparable to the ones offered to local firms in the oil extracting link in the chain.

Botswana

The Government of Botswana has a well-developed vision for the development of forward linkages from the diamond mining industry. This sector specific strategy was clearly defined in the National Development Plans (2006 and 2009), which in addition to diamonds, identified five other strategic foci to guide future development of the economy - education, innovation, agriculture, health and transport. It is intended that there will be strong links between these strategic interventions. For example the diamond value chain – which is seen as the key sector for development - will be supported by the education hub which will produce skills for the different industries in the diamond hub, whilst the innovation hub will attract business to perform research for the diamond industry and the transport hub will ensure that the all the necessary transport infrastructure needed by the industry is in place.

This is not the first time the Botswana government has targeted downstream beneficiation. Faced with the likely exhaustion of low cost near to the surface diamond mines, attempts were made in the early 1980s to promote a cutting and polishing industry. De Beers did not support the government's ambitions at that time, arguing that cutting and polishing activities were not economically viable in Botswana. However, after political pressure was exerted on De Beers, three cutting and polishing factories were started between 1980 and 1990. However, government policy at that time was not backed by clear monitoring or strong sanctions and none of these factories ever reported a profit or showed any signs of expanding. Although this early attempt was a failure, it proved to be an important learning experience.

After employing consultants to map the value chain and determine an appropriate path to deepening forward linkages, an ambitious Vision for diamond beneficiation was developed in 2005, this time backed by clear supportive policies and by strong sanctions. An opportunity was provided for this Vision by the expiry of De Beers' 25-year diamond mining lease. The fact that De Beers sourced more than half of its diamonds from Botswana through a 50-50 joint venture with the government (Debswana) gave the government significant bargaining power.

As part of the new agreement, a 50-50 joint venture between the government and De Beers, the DTC Botswana was established and clear performance targets were set. The agreement stipulated that clearly stated sales and employment targets were to be achieved by 2010. The penalty clause for non-performance for De Beers was such that the employment target was met rapidly. In 2010, $482 million of rough diamonds were sold to the 16 sight holders by the DTC Botswana and according to the agreement, at least 80 per cent of the rough diamonds have to be cut and polished domestically.

In order to implement this strategy, the Botswana government established two sector specific institutions, the Diamond Office and Diamond Hub. The Diamond Hub is the sector executive agency tasked with the practical implementation of policy. The Diamond Hub has implemented five policies designed to provide a favourable business environment for the industry. The first is a reduced corporate tax rate (15 per cent rather than 25 per cent) for the cutting and polishing firms. The second provides for the fast tracking of Work Permit applications for skilled labour used to train locals and for labour visiting to maintain and repair their equipment. The third is an exemption from paying the economy wide training levy if firms have their own training programmes (which have to be accredited with the Training Authority). The fourth is an exemption from paying taxes on polished diamonds exports and the fifth is that the cutting and polishing firms do not have to pay import duties on their technology imports. The Diamond Office is responsible for inspecting diamond exports, issuing Kimberley Process certificates (certifying that the diamonds do not emanate from conflict zones) and, together with

DTC, for monitoring the activities of the companies by undertaking six monthly audits.

Thus, the government has a clear vision, backed by policies that embody both negative sanctions (exclusion from rough diamond supply) and positive sanctions (exemption from work permits, import duties and lower taxes). However, what happens on the ground and does the government have the capacity to implement and monitor these policies? It is only five years since the programme was introduced, but the trajectory is in general a positive one. Based on interviews with three senior government respondents and seven senior industry managers (five of the 13 cutting and polishing firms and two brokers), it seems that there is a clear dialogue between the public and private sector, since in general both sets of respondents weighted the coherence of the government's vision and policies similarly (Figure 5.4). Moreover, as one senior private sector executive observed, 'Policy is working with and not against the industry, the culture is very open and we can recommend things to the Diamond Hub'. The major difference in perspectives was that the private sector felt that government policies were more promoting of backward linkages than did the government officers themselves.

Figure 5.4 Industry and government responses on government's policy in Botswana

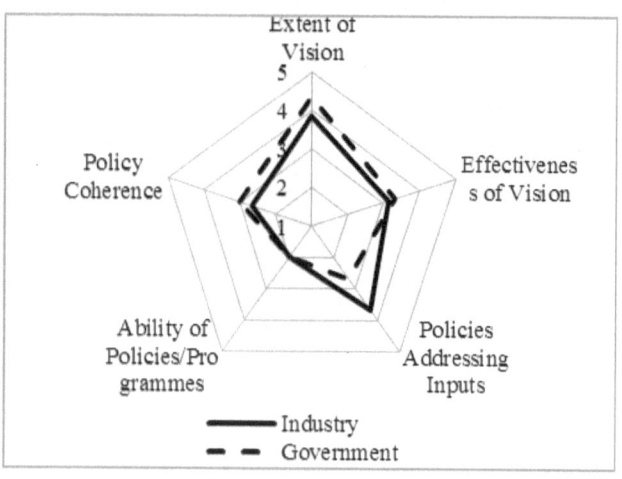

1 = not at all, 5 = extremely

Source: Mbayi (2011)

Having a vision and complementary policies is of course one important strand in effective policy design and implementation. However, it needs to be backed by the capacity and the will to implement these policies adequately. Here there is agreement between the government and private sector respondents on the integrity of government officials and, in general the will of government to execute its policy. Not surprisingly, however, government respondents tended to rate their capacities to implement these policies more highly than did the private sector (Table 5.15).

Table 5.15 Industry and government responses on government's capacity (% response) in Botswana

	Government (n=3)		Industry (n=7)	
	Yes	No	Yes	No
Do you think the government has the *capacity* to implement its policies for the cutting and polishing industry?	100	0	29	61
Do you think it *really wants to*?	100	0	86	14
Do you think issues of personal integrity amongst the relevant government officials affect the Government's ability to implement its policies for the industry?	0	100	0	100

Source: Mbayi (2011)

Most often 'policy' is seen as an agenda for government alone, rather than the effective product of a public-private partnership, driven by government but with the active support of the firms in the sector. It is firms that manufacture rather than the government, so it is also important to interrogate firm policy in the same way as that of governments. Do firms have a vision, is this backed by consistent 'policies' (for example, supply chain development policies), do these policies have sanctions (suppliers are rewarded or 'fined' for poor performance) and do they have the will and the capacity to implement these firm specific routines? Again, it is of interest to assess the views of both government and private sector respondents on these issues, in the same way as we have done for government policies.

Figure 5.5 shows a much greater divergence in assessment between these two sets of respondents than was the case for government policies. The private sector believed that it scored highly on all the relevant counts, whilst government officials were more sceptical of these firm specific capabilities. Neither of the two government officials polled on this issue believed that the firms really wanted to implement their beneficiation strategies, whereas four of the five companies responding to this question believed that the private sector as a whole did indeed want to push through their commitment to cutting and polishing. This reflects the lack of a joined up policy, the hallmark of effective industrial strategy, which involves both government and industry in the joint development and implementation of such policy initiatives.

Figure 5.5 Industry and government views on corporate beneficiation policies in Botswana

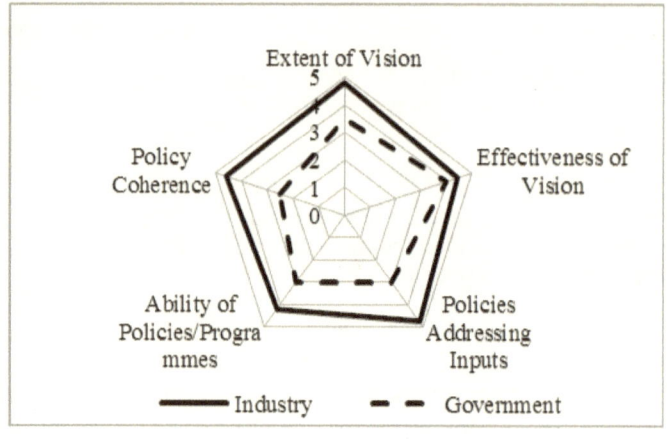

1 = not at all, 5 = extremely

Source: Mbayi (2011)

Gabon

Gabon has a clear vision -for the broadening and deepening of forward processing. The 2001 Forestry Code established direct local processing requirements in which 75 per cent of timber production needed to be processed domestically before exportation by January 2012. Prior to that, beneficiation had largely been driven by the private sector reacting to changes in European consumption patterns. Timber beneficiation was also central to the 2006 Growth and

Poverty Reduction Strategy Paper, which aimed to develop a diversified private sector driven economy and to reduce poverty. As part of the 'reform' process, the government issued a Sectoral Program for Forests, Fisheries and the Environment that, inter alia, focused on environmental considerations and the maintenance of a sustainable and regulated tropical timber logging and processing industry.

After the entry of Asian firms in the timber value chain, the close fit between government and private sector policies (in which both stakeholders were driving forward linkages) weakened. Between 2004 and 2007, the volume of plywood exports decreased by over 40 per cent. In particular Asian owned and small Gabonese firms concentrated on the export of raw, unprocessed logs to China, contrary to the objectives of the Forestry Code. At the same time, there is evidence to suggest that logging which does occur in parts of Gabon flouts the Code's provision on sustainable logging practices. It was thus clear that the objectives of the 2001 Forestry Code were being undermined by the actions of the private sector. The government responded in August 2010 with a total ban on log exports, a sledgehammer approach whose consequences are as yet unknown.

We can thus observe a policy environment where there is a clear vision (forward linkages and sustainable logging). However, whilst the Forestry Code set explicit targets, rules and incentives, the translation of these into day-to-day routines has been weak. This is a result of government failure, the political economy of Gabon and poor private sector compliance (though varying by ownership). The response of the government was a heavy handed sanction with untold economic consequences but even then, weak will and capacities in government threaten to undermine what policy coherence exists.

Ghana

The Government of Ghana has a vision for backward linkages from the gold mining industry that has two components. The first is to promote domestic value added, articulated as giving preference to 'made in Ghana' products. The second is to promote local ownership and the employment of citizens. Detailed legislation included provisions for local content, but these were not articulated as part of a vision for linkage development. Nor was it supported by detailed targets or backed by specific sanctions and, as an instrument of industrial policy, has had little impact on either the breadth or the depth of linkages. The most detailed of these poorly specified policies on local content were those that required the mines to submit detailed programmes for the recruitment and training of Ghanaian personnel.

In recent years there has been a groundswell of concern that the mines have been operating as enclaves even though, as was shown in chapter 4, local content has grown (more as a consequence of market forces rather than of government policy). This has led the Ghana Chamber of Mines (GCM) and individual companies to commit themselves to a policy to develop local business through the Local Business Development Programme (LBDP). This programme also overlaps with a series of CSR policies designed to promote near sourcing into the mines and in so doing to benefit the local communities in which the mines are located.

This is an embryonic policy. However, it does not function effectively, for four sets for reasons. First, there is a lack of coordination between industrial policy and the policy framework affecting the mines. The Investment Promotion Agency that is responsible for industrial policy implementation is, by law, banned from working with the mining and oil sectors.

Second, the tariff structure exempts mining companies from import duties on a wide range of inputs. This does not apply however to the mining supply firms, who continue to pay tariffs on the import of their inputs. This has the effect of favouring the importation of inputs rather than in obtaining them from domestic suppliers.

Third, suppliers and service companies, notably SMEs, confront difficulties in accessing finance and generally pay higher interest rates than large firms pay. The local banking system also has only a limited developmental capability and SMEs are poorly supported.

Fourth, there seems to be a misalignment between the government's policy framework and the supply chain procurement and development policies of some of the gold mines themselves. For example, Newmont Ghana has a clearly articulated vision and implementation steps for a local procurement strategy (although it is not clear to what extent this strategy has been implemented) (Figure 5.6).

Figure 5.6 Newmont Ghana vision for backward linkage development

Objectives

- Strive to increase local expenditure year after year
- Strive to place more business with companies with a higher level of Ghanaian ownership, including use of local authorized distributors and agents of international companies, where a value-added service is being provided

Areas of support

- Increasing Newmont's awareness of goods manufactured in Ghana through:
    o A supplier open day
    o A formal process of supplier registration
    o Identifying products currently being purchased by other mining companies
- Broaden access to opportunities for potential suppliers:
    o Supplier open days
    o Greater use of open tendering, including for all major longer-term service contracts for mining operations as existing agreements expire
    o Advertise available work and goods requirements via the Internet
    o Publish local spend profile data on a quarterly basis
- Apply preference in assessing tenders, giving preference in the following order (all else being equal):
    o Local-Local Company
    o Ghanaian Owned Company
    o Ghanaian Participation Company
    o Ghanaian Registered Company
    o International Company
- Build capacity of local companies through the development of collaborative partnerships between

- industry, NGOs, existing foreign and Ghana-registered companies
- Apply the policy across operational and capital spending:
  - Include provisions for policy to be cascaded by contractually obliging vendors to implement this policy
  - Ensure EPCMs implement the policy
- Newmont also specifies where local procurement may not be feasible, including:
  - Goods and services of a proprietary nature
  - Items covered by Newmont Global Agreements and Alliances determined by need for security of supply for strategic commodities and economies of scale
- Effectively communicate policy and achievements, including through supplier open days, WAMPOC, and online reporting on local spend

Implementation principles

- Develop metrics, monitor and publish performance against strategic goals
- Work together with other mining companies, government, and agencies
- Assess the effectiveness of the policy yearly

Newmont Ghana. (2010). Local Procurement Policy and Action Plan

Nigeria

Nigeria has a long history of policy development focusing on an increase in backward linkages and local content legislation dates back to the late 1960s. The first provisions were found in the Petroleum Act of 1969. Later, the Joint Operating Agreements (JOA) and the Production Sharing Contract (PSC) between the Nigerian government and the foreign oil companies in 1991 and 1993 respectively, included provisions for the involvement of indigenous firms in the supply of commodities. In 2005, a Nigerian local content policy involved the issuance of 23 directives designed to promote backward linkages through provisions on the domestic supply of goods and services and the sourcing of low-tech on-shore supply of goods and services from indigenous firms. The government set targets of 45 per cent local content in the oil and gas sector in 2009 and 70 per cent in 2010. There has thus been a sustained policy environment designed to promote a greater breadth of input provision. As we saw in chapter 4, the Vision for the promotion of backward linkages was strengthened in 2011 when the Nigerian Content Act (2010) was enacted.

This strengthening of local content policy was embedded in a wider Vision for the economy as a whole. Vision 2020 specified particular targets and sanctions for the oil sector, including for backward linkages. The First Implementation Plan covered the period 2010-2013 and included provisions for the promotion of private sector investment in both upstream and downstream links of the oil and gas industry and the growth of national content in value added. The very ambitious target set was to increase local content in oil and gas from two per cent in 2009 to 35.5 per cent in 2010 and to 70 per cent by 2013. Thus, whereas the earlier legislation focused on national ownership and the breadth of linkages, the 2010 legislation also explicitly targeted the deepening of value added.

These ambitious targets for local content have not been met. This was partly because local capabilities did not allow for production costs at a premium of less than 10 per cent above the import price and partly because there was no systematic monitoring of these targets by the Nigerian National Petroleum Company (NNPC). Moreover, the ultimate target of 70 per cent local content is almost certainly unrealistically high. Probably even higher than the value of purchases in the UK's North Sea offshore industry. Nevertheless, as can be seen from the comparison of local content in Nigeria compared to other SSA economies (chapter 4), there has been a substantial growth in domestic content, at least in the sub-sectors that we have examined. Two thirds of the Nigerian supplier firms we interviewed said that local content policies had been an important driver of their linkages to the oil and gas sector. Nevertheless, despite the general strategic thrust of local content policy, there are significant inconsistencies between different government policies (Table 5.16). Suppliers to the oil and gas industry reported that there was greatest conflict between deepening their linkages and the need to respond to policies on import tariffs and taxation.

Table 5.16 Consistency of government regulations with meeting objective of increasing local content (%) in Nigeria

Regulations	Consistent	No opinion	Inconsistent	Mean
Ownership regulations	37.5	45	17.5	2.20
Labour market regulation	32.5	42.5	25	2.08
Taxes/tax holidays/duty rebates	26.3	36.3	37.5	1.89
Licensing	33.8	41.3	25	2.09
Import tariff	18.8	38.8	42.5	1.76
Business registration and start up	32.5	46.3	21.3	2.11

Source: Oyejide and Adewuyi (2011)

Thus the Nigerian policy environment is one in which the government has gradually developed a strategic Vision for linkage development. The early focus on local content policy has been sustained and is now complemented by a clearer understanding that localisation does not only refer to ownership of suppliers, but also to the depth of value added. The policy environment has a number of inconsistent elements to it, in the past has been poorly monitored and is almost certainly over ambitious. Nevertheless, notwithstanding the weaknesses in policy integration and implementation, local content policies have been an important driver of the increasingly broad and deep participation of local suppliers in the oil and gas value chain.

South Africa

South African mining equipment and specialist services suppliers have developed progressively over many years to serve a long established local mining industry. The scale of mining allowed for local supply firms to exploit economies of scale while the diversity of South African mining allowed local firms to exploit economies of scope with many buyers who found it advantageous to source specialist expertise from external and locally situated suppliers. Further, the extraction and processing of South African minerals presented very significant and specific technological challenges that promoted the development of local expertise and technological capacities. Over the decades, state support took a number of forms including policies to encourage import replacement through tariff protection, extensive support for world class training in mining engineering and artisanal skills and the development of significant research institutions and funding.

However, in recent years, governmental policies have not been supportive of mining or mining equipment and specialist services. While the prices for South African commodities have risen, by contrast with other countries with a well-developed and diversified mining sector such as Australia, South Africa's mining output stagnated. Output growth was constrained by uncertainty - over property rights (a combination of government changes to existent mining rights and the active promotion of black empowerment programmes), perceived uncertainty and corruption in the awarding of mining rights and threats of nationalisation. Output was further constrained for some minerals, notably coal, by infrastructural bottlenecks. Not only were ports and rail failing to invest in additional capacity to handle increased tonnage, but there was a deterioration in existing capacity. Mines have also been increasingly threatened in recent years by power shortages.

In regards to the mining equipment and specialist services sector specifically, government support has been very limited. The sector receives no financial support and it does not appear in the technologies identified for support in the Department of Science and Technology's recent 10 year plan (DST, 2008). The DST has instead chosen to support science intensive activities – including space science, energy, climate change, biotechnology and human and social dynamics. None of the supplying companies interviewed made extensive use of any of the government technology support programmes for firms. Some companies did claim the R&D tax credit administered by the DST, but the applied nature of the research and design in mining equipment and specialist services meant that many of the expenditures related to applied technology development in mining did not qualify for support.

Mining equipment and related services was not included in the National Industrial Policy Framework or in the Industrial Policy Action Plan (IPAP). Instead, industrial policy has focused on beneficiation rather than developing backward linkages or extending the technological capacities developed in mining equipment and specialist services laterally into new non-mining markets and products

Tanzania

In the heady post-independence years of Ujamaa, the government of Tanzania had grand ambitions for the development of the economy as a whole, and within this, for the exploitation of its natural resources. As part of this, the mineral sector was reserved for the state. Years of successive economic stagnation led to the abandonment of the Ujamaa policies from the mid-1980s and, after some years of policy stagnation, the minerals sector was subject to a major change in policy environment. This reflected a more general trend in which domestic policy-making capacities were replaced by externally inspired structural adjustment policies.

The 1997 Mineral Policy of Tanzania was an attempt to provide for the development of the minerals sector. Its prime purpose was to attract inward FDI into the mining sector. However, beyond a vague commitment to local sourcing, it failed to address either the breadth or the depth of linkages. Whilst it articulated a general vision of 'developing the country's ability to provide essential inputs to the mining sector', the objectives of these and other sections of the Mineral Policy lacked specific targets. In addition, there were no specific positive incentives or negative sanctions promoting the achievement of this broad goal. No targets were set and no clear monitoring mechanisms were developed to ensure the local content could be encouraged. The primary concern of local content policy – to the extent that there is any – is one that conflates local content with local ownership. Key steps in the exploration sector are reserved for Tanzanian companies and (somewhat eccentrically) Tanzanian control is defined as 100 per cent ownership by local citizens, rather than majority ownership.

The failure to develop policies designed to promote directly backward linkages was reflected in similar policy failure with regard to the drivers of linkages that were considered above. Tanzania's infrastructure is in a woeful state and recent improvements have been limited. Roads leading to some mines remain unpaved and some mines, like the Geita Gold Mine, are yet to be connected to the national electricity grid. The supply of utilities services is highly erratic and they are of poor quality. Skill development is poor and inadequate. Moreover, to compound these weaknesses, policies are inconsistent. Most mines have access to duty free imports of inputs, but this does not apply to their suppliers, who therefore face a double disadvantage – a weak infrastructure and disadvantageous tariffs on their own imported inputs. Further, each of the new mines strikes bilateral agreements with Government on specific provisions and rather than this resulting in increasing obligations on foreign investors, in general these have led to individual TNCs bargaining for specific exemptions on the employment of expatriates, on tax and on duty free imports. All of these have the effect of reducing rather than increasing backward linkages.

Recent changes to the Mining Act in 2010 contained some provisions, which might improve the environment for suppliers to the mines. In applications for prospecting licenses and mining licenses, mining companies are expected to provide a list of goods and services that might be supplied by local firms. However, no targets have been set, there is a total absence of incentives and sanctions and there are no provisions for monitoring progress. Exacerbating the situation is a milieu of pervasive corruption, with various provisions in the legislation allowing for individual discretionary decisions, chaotic physical infrastructure and weak soft infrastructure (such as customs clearance). All of this provides ample scope for the exercise of discretion by individual gatekeepers of permits and certification. Thus, policy will and policy capabilities are weak.

Zambia

As in the case of Tanzania, the early post-independence policy agenda in Zambia was characterised by a strong commitment to a nationalist agenda. In 1969, Zambia nationalised the copper mines and placed them under the umbrella of Zambia Consolidated Copper Mines (ZCCM). The long history of mining in Zambia had led to a situation in which there were extensive backward and forward linkages. However, economic decline led to stagnation and then a fall in mining output after the mid-1970s. As was the situation in much of continent, the consequences was a series of Structural Adjustment Programmes, reflecting a policy agenda set by parties external to Zambia, and leading to major programmes of privatisation and liberalisation. By 2001, all of the copper mines bar one (KCM) had been privatised. The liberalising of mine ownership was associated with the liberalisation of imports and this policy environment led to a major increase in the import of inputs and a reduction in backward linkages. In other words, a policy environment that had led to the development of extensive linkages being swept away, removing the incentives for the broadening and deepening of backward linkages.

Economic policy in the years following privatisation was geared towards private sector development. Within this, policy makers failed to see the potential for private sector development in the localisation of backward linkages. These were not included in any industrial and private sector development programmes. In 2007, the World Bank, through the IFC, undertook a supplier development programme in the copper-belt Province. This was, and remains, a donor and private sector funded programme, with little policy ownership from government. Staff from the relevant ministries attended only a few initial meetings.

The legal framework for the mining sector privatisation process was set by the 1995 Mines and Minerals Act. The Act liberalised the investment regime and provided for fiscal incentives to be negotiated with each mining company and enshrined in Development Agreements (DAs). The 1995 Act, and later the 2008 Act, granted the mines VAT exemption and eliminated customs and excise duties on all machinery and equipment. This incentivising tax regime only applied to the firms holding mining rights and not their suppliers. Suppliers of capital goods, therefore, paid a customs duty ranging from 15 to 25 per cent for some goods (unless these goods qualified for preferential regional trade agreements under SADC), plus VAT on all imports. This measure conferred a cost penalty on local suppliers since as in the cases of Ghana and Tanzania imports by the mines were duty and quota free.

All the Development Agreements included provisions for local procurement, to be monitored by an inter-ministerial committee comprising the Ministry of Mines and Mineral Development and Ministry of Commerce, Trade and Industry. However, these provisions were largely disregarded by both the mines and government, with the exception of a limited IFC led suppliers' development programme. Poor institutional capacity in the Ministries involved meant that no comprehensive assessment of the supply chain was conducted, nor were monitoring mechanisms established or support programmes designed. This was due to, among other reasons, high staff turnover in the Ministries, lack of clear implementation and monitoring mechanisms, and a highly personalised style of management, which built on individual rather than institutional, capabilities.

Thus, Zambia's policy towards linkages in the mining sector involves a poorly developed vision and an absence of detailed supportive policies embodying either positive or negative sanctions to promote backward linkages. Policies were inconsistent insofar as the policy commitment to linkage development was undermined by trade policies putting local suppliers at a disadvantage. Implementation and monitoring capabilities in government have been weak and to the extent that any of the Development Agreements had any specific linkage commitments by individual mines (a rare occurrence), even this was lost when the 2008 Mining Act removed the legal obligation (which was not reflected in practice) of the mines to develop local supply chains.

In conclusion, in this chapter we have summarised the findings of our individual studies focusing on the roles played by key drivers in linkage development. However, is there a general story to be told, drawing together these individual experiences, and providing a generalizable picture of the determinants of linkage development across sectors and countries? Moreover, what policies might be appropriate and effective in hastening the process of market-led linkage development that we charted in chapter 2. These are the issues that we will now consider in chapter 6.

Chapter 6

Does One Thing Lead to Another and if Not, Why Not?

In chapter 2, we drew on the seminal analysis of linkages by Albert Hirschman. Writing in the 1960s and 1970s, Hirschman argued that there were three categories of potential linkages arising from the resource sector – financial linkages (appropriating commodity rents and investing them in unrelated sectors); consumption linkages (demand for domestic production arising from the incomes earned in the commodities sectors); and production linkages (forward and backward linkages into the commodities sectors). He believed, and in our analysis we have adopted the same approach, that production linkages provided a fruitful path for the diversification of resource rich economies, for employment creation and for the spreading of resource rents. Hirschman also argued that there would be a natural process whereby linkages would unfold, arising from externalities in the supply chain which would spur the development of further linkages. He described this process graphically - '…development is essentially the record of how one thing leads to another' (Hirschman, 1981:75).

So, what have we found in our analysis of production linkages across a range of sectors and economies in SSA at the end of the first decade of the twenty-first century? We begin by reviewing the extent of production linkages, considering both the breadth and depth of linkages into and out of the commodities sectors. This is followed by an analysis of the extent to which four key contextual drivers determine the breadth and depth of these production linkages. Thereafter we will consider the key lessons that emerge from this analysis and conclude with a discussion of the policy implications for a more rapid unfolding of linkages into and out of the commodities sector.

Has one thing led to another?

In chapter 2, we challenged the hegemonic conclusions of the Resource Curse and Enclave schools of thought. They asserted that there have been, and would continue to be, only limited production linkages from the commodities sector. Moreover, they also concluded that a specialisation in commodities would undermine and erode the development of other traded goods sectors such as manufacturing and traded services. We argued, by contrast, that this was a misreading of the industrial history of the high-income economies.

Further, whatever might have been the case prior to the mid-1990s, the increasingly rapid adoption of corporate strategies focusing on specialisation in core competences mean that contemporary lead commodity producers have a vested interest in outsourcing. Enclave development is as sub optimal to these lead firms as it is for governments, suppliers and processors and the communities surrounding commodity extraction sites. However, we concluded, the extent of linkage development would reflect the passing of time (long standing commodity production is more likely to have led to linkage development), the technological complexity of individual sectors, the capabilities in the local economy and the impact of four key contextual drivers (which we will discuss in below).

What general trends in linkage development did our analysis, as reported in detail in chapter 4, show? Bearing in mind the uneven and largely qualitative nature of the evidence that we have been able to collect, our assessment of the depth, breadth and trajectory of linkages in the eight country studies is summarised in Table 6.1. This shows a range of experiences, beginning with the breadth and depth of linkages, at the one extreme lie Angola, Botswana and Tanzania. In each of these countries, linkages are very limited, although there seems to be a more positive trajectory in Angola and Botswana than in Tanzania. At the other extreme is South Africa, where there is a very broad spectrum of linkages, in some cases of a globally leading character. There are also, less substantial, but nevertheless well-developed linkages in Gabon, Ghana, Nigeria and Zambia.

It is notable that the extent of the depth of linkages was more limited than the breadth of linkages. In an era of international specialisation and globalisation, this is a near universal phenomenon, since suppliers invariably import some of their own inputs. However, the shallowness of linkages in SSA is more evident than in most other regions of the global economy. In three of our case studies (Angola, Botswana and Tanzania) the only effective addition to local value addition was the labour content, although in two of these countries (Angola and Botswana) there was an increase in the level of skills employed. In Nigeria and Zambia where the depth of linkages was greater, and especially in South Africa, there is also evidence of horizontal linkages, that is, competencies developed in meeting the needs of the commodities sector are also applied to serving the needs of other sectors.

The duration of commodity exploitation emerges strongly as an important factor in this summary table. South Africa, where large-scale mineral exploitation stretches back for more than a century, is a clear indicator of this. The depth and breadth of linkages in Zambia and Nigeria (particularly when contrasted with the pattern of linkages in the same sector in Angola) also shows a positive association with time, as do the respective patterns of linkage in the gold sectors of Ghana (relatively high) and Tanzania (relatively low). Gabon, too, reflects the deepening of linkages over time. On the other hand, despite the diamond industry having a fifty year history in Botswana, linkages only really began to develop after 2005. Thus whilst the age of the sector may have an important role to play in linkage development, in itself, the simple passage of time, will not lead to an optimal unfolding of linkages.

In all countries, there are important capability gaps that hinder the extension of linkages. As we have observed, this is an intrinsic character of production in the global economy. However, the nature of this gap differs across our sample of countries. In some cases, such as South Africa and to a lesser extent Nigeria and Ghana, this capability gap is reflected at a relatively high-level of knowledge intensity. In other cases, such as Angola and Tanzania, the gap surfaces at very basic levels of industrial capabilities and knowledge capabilities.

Finally, the trajectory of linkages was not always positive. In some countries –Angola, Botswana, Ghana and Nigeria - there is evidence of linkage growth (with varying degrees of local content). By contrast, in other countries the degree of linkages is static. This is the case for Tanzania as well as in Gabon (where the tendency for linkages to become shallower has only been arrested due to government fiats limiting the export of logs). In the two most advanced cases of linkages – South Africa and Zambia – there is evidence of a shallowing of linkages.

Why does one thing not always lead to another?

Given this uneven, and in some cases rather slow evolution of linkages, we have sought to understand the factors which have driven this unfolding scenario. In chapter 2, we distinguished two primary sets of linkage drivers. The first are of an intrinsic nature - notably the age of the commodity exploiting sector and sectoral factors such as the requirement for just-in-time and flexible logistics, the specificity of individual commodity deposits, and the technological complexity of the sector. We have briefly considered these intrinsic drivers in the preceding discussion of the extent of linkages above.

The second category of drivers is contextual and reflects the particular circumstances in which commodity production occurs. Unlike the technological character of a particular commodity sector and the individual nature of deposits, contextual factors are more easily open to influence and therefore pose the question of what are the most effective forms of policy intervention. In chapter 5, we analysed four of these contextual drivers of linkage development, namely:

1. The nature of ownership of lead commodity firms, and their suppliers and customers
2. The nature and quality of infrastructure
3. The nature of capabilities, as reflected in skills and the National System of Innovation

4. Policies and their implementation.

From a comparative analysis of linkage development across the sectors and economies, we drew the following broad conclusions on the influence of these contextual drivers.

The role of ownership in promoting linkages

Outside South Africa, as a rule the lead firms in SSA's hard commodities sectors are foreign owned. The exception is in oil and gas. But, whilst governments have an active presence as equity holders in oil and gas, in most cases these are 'sleeping', rentier equity holdings, and the core sourcing decisions are made by TNCs. Only in soft commodities do locally owned producers exercise control over the sourcing of inputs and the destination of outputs. There are important differences between the origin of foreign investors, their modes of ownership, their insertion into their home markets, and the distinctive character of individual firms. To what extent, and in what ways, have these ownership attributes affected the pattern of linkage development?

Table 6.1 Summary of findings on the breadth, depth, and trajectory in linkages from commodities to other sectors in eight SSA economies.

Country	Sector	Linkage type	Breadth of linkage	Depth of linkage	Horizontal linkages	Maturity of the Commodity Sector	Gap between capabilities, sectoral complexity and capital cost	Trajectory of linkages
Angola	Offshore oil	Backward	Thin	Thin (labour only)	None	Mid 1990s	Complex and capital intensive sector vs. low domestic capabilities	Increasing depth
Botswana	Diamonds	Forward	Thin	Thin (largely labour)	None	1960s	Craft intensive processing and weak skills	Increasing breadth and depth
Gabon	Timber	Forward	Thick	Transformation of commodities	None	Early 1960s	Capital intensive processing, weak skill and supplier base	Resistance to shallowing

Country	Sector	Linkage type	Breadth of linkage	Depth of linkage	Horizontal linkages	Maturity of the Commodity Sector	Gap between capabilities, sectoral complexity and capital cost	Trajectory of linkages
Ghana	Gold	Backward	Beyond thin	Some transformation of inputs, and knowledge intensive services	Not fully known, but probable	late 19th Century	Capital intensive processing, moderate skill base	Increasing breadth and depth
Nigeria	Oil	Backward	Approaching thick	Knowledge intensive services	Not fully known, but probable	1950s	Capital intensive processing, improving skill base	Increasing breadth and depth
South Africa	Mining capital equipment and specialist services	Backward	Thick	Transformation of inputs, and considerable knowledge intensive services	Substantial	1880s	Knowledge and capital intensive, well-developed industrial skill and knowledge base	Becoming shallower?

194 One Thing Leads to Another

Country	Sector	Linkage type	Breadth of linkage	Depth of linkage	Horizontal linkages	Maturity of the Commodity Sector	Gap between capabilities, sectoral complexity and capital cost	Trajectory of linkages
Tanzania	Gold	Backward	Thin	Thin	Unlikely	1998	Capital intensive processing, weak skill base	Static
Zambia	Copper	Backward	Approaching thick, but diminishing	Approaching thick transformation of inputs and outputs, but diminishing backward linkages	Not known, but probable	Early 20th Century	Capital intensive processing, moderate industrial base	Shallowing

The first ownership specific driver of linkages arises from the transnational operations of lead commodity foreign investors in SSA's commodity sectors. The fracturing of value chains in many sectors, particularly those involving a large number of links in the value chain, has led to the development of what has come to be called a 'global sourcing follower supply' pattern of chain organisation. In this, the lead chain driver expects its TNC first tier global suppliers (OEMs) to satisfy its needs locally in their global operations. Developed in the auto industry and rapidly extending to the electronics industry, this form of chain organisation has spread to the global operations of lead commodity producing TNCs. First tier suppliers such as Caterpillar follow the mining firms into their operations in Africa, adding value locally through skills and services, but with a very limited deepening of the domestic supply chain into the second and third tiers. Locally owned firms tend to be excluded from these TNC owned first tier supply chains, which provide complex and key inputs to the lead commodity firms. These locally owned suppliers are instead relegated to other sub chains, such as the provision of low technology and/or non-scale intensive inputs to the lead commodity producers (for example in Zambia, steel fabrication, gas and welding products, castings, personal protective equipment, plastic pipes/fittings and tanks, injection moulding, simple engineering, as well as security and fresh food). Global sourcing and follower supply does not mean that there is no local production, but rather that local production is in the hands of foreign firms and is affected by the policies of these global suppliers. In this sense, the sourcing patterns of TNC first tier suppliers and users may be similar to those of lead commodity firms.

Second, the dominance of foreign ownership amongst lead commodity firms may not be bad news for linkage development, since TNC lead firms and very large TNC first tier suppliers tend to have developed structured programmes for supplier and customer development in their global operations. Although these programmes in the commodities sectors lag some way behind the frontier of chain management in the auto and electronics sectors, they do embody routines for supplier and customer development, which hold considerable potential for linkage development. Our studies show widespread strategic commitment at senior corporate levels to supplier development (and to a lesser extent customer development) by these large TNCs. However, there was less evidence of implementation and in most cases we observed a large gap between corporate vision and execution. But where TNCs do have supply chain development capabilities (as, for example in Zambia), these are promoting of linkage development

Third, foreign owned lead commodity firms with their roots in the OECD economies are vulnerable to pressures from civil society organisations in their home countries. This has led to increasing pressures to shape their commodity operations in SSA to take account of social and environmental considerations through the introduction of CSR programmes. Some of these CSR programmes have resulted in the development of backward linkages in the local communities adjacent to the commodity deposits, and this has been a major driver of what linkages have developed in Ghana and Tanzania. There is little evidence that Chinese, Indian and Malaysian owned lead commodity firms have been subject to similar pressures from their home environment. In South Africa, the current drive to widen ownership to the formerly disadvantaged black population has also increasingly led to the development of black empowerment supplier and user firms.

A fourth and related conclusion to emerge from our case studies is the distinctive character of Chinese lead firms' rapidly growing presence in Africa's commodities sectors. Unlike northern countries where the Washington Consensus has led to the separation of aid, trade and FDI, China's growing presence in Africa's resource sector has been characterised by a process of strategic bundling, in which access to Africa's resources has been achieved through complementary aid and FDI. A consequence of these aid related commodity investments is that the use of the 'Angola mode' financing of operations through China's Exim Bank is associated with low levels of domestic content as the financial facility specifies the use of Chinese inputs on a large-scale. Thus, in infrastructural investments in Angola, Chinese firms tend to have much lower levels of local content than do northern and Brazilian and South Africa firms. However, this is not always the case. In Zambia, Chinese lead firms appear to be willing to use local suppliers, but they lack experience with structured supply chain upgrading routines and do not invest in the upgrading of their suppliers in the same way as northern and South African lead commodity producers. They are also more prone to delisting, as opposed to assisting, weak suppliers.

Where Chinese firms are prepared to source domestically, this seldom extends into the mobilisation, development and promotion of locally owned suppliers. In many cases, their locally based suppliers are Chinese owned. That is, they are following the follower supply model of lead northern firms, but not just with respect to technology and scale intensive inputs provided by TNC first tier suppliers, but also in relation to the provision of relatively simple inputs which are characteristically supplied by small-scale, privately owned, second and third tier Chinese suppliers. However, these firms differ from the classic northern follower supply OEM pattern insofar as they are generally examples of private Chinese firms migrating with their families and relocating to live in African countries. The industrial processing zones under construction in Zambia and other African countries are a vehicle for the promotion of this model. In Sudan, the Chinese lead oil firms have brought nearly 100 Chinese supplying firms with them, employing more than 4,600 people (Suliman and Badawi 2010).

Chinese firms are also not homogeneous and there are signs that independent private sector firms operate differently to state owned firms in their sourcing patterns. As a rule, private sector firms are more deeply imbedded in African economies and appear to show a greater willingness to source locally, and from locally owned firms. However, within the category of private Chinese FDI, the large private sector firms are less likely to source locally than the smaller Chinese private firms are. This evidence on the difference in sourcing behaviour of private sector firms is only suggestive, as is the evidence that there may be a growing convergence in the behaviour of Chinese lead commodity producers with those of northern investors.

Fifth, an important component of ownership that affects the nature, breadth and depth of linkages from the commodities sector is firm specific attributes. Individual firms have specific capabilities and trajectories and are inserted differentially into global value chains. Not all firms operate in the same way, even when they produce in the same sector and the same country, and have the same country of origin as their competitors. There is widespread evidence of this firm specific factor, including in backward linkages in Angola, the gold mining industry in Tanzania and the DRC and the diamond industry in Botswana. There is nothing unique to the significance of these firm specific characteristics, but they provide scope for host country governments to exploit firm differences and firm specific strengths and weaknesses in order to maximise linkage development.

Finally, although limited to a single study, we are able to draw reasonably clear conclusions on how the ownership of the lead commodity firm and its insertion in its home market influences both forward and horizontal linkages. The insertion of China based buyers in the timber value chain has led to a thinning out of forward linkages in Gabon and to a diminution of the possibilities for horizontal linkages promoting the development of other sectors. This outcome in Gabon is mirrored in Thailand's cassava industry (Kaplinsky et al., 2011) and in other soft commodity sectors exporting to China such as Malaysian palm oil and Vietnamese tea and vanilla exports.

The role of infrastructure in linkage development

It is clear that the nature of the commodity affects the types of infrastructure that is required. At the one extreme are those elements of export infrastructure that are highly commodity specific such as the oil pipelines and loading facilities in Angola and Nigeria, and the export infrastructure for gold in Ghana and Tanzania, and diamonds in Botswana. In other sectors, the infrastructure required to export commodities will have important spill-overs into other sectors, as well as to linkage firms. This is the case in the transportation of copper from Zambia and coal from Mozambique to the East African coast, and potentially also for the export of timber from Gabon.

Infrastructural requirements on the input side are much less specifically tailored to particular commodities. All of the sectors that we have examined are heavy users of imported inputs and these are impeded by weak infrastructure. This poses both threat and opportunity for linkage firms. On the one hand, the difficulty of importing inputs is a form of natural protection favouring local suppliers. This is evident in the supply of fresh fruit and vegetables to lead commodity firms in the DRC and, to a lesser extent, in Ghana and Tanzania. On the other hand, the operations of domestic linkage firms is also hindered by weak infrastructure and this often has particularly adverse implications for small and medium sized firms. This is evidenced in relation to poorly developed power utilities in Angola, Botswana, Nigeria and Tanzania. Linkage firms are forced to invest in their own power generating capacity, which is invariably much more costly than grid based supplies. This creates additional costs for these linkage firms, undermining their capacity to link effectively to lead commodity firms.

Turning to soft infrastructure – that is, the facilitating environment that reflects enterprise efficiency and trade – there is evidence of significant shortcomings in virtually all of our case studies, bar diamonds in Botswana. These reflect a number of infrastructural weaknesses. High amongst these in some economies (notably Angola, Gabon and Tanzania) is the corruption that wastes entrepreneurial energies and biases investment decisions. More generally, the development of linkages with the commodity sector is severely impeded by what the World Bank refers to as 'the Business Environment' reflecting factors such the time taken to establish enterprises and other barriers to entry and exit. However, as in the case of weak physical infrastructure, in principle weak soft infrastructure may favour local production and local linkage development. Lead commodity firms and their first and second tier suppliers and users face considerable logistic difficulties in importing inputs and are therefore predisposed to draw on local providers.

As a rule, outside of the very specific export conduit routes of oil and precious minerals, almost all hard and soft infrastructure is of a public good nature. As a consequence, it is unlikely that the private sector will invest in their provision, or if they do so, the level of investment will be socially suboptimal. By 'socially suboptimal' investment, we refer to a situation where potential externalities which have a high benefit-cost payoff will not be maximised, thereby undermining linkage development. Therefore, in all of these cases, it is the efficiency of government provision – and, where infrastructure spans national boundaries, of inter-government provision - which has a bearing on linkage development. Again, Botswana stands out as a country where the state has taken action in the face of market failures in infrastructure provision and this is reflected in the positive trajectory of forward linkage development. In Nigeria, government has been effective in some sets of infrastructure such as telecommunications and weak in others such as power. Both of these sets of infrastructure have a demonstrable bearing on linkage development. In general, the low level of public provision in some of the economies such as Tanzania and Angola places severe penalties on all users of infrastructure. However, whilst the lead commodities firms have some capacity to cover their own infrastructure needs and to solve their own problems, their suppliers and users find this more difficult. This means that whilst the lead commodity producers may wish to increase outsourcing, weak infrastructure forces them to either internalise these noncore value added activities or import from stable foreign suppliers. In the extreme case of Angola, state-provision of infrastructure is so weak, that the only viable location for linkage firms is in the compounds of the lead commodity firms who have invested heavily to meet their own infrastructural needs. These compounds are not open to second- and third-tier suppliers.

This pervasive state failure in infrastructural provision throughout our case-studies is exacerbated when a number of countries and donors are involved. This is particularly evident in the case of the Central Development Corridor, which links the Great Lakes interior to the East African seaboard. There are enormous potential gains for production linkages from this Corridor, perhaps even greater for horizontal linkages to other sectors than for backward and forward linkages from the commodities sector. However, there appears to be a chronic incapacity of the governments involved in this collective effort to work together in an effective and timely manner. This contrasts sharply with the southern Corridor in Mozambique, which has potential regional spill-overs to externalities in Malawi and southern Tanzania. In this latter case, and partly as a consequence of the nature of the commodity (coal, which in itself will cover the costs of infrastructure development), the primary government in question (Mozambique) and the involvement of an emerging company firm which has deep experience both in mining and infrastructure (Vale), progress seem much quicker and better directed.

The role of capabilities in linkage development

In all of the industrialised economies that emerged out of commodity intensive production activities, there were accompanying major investments in education – more especially technical education. It would seem that enhancing human resources is a *sine qua non* for building linkages – and particularly horizontal linkages i.e. the movement of capabilities initially developed in commodity production into new areas. Capabilities, and the growth of capabilities, are therefore the essential ingredients for a broadening and deepening of linkages between the commodities sector and other sectors of the economy. In turn, capabilities depend on competences, that is, the availability of knowledge intensive inputs that make it possible for firms to operate effectively. Our research explored two sets of competences relevant to the capabilities of linkage firms feeding into the commodities sector. These were skills – their number and quality, the training programmes that created them, and their mobility – and the range and quality of institutions in the NSI.

Across the board, and to varying degrees, the skill constraint was reported as being a critical determinant of linkages both by lead firms and their suppliers and customers. Although the shortage of skills is not unique to SSA or to the commodities sector, for historical reasons the skills deficit is particularly marked in SSA. The extent of this skills deficit varies across countries, a function of both skills supply and demand. Nigeria with a relatively long history of independent government tends to have relatively developed human resources, for example when compared to Angola. Of all our case studies, supplier firms to the Nigerian oil sector reported the lowest levels of skills shortage. In Gabon, the skills constraint was so acute that even some low levels skills were imported from neighbouring countries. In most cases, though, the primary skills gaps arise with regard to vocational production skills (such as welders, fitters and turners, drivers of specialised equipment, gemstone cutters) and more advanced engineering skills. The absence of adequate numbers of engineering skills was especially evident in the firms supplying control lines to the offshore oil firms in Angola and at higher levels of technological knowhow in South Africa's mining services providers.

In all of the countries in which we undertook research, governments were aware of the importance of skills and this was reflected in their high-level policy visions. Yet the recognition of this skill deficit was in practice expressed in different ways. In Angola, government set targets for the recruitment of skills by the lead commodity firms, but at the higher ends of skill spectrum, these targets were unrealistic. Moreover, the quantity of skills being developed in Angola, even in prioritised engineering skills, was inadequate to meet the needs of the industry. In Gabon and Tanzania, the shortage of skills at all levels meant that the government allowed the lead commodity firms to import skills without any effective limits. By contrast, in South Africa, despite the acute shortage of high-level skills, commodity firms encountered great obstacles in recruiting skilled labour from abroad. In Botswana, government targeted skill development as a major objective of policy.

The picture with regard to capacities available in the National Systems of Innovation tells a similar story. Whilst each of our sample countries had institutions in the NSI, which nominally addressed the needs of the commodities sector and its linkage firms, only in Nigeria was there evidence of the required scale of effort or a systematic attempt to build industry specific skills and research capacities. In Angola, Gabon, Tanzania and Zambia there were only token efforts to build innovative capacities. In South Africa which historically had global class-leading mining industry research capacities, these institutions are stagnating, and research skills are being exported to other countries, notably Australia.

Turning to capability growth in linkage firms, in none of the countries was there any evidence of effective programmes designed to upgrade suppliers and processors. If anything, in some cases such as Angola and Ghana, the Ministry of Industry that was responsible for this upgrading agenda was specifically debarred from working with the commodities sectors. These were instead the responsibility of ministries responsible for resources, with little history and very limited capabilities for strengthening industrial competences. In Angola, Ghana and Zambia, aid funded programmes of SME upgrading agencies nominally focused on linkage firms in the commodities sector. However, not only were these inputs fragmentary and small in scale, but their usefulness was often dismissed by both lead commodity firms and linkages firms.

This uneven picture of capacity building in skills and institutional support is only part of the story. Competences may be developed but they may not be translated into the capabilities that govern the effectiveness of supplier and user firms. This reflects a combination of two factors – the misguided nature of capacity building and poorly developed routines in user firms and institutions. In all of the countries that we researched, to a greater or lesser degree capacity building was either not focused on the needs of the sector, or misguidedly focused. In South Africa, for example, the new industrial policy makes no mention of the promotion of the commodities sector or its linking firms, despite their global competiveness and high levels of local value addition. Similarly, in Tanzania, despite a stated vision of supporting commodities production, neither the educational system nor the NSI was focused in any meaningful way on the sector's needs. In Angola, as noted, the provision of specialised professional skills was inadequate. The disciplines taught were not attuned to the specific needs of the commodities sector, the levels of training were insufficient and there was generally an inadequate intercourse with the users of skilled labour on what types of skills were required. Only in Botswana was there any evidence of targeting the specific skill needs of firms supplying inputs into the commodities sector and beneficiating the outputs of the sector, an exercise being carried out in collaboration with the private sector. Where skills were available, the routines governing their use led to suboptimal capability building. This was particularly evident in most of the lead commodity firms. They had trained purchasing managers (generally recruited from abroad), but the routines governing their performance and reflected in the firms' incentive structures were such that the purchasing managers invariably chose to import inputs from abroad rather than to engage in the long-term development of supplier capabilities.

Finally, and perhaps not surprisingly, in none of our case studies did we identify beyond-the-horizon thinking on skills and NSI development. This was true even in the most strategically focused case of Botswana, where no thought appears to have been given to the impending electronics and laser revolutions which seem likely to undermine the centrality of tacit knowledge and craft based skills in diamond cutting and polishing.

The role of policy in linkage development

In chapter five we identified a number of factors which were critical for successful policy design and implementation. We begin by asking whether governments have a Vision for the promotion of linkages from commodities? Here we can identify three broad overlapping strands in our case study countries.

The first comprises a group of countries that have a general vision for making the most of commodities - both by maximising the growth of this sector and by promoting linkages – but who fail to articulate this vision in any specific meaningful way. This is particularly evident in the case of countries such as Ghana, Tanzania and Zambia, which have implemented Structural Adjustment Policies under the behest of the international financial institutions. It also includes Gabon and South Africa. In each of these countries, there is a stated wish to promote the commodities sector and to spread the benefits, but there is little strategic thinking beyond these broad commitments. The visions are thus largely vacuous.

The second group of countries are those where the vision – to the extent that it exists - conflates the development of local content with the development of local indigenous participation in linkages to the commodities sector. In these countries, 'localisation' is interpreted as greater participation by citizens as owners and employees rather than as a deepening of domestic value added. It is not that these visions are indifferent to the depth of linkages, but this is a subsidiary priority of an indigenisation policy, which, it is assumed, will in time lead to a greater degree of domestic content in the commodity value chains. South Africa, Angola, Nigeria and Tanzania have all prioritised indigenisation in the development of linkages.

The third strand is one of a coherent and well worked vision for expansion of linkages, backed by informed analysis and setting a timetable with clear benchmarks. This is best exemplified by Botswana's strategic vision for forward linkages in the diamond chain. The Nigerian policy framework has been both dynamic and facilitative of linkage development. Policy has given increasing prominence to the deepening of domestic value added and the associated need to grow relevant capacities in skill development and the NSI.

Beyond strategies, lies the question of policy development. Is the vision backed by detailed policies, do these policies embody positive and negative sanctions, and do these policies cohere or are they contradictory in nature? Not surprisingly, the picture that emerges in these respects is similar to the degree of development of each country's strategic vision. Botswana's vision is backed by a series of mutually consistent policies, although its framework for promoting skill development is still at an embryonic stage and fails to capture the dynamic nature of technological change in the sector. Gabon, too, has a sharply focused specific policy for linkage development – a blanket ban on exports of unprocessed logs – but this is less informed by the detailed steps required to build competitive dynamic capabilities in this chain. Similarly, the list of inputs subject to a local content cost premium in Angola's oil sector does not appear to be backed by an informed analysis of the gap between local capabilities and technological challenge. At the other end of the spectrum lie Ghana, Tanzania and Zambia who have failed to develop any meaningful specific policies to promote linkage development. Moreover, some of the policies which have been implemented and which are relevant to linkage development are counterproductive, notably special bilateral agreements with the lead mining firms which allow them duty and quota free importation of inputs and skilled labour but force linkage suppliers to pay duties and to struggle to obtain work permits for expatriate skills. Between the ends of this spectrum lie Angola and South Africa. Each of these countries has a clear set of policies, but these have limited efficacy with respect to the broader goal of deepening local content.

To what extent do the governments in these economies display the will and the capacity to implement their strategic vision and policies to promote linkage development? There is a major capacity gap in government in all the countries that have been considered and this is reflected in the failure not only to develop a vision and supporting policies, but also to monitor and implement these policies. In some cases, the capacity gap is exacerbated by a 'will gap' for a combination of reasons which include an undermining of legitimacy and morale in government, and the pervasiveness of corruption. Policies that exist on paper are very poorly implemented. This affects not just policies directly related to the commodity sector and the development of linkages, but also policies that indirectly affect linkage development such as those on human resource development and infrastructure. The extreme cases are Gabon, where the Forestry Code's provisions on sustainable logging and the ban on log exports have been routinely flouted, and Tanzania where policy implementation has been undermined by a combination of lack of will and corruption. Angola and Nigeria, too, are states that are widely believed to be bedevilled by corruption although this did not surface in our research as a factor directly affecting the implementation of policies towards the commodities sector and its linkages. Again, as in so many respects, the outlier has been Botswana where there has been a recognition that the gap in domestic capacities in government needs to be filled by buying in the external expertise which is required to develop evidence based policy.

This is in many respects a damming critique of the policy environment in the SSA economies in which we have researched. Misalignments both between and within the visions and programmes of government and the private sector are pervasive. However, as we noted in chapter 5, the challenges of developing a vision, backed by policies with teeth and are implemented effectively are not confined to government. They are also central to the operations of the private sector. In all of the sectors and countries in which we undertook research we encountered a corporate sector, which was aware of the potential offered by near sourced linkages for cost reduction, particularly in the medium and long-term. The northern origin TNCs in particular had well-developed corporate visions on linkage development and, on paper, had structured programmes ('policies') for supplier (and in some cases, customer) development. Yet the reality has been that these visions and policies have seldom been implemented. There is an enormous gap between what happens on the ground and what exists on paper. Therefore, here, too we can identify a major policy shortfall, which means that the opportunities for win-win linkages from the commodities sectors are not being grasped.

An accompanying element in this shortfall in policy as a driver of linkage development is the pervasive failure of private and public sector stakeholders to work together in the development of a collective vision, and mutually reinforcing and implemented policies. In most cases, we observed an absence of dialogue on the specifics of linkage development. In Tanzania, this absence was not an accident of omission but arose as a direct consequence of hostile negotiations between government and the private sector on the fiscal regime that governed the minerals sector. Similarly, in South Africa, debate on policy towards the mineral sector has been overwhelmed by the issue of property rights and indigenisation of ownership. Respect for, and recognition of, the visions and policies of other stakeholders on linkage development was highest in Botswana, but even here this did not translate into the structured programmes of multi stakeholder strategic development which have aided the deepening of value added in other sectors and in other countries.

How can policy help make one thing lead to another?

The story that we have told in the preceding discussion in this and earlier chapters has been one of missed opportunities and misalignments. We have argued that in the context of contemporary business strategies, lead commodity producers have been unable to give effect to policies by implementing effective strategies to maximise outsourcing of non-core competences, preferably to local suppliers. These strategies are bounded, of course, by the capacity of suppliers to deliver reliably adequate quality at competitive prices. Where local inputs are sought and acquired, most lead commodity firms accept that they might have to pay a higher price in the short run, but with the expectation that local capabilities will grow and reduce these price premiums over time. Governments in host countries, as well as existing and potential suppliers and local communities, clearly have a vested interest in fostering this process of local outsourcing. This is in principle a win-win world of mutual interest in backward linkage development. With regard to forward linkages, lead commodity producers have less of an interest in promoting this form of linkage development, but it is of central interest to host governments, local processors and beneficiators, and local communities.

Yet our case-studies evidence a mixed picture in linkage development. We have recorded varying degrees of local outsourcing and forward linkages, driven by a variety of market-led, sector-specific and contingent factors. Yet, in almost all cases, we observe sub-optimal outcomes. Generally, we have observed an absence of potentially viable linkages. However, we also have encountered the 'overdevelopment' of some beneficiation linkages, that is, focusing on local linkage development, which has little chance of competitive production even in the medium and long-term. We have charted a number of factors that explain these suboptimal outcomes. Some of these factors are very difficult to influence, such as the intrinsic technological intensity of manufacturing processes and knowledge intensive services. However, others are subject to change. It is these which we now address, focusing on the implications which this holds for government policy in host countries, for corporate strategy and policy, and for the dialogue between public and private actors in commodity value chains.

The key theme underlying a strategic response to linkage development is to develop a roadmap. This involves an *informed* process in which stakeholders cooperate in identifying three broad families of linkages in the context of a moving global innovation frontier. The first family are the '*low hanging fruit*', linkages that provide short term returns to lead commodity firms (Figure 6.1). In these cases, suppliers and customers are able to produce quality products reliably at prices that are near the global price frontier. In the case of backward linkages, we can term these 'commodity gate prices', that is the cost of inputs at the mine/farm/well gate, including both the costs of transforming inputs into products and the costs of hard infrastructure (for example, transport) and soft infrastructure (for example, import permits). In the first instance, linkage development policies should be designed to grasp these win-win low hanging fruit opportunities. Beyond this are linkages where *embryonic* capabilities exist and where there is some prospect, that with reasonable time-bound support, local producers are able to compete with foreign producers. The response in this category of products is to develop targeted interventions that enable local producers to compete with foreign producers over time. The final family are ambitious and often high profile linkages that are *beyond feasible reach* in the short to medium term. Policy here should be focused on resisting the political pressures often exerted by local stakeholders (such as segments of industry, local scientists and engineers and politicians) to promote these overly ambitious linkages.

Figure 6.1 The trajectory of local supply

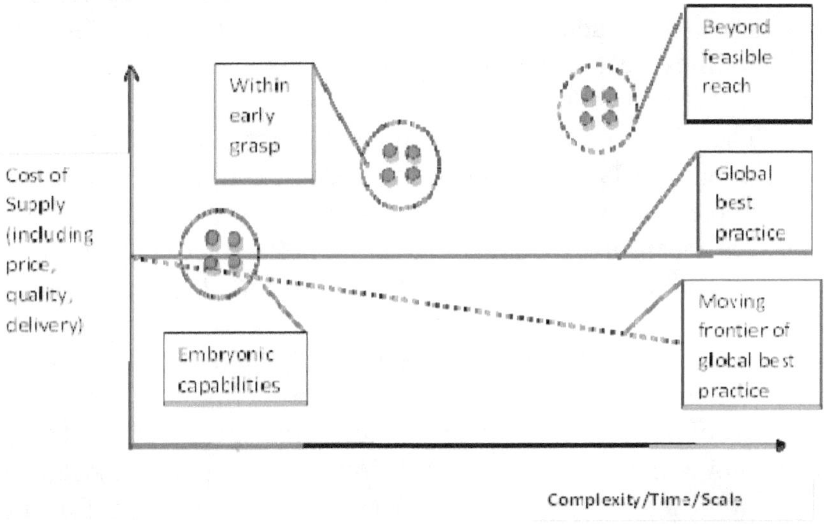

It is critical that this roadmap be developed as an outcome of a cooperative, on-going and informed interaction between key value chain participants. Although the composition of these restructuring coalitions will inevitably reflect context (the sector, the country and the lead firms), in principle it should include all the major participants in the value chain (lead commodity firms, first and some second tier suppliers and customers), governments, representatives of the NSI, and in some cases representatives from the local communities. This multi stakeholder coalition is important for two reasons. First, typically, each of the parties has specific knowledge sets, which they can contribute to an informed understanding of realistic and effective policies for linkage development. Second, since successful policy implementation requires the active participation of each of these key stakeholders, this is most likely to occur if they are actively involved in the development of the linkage strategy.

Beyond this need for a continuing and constructive dialogue of value chain stakeholders are a series of specific responses that are required of each of the key parties in the public and private realms.

Implications for government policy

Government policy to promote linkages needs to address both policies directly, addressing the development of linkages from the commodities sector and those that have an indirect effect on linkage development.

The first and most critical task is for the government to initiate and sustain a process of strategic visioning and policy development drawing in a range of relevant stakeholders. This does not mean that the government should actively run this value chain coalition – indeed in many cases, this might be an obstacle to its efficient functioning – but rather that it should ensure that this value chain coalition operates effectively. Government's prime role here is as a broker. Critical to this brokering role is the need for government to have an informed picture of the strengths and vulnerabilities of the major global firms operating in the sector. As we saw in the case of linkages from the gold sector in Tanzania and the DRC and the oil sector in Angola, there are important differences in the sourcing behaviour of individual lead commodity firms and in the strategic locational decisions of key first tier suppliers. An informed government can not only make sure that the lead firm offered access to the commodity deposit is most likely to actively promote local linkages, but also use this (as in the recent case of the DRC's copper sector – Kaplinsky and Farooki, 2009) as a bargaining chip with other foreign investors to get them to broaden and deepen their forward and backward linkages.

A second major direct policy initiative that is of proven efficacy in linkage development in SSA and elsewhere is local content policy. As we saw in previous chapters, this has probably been the single most important policy driver of linkages from the commodity sector. Although in principle prescribed by the World

Trade Organisation, *de jure* leeway is given to least developed economies for some years, and *de facto*, many countries find ways of sustaining local content policies for some years. However, it is possible to get this wrong. In many cases in the SSA context, local content policies designed to promote domestic value added have been conflated with indigenisation policies designed to transfer ownership of linkage firms to 'indigenous' citizens, in some cases not only to citizens, but to citizens of a particular racial or ethnic group. Where there is evidence that nationally owned firms are more deeply embedded than foreign firms are and thus are likely to sustain linkage development, this makes for sensible policy. However, where this is not the case, this policy conflation can often lead to a diminution of linkages or to the supply of high cost and poor quality inputs to the commodities sector and inefficiencies in processing and beneficiation. (It is notable that linkage development in most of the high-income resource intensive economies such as Norway and Australia does little to privilege local ownership of linkage firms). It is also critical that local content policies be informed, that is that they privilege sub-sectors that are within easy grasp or are embryonic linkage sectors rather than in sectors beyond feasible reach (see Figure 6.1 above). We see evidence of both phenomena in our case studies. Botswana's strategy towards linkage development is well informed and based on a series of on-going studies commissioned from external industry experts. By contrast, the local content directives issued in Angola to promote backward linkages are not informed by detailed knowledge of the sector. Fortunately, the Angolan government lacks the competences to enforce this local content policy, limiting the potential damages resulting from poor policy development.

A third category of government support is that directed to enhancing the development of local supplier firms and processors, particularly second and third tier firms. Typically, government support policies for value chain upgrading are located in the Ministry of Industry and implemented through institutions such as Investment Promotion Agencies. There is considerable international experience and expertise to draw on in supporting supply and customer chain development, much of which is generic across sectors. However, some support will be specific to the resource sector and, moreover, to the extent that there are limited restructuring capabilities available, these may need to be privileged towards the resource sector if linkage development is to be optimised.

Related to this is a fourth element to government support, which addresses the development of appropriate local capabilities. This will involve investments in skill development – at all levels – and also institutions in the NSI, which can support both the lead commodity firms and particularly their suppliers and customers. The skills component of capability building is critical at all stages of the commodity sectors development. The strengthening of the NSI represents a less immediate task for policy, having greater and increasing relevance as the commodity sector matures and draws on more knowledge intensive manufactures and services, both upstream and downstream.

A fifth area of policy is support for infrastructure. This is often the most important set of policies aiding the development of both the commodity sector itself and its linkages. It involves both hard infrastructure such as roads, telecoms and utilities and the soft infrastructure required to support businesses such as customs clearance and ease of entry and exit for firms. In principle it is possible that local linkages benefit from poor infrastructure, since the more difficult it is to source inputs from abroad or to export commodities for processing, the greater the degree of 'natural protection' offered to local linkage firms. However, promoting local linkages by increasing the costs of supply is a poor way of fostering an efficient and competitive diversified economy. There can be little justification for promoting poor infrastructure or for allowing it to continue to undermine cost effective linkage development.

Underwriting each of these five elements of policy is the capacity which government has to develop and effectively implement its policy towards linkage development. Earlier in this chapter, we identified a series of policy capabilities, beginning with the capacity to develop a coherent and informed strategy towards the commodities sector itself and to linkage development in particular. Beyond strategy lies the design of effective policies which embody positive and negative sanctions, and which are mutually reinforcing rather than contradictory. These policies need to reflect accurately the capacity of government to implement them. This in turn has to be backed by government 'will', that is, an administrative system which is (relatively) free from corruption and in which reflects government's legitimacy to push through policies that might sometimes be controversial. Legitimacy has to be earned, though, and without this, policies designed to promote linkage development may look good on paper, but have little impact in the real world of production. Finally, policy is a dynamic process and the panoply of policies that directly and indirectly influence linkage development need to be monitored regularly and to evolve over time as circumstances change.

Implications for corporate policy

The discussion of 'policy' usually starts and ends with government policy. However, the studies of linkage development presented in earlier chapters show that the corporate sector, too, has a policy problem that inhibits the extension of linkages. These corporate weaknesses mirror those in government. That is, not all lead commodity firms have a well-worked and informed strategy to foster linkage development, despite the fact that this is in their commercial interest. Even where they do have strategies, these may not be backed by effective policy instruments, for example, the failure to institutionalise supply chain development within their operations, particularly those targeting second and third tier suppliers. The various policy instruments that they have are often toothless, failing to identify and then reward and support potential local effective linkage firms. Various elements of corporate policy may also be contradictory. For example, as we saw in the case of Tanzania's gold mining industry, many lead firms task their purchasing departments with increasingly local inputs, but back these objectives with employee work performance targets and incentives, which privilege short term over long-term results. Purchasing officers generally work on short term residential cycles and are 'encased' in compounds. This makes it very difficult for them to develop the local contacts and trust required to promote supplier development. Capabilities may also be lacking in purchasing departments, where personnel are not professionally equipped to work with nascent suppliers and processors. Moreover, purchasing functions in lead firms are also not devoid of the corruption problems which confront government and which undermine linkage development. 'Legitimacy' can often be as big a problem for lead commodity firms as it is for governments.

Might one thing lead to another?

If linkage development truly is a matter of 'one thing leading to another' and offer win-win outcomes for both the public and private sectors, how is it that we have landed in a world of suboptimality where we observe unexploited scope for the extension of local linkages? One primary explanatory factor is that the key actors are caught in trajectories of behaviour that do not allow them to acknowledge the scope for win-win linkage development. Whilst this is true of some lead firms in the commodity sector, our evidence suggests that this is primarily a failure in public policy. Many governments are locked into a worldview in which they are convinced that lead firms have no intrinsic interest in broadening and deepening linkages. This may have been the case in the past, but over the past two decades the fracturing of value chains as firms seek to outsource noncore competences belies the enclave mentality that, as Singer and others documented, dominated corporate policies in the preceding decades.

A second reason why we have landed in a paradoxical and suboptimal world is that stakeholder cooperation in linkage development has been bedevilled by disputes over the sharing of resource rents. This is graphically evidenced in Tanzania (and, to a lesser extent Zambia) where taxation policies introduced in the Structural Adjustment Programme during the 1990s have resulted in situations in which governments have reaped very little of the resource rents generated during the post-2002 commodity booms. This has led to on-going conflict between government and the private sector and to an atmosphere in which the two parties find it difficult to sit down and discuss areas of win-win benefit (such as in linkage development) when they are engaged in win-lose disputes over revenue sharing.

However, third, these suboptimal outcomes are not confined to the commodities sector, or to SSA. They are an intrinsic feature of much of economic activity everywhere. As Rodrik has pointed out, it is not just that there is widespread state-failure, which calls for effectively functioning markets, but the world is also characterised by firm-failure, which calls for effective and nuanced state support (Rodrik, 2004). In the face of this simultaneous state and firm level failure, effective economic restructuring requires that both parties join hands and walk the path together. In this case, their combined task and interest lies in making the 'most of commodities' and ensuring that indeed, 'one thing leads to another'.

References

Al Jazeera. (2011, 18 June). 'Transparency' hides Zambia's lost billions. Retrieved from http://www.aljazeera.com/indepth/opinion/2011/06/20116188244589715.html

Arvis, J. F., Mustra, M. A., Ojala, L., Sheperd, B., & Saslavsky, D. (2010). *Connecting to compete 2010: Trade logistics in the global economy*. Washington, D.C.: The World Bank.

Aryeetey, E., Owusu, G., & Mensah, E. J. (2009). *An analysis of poverty and regional inequalities in Ghana*. (Working Paper Series No. 27). Washington/New Delhi: GDN.

Barnes, J., & Kaplinsky, R. (2000). Globalisation and the death of the local firm? The automobile components sector in South Africa. *Regional Studies, 34*(9), 797-812.

Barnes, J., Kaplinsky, R., & Morris, M. (2004). Industrial policy in developing economies: Developing dynamic comparative advantage in the South African automobile sector. *Competition & Change, 8*(2), 153-172.

Barnett, A., & Bell, M. (2011). *Is BHP Billiton's Cluster-Programme in Chile relevant for Africa's mining industry?*. (Policy Practice Brief No. 7). Retrieved from www.thepolicypractice.com.

Bessant, J., Kaplinsky, R., & Lamming, R. (2003). Putting supply chain learning into practice. *International Journal of Operations & Production Management, 23*(2), 167-184.

Best, M. H. (1990). *The new competition: Institutions of industrial restructuring*. Oxford, UK: Polity Press.

Bleaney, M., & Greenaway, D. (1993). Long-run trends in the relative price of primary commodities and in the terms of trade of developing countries. *Oxford Economic Papers, 45*(3), 349-363.

Bloch, R., & Owusu, G. (2011). *The drive to increase local procurement in the mining sector in Ghana: Myth or reality?*. (MMCP Discussion Paper No. 1). Cape Town, South Africa, and Milton Keynes, UK: University of Cape Town and the Open University.

Blomström, M., & Kokko, A. (2007). From natural resources to high-tech production: The evolution of industrial competitiveness in Sweden and Finland. In D. Lederman, & W. F. Maloney (Eds.), *Natural resources, neither curse nor destiny* (pp. 213-256). Washington, DC: Stanford University Press and World Bank.

Bova, E. (2009). *The implications of mine ownership for the management of the boom: A comparative analysis of Zambia and Chile.* (NCCR Working Paper 2009/13). Bern, Switzerland: Swiss National Centre of Competence in Research.

Braczyk, H.-J., Cooke, P. N., & Heidenreich, M. (1998). *Regional Innovation Systems: The role of governances in a globalized world.* London, UK: Routledge.

Bravo-Ortega, C., & de Gregorio, J. (2007). The relative richness of the poor? Natural resources, human capital and economic growth. In D. Lederman, & W. F. Maloney (Eds.), *Natural resources, neither curse nor destiny* (pp. 71-99). Washington, DC: Stanford University Press and the World Bank.

Broadman, H. G. (2007). *Africa's silk road: China and India's new economic frontier.* Washington, DC: The World Bank.

Brunnschweiler, C. (2008). Cursing the blessings? Natural resource abundance, institutions, and economic growth. *World Development, 36*(3), 319-419.

Buckley, P. J., Clegg, L. J., Cross, A. R., Liu, X., Voss, H., & Zheng, P. (2007). The determinants of Chinese outward foreign direct investment. *Journal of International Business Studies, 38*(4), 499-518.

Burke, C., & Corkin, L. (2006). *China's interest and activity in Africa's construction and infrastructure sectors.* (Paper prepared for DfID China). Stellenbosch: The Centre for Chinese Studies, Stellenbosch University.

Business Monitor International (2009). *Angola Infrastructure.* (Report Q2 2009 March). Retrieved from http://www.businessmonitor.com

Callender, G. S. (1909). *Economic history of the United States.* Boston, MA: Ginn and Company.

Cashin, P., & McDermott, J. C. (2002). *The long-run behaviour of commodity prices: Small trends and big variability.* (IMF Staff Papers 49:2). Washington, D.C.: The International Monetary Fund.

Chamberlin, E. H. (1933). *The theory of monopolistic competition.* Cambridge, MA: Harvard University Press.

Chang, H. J. (2002). *Kicking away the ladder.* London: Anthem Press.

Chenery, H. B. (1960). Patterns of industrial growth. *American Economic Review, 50*(4), 624-654.

Cheung, Y. W., & Qian, X. (2009). Empirics of China's outward direct investment. *Pacific Economic Review, 14*(3), 312-341.

Corkin, L. (2011). *Chinese Construction Companies in Angola: A Local Linkages Perspective.* (MMCP Discussion Paper No 2). Cape Town, South Africa, and Milton Keynes, UK: University of Cape Town and the Open University.

Corkin, L. (2012). Backward linkages in Angola: Insights from the infrastructure sector. *Resource Policy (forthcoming).*

Currie, A. W. (1951). *Canadian economic development.* Toronto, Canada: Thomas Nelson and Sons.

Davies, G. A. (1995). Learning to love the Dutch disease: Evidence from the mineral economies. *World Development, 23*(10), 1765-1779.

Davies, K. (2009). While global FDI falls, China's outward FDI doubles. *Columbia FDI Perspectives, 5,* 1-3.

Diakosavvas, D., & Scandizzo, P. L. (1991). Trends in the terms of trade of primary commodities, 1900-1982: The controversy and its origins. *Economic Development and Cultural Change, 39*(2), 231-264.

Dunning, J. (2000). The Eclectic Paradigm as an envelope for economic and business theories of MNE Activity. *International Business Review, 9*(1), 163-190.

Even-Zohar, C. (2007). *From mine to mistress: Corporate strategies and government policies in the international diamond industry.* London, UK: Mining Communications Ltd.

Farooki, M., & Kaplinsky, R. (2011). *The impact of China on global commodity prices: The global reshaping of the resource sector.* London, UK: Routledge.

Fessehaie, J. (2011). *Development and knowledge intensification in industries upstream of Zambia's copper mining sector.* (MMCP Discussion Paper No. 3), Cape Town, South Africa, and Milton Keynes, UK: University of Cape Town and the Open University.

Fowke, V. C. (1946). *Canadian agricultural policy.* Toronto, Canada: University of Toronto Press.

Freeman, C. (1995). The National System of Innovation in historical perspective. *Cambridge Journal of Economics, 19*(1), 5-24.

Fu, X., Kaplinsky, R., & Zhang, J. (2009). *The impact of China's exports on global manufactures prices.* (Working Paper 32). Sanjaya Lall Programme for Technology and Management for Development, Queen Elizabeth House. Oxford, UK: Oxford University.

Gereffi, G. (1994). The organization of buyer-driven global commodity chains: How U.S. retailers shape overseas production networks. In G. Gereffi, & M. Korzeniewicz (Eds.), *Commodity chains and global capitalism* (pp. 95-122). Westport, Conn.: Praeger.

Gereffi, G., Humphrey, J., & Sturgeon, T. (2005). The governance of global value chains. *Review of International Political Economy, 12*(1), 78-104.

Girvan, N. (1987). Transnational corporations and non-fuel primary commodities in developing countries. *World Development, 15*(5), 713-740.

Green, A.G. (1971) *Regional aspects of Canada's economic growth.* Toronto, Canada: University of Toronto Press

Grilli, E. R., & Yang, M. C. (1988). Primary commodity prices, manufactured goods prices, and the terms of trade of developing countries: What the long run shows. *The World Bank Economic Review, 2*(1), 1-47.

Gu, J. (2009). China's private enterprises in Africa and the implications for African development. *European Journal of Development Research, 21*(4), 570-587.

Hamel, G., & Prahalad, C. K. (1994). *Competing for the future.* Cambridge, MA: Harvard Business Press

Hanlin, C. (2011). *The drive to increase local procurement in the mining sector in Africa: Myth or reality?.* (MMCP Discussion

Paper No. 4). Cape Town, South Africa, and Milton Keynes, UK: University of Cape Town and the Open University.

Hausmann, R., Klinger, B., & Lawrence, R. (2008). *Policy Brief - Examining beneficiation* (May). Cambridge, MA: Center for International Development, Harvard University.

Heum, P., Quale, C., Karlsen, J. E., Kragha, M., & Osahon, G. (2003). *Enhancement of local content in the upstream oil and gas industry in Nigeria: A comprehensive and viable policy approach*. (SNF Report No. 25/03, August). Bergen, Norway: SNF-Institute for Research in Economics and Business Administration.

Hirschman, A. O. (1981). *Essays in trespassing: Economics to politics and beyond*. New York, NY: Cambridge University Press.

Hummels, D. (1999). *Have international transportation costs declined?*. Mimeo, University of Chicago. Retrieved from http://www.krannert.purdue.edu/faculty/hummelsd/research/decline/declined.pdf

Hymer, S. (1976). *The international operations of national firms: A study of direct foreign investment*. Cambridge, MA: MIT Press.

Innis, H. A. (1930). *The fur trade in Canada: An introduction to Canadian economic history*. New Haven, CT: Yale University Press.

Innis, H. A. (1940). *The cod fisheries: The history of an international economy*. Toronto, Canada: University of Toronto Press.

Innis, H. A. (1956). *Essays in Canadian economic history*. Toronto, Canada: University of Toronto Press.

Kaplan, D. (2011). *South African mining equipment and related services: Growth constraints and policy*. (MMCP Discussion Paper No. 5). Cape Town, South Africa, and Milton Keynes, UK: University of Cape Town and the Open University.

Kaplinsky, R., & Farooki, M. (2009). *Africa's cooperation with new and emerging development partners: Options for Africa's development*. New York, NY: The United Nations Office of Special Advisor on Africa.

Kaplinsky R., & Mhlongo, E. (1997). Infant industries and industrial policy: A lesson from South Africa. *Transition, 34*, 57-85.

Kaplinsky, R., & Morris, M. (2001). *A handbook for value chain research*. Retrieved from www.globalvaluechains.org.

Kaplinsky, R & M. Morris, (2008), 'Do the Asian Drivers Undermine Export-Oriented Industrialisation in SSA?' *World Development*, 36, 2

Kaplinsky, R., & Morris, M. (2009). Chinese FDI in sub-Saharan Africa: Engaging with large dragons. *European Journal of Development Research, 21*(4), 551–569.

Kaplinsky, R., & Morris, M. (2010). *The policy challenge for sub-Saharan Africa of large-scale Chinese FDI*. Elcano Royal Institute of International and Strategic Studies, Madrid, Spain 2010

Kaplinsky, R., & Readman, J. (2005). Globalisation and upgrading: What can (and cannot) be learnt from international trade statistics in the wood furniture sector?. *Industrial and Corporate Change, 14*(4), 679-703.

Kaplinsky, R., & Santos-Paulino, A. (2005). Innovation and competitiveness: Trends in unit prices in global trade. *Oxford Development Studies, 33*(3-4), 333-355.

Kaplinsky, R., & Santos-Paulino, A. (2006). A disaggregated analysis of EU imports: Implications for the study of patterns of trade and technology. *Cambridge Journal of Economics, 30*(4), 587-612.

Kaplinsky, R., Terheggen, A., & Tijaja, J. P. (2011). China as a final market: The Gabon timber and Thai cassava value chains. *World Development 39*(7), 1177-1190.

Larsen, M. N., Yankson, P., & Fold, N. (2009). Does Foreign Direct Investment (FDI) create linkages in mining? The case of gold mining in Ghana. In A. Sumner, D. Sanchez-Ancochea, & E. Rugraff (Eds.), *Transnational corporations and development policy: Critical perspectives* (pp. 247-273). London, UK: Palgrave Macmillan.

Lederman, D., & Maloney, W. F. (2007). Trade structure and growth. In D. Lederman, & W. F. Maloney (Eds.), *Natural resources, neither curse nor destiny* (pp. 15-39). Washington, DC: Stanford University Press and World Bank.

Lundvall, B. A. (1992). *National Systems of Innovation*. London,UK: Frances Pinter.

Mackintosh, W. A. (1923). Economic factors in Canadian history. *Canadian Historical Review, 4*(1), 12-25.

Mackintosh, W. A. (1939). *The economic background of dominion-provincial relations: Appendix III of the royal commission report on dominion-provincial relations.* Ottawa, Canada: King's Printer.

Malerba, F. (2002). Sectoral systems of innovation and production. *Research Policy, 31*(2), 247-264.

Manzano, O., & Rigobón, R. (2007). Resource curse or debt overhang? In D. Lederman, & W. F. Maloney (Eds.), *Natural resources, neither curse nor destiny* (pp. 41-70). Washington, DC: Stanford University Press and the World Bank.

Marin, A., Navas-Aleman, L., & Perez, C. (2009). *The possible dynamic role of natural-resource based networks in Latin American development strategies.* Mimeo prepared for the CEPAL-SEGIB Project (July).

Mbayi, L. (2011). *Linkages in Botswana's diamond cutting and polishing industry.* (MMCP Discussion Paper No. 6). Cape Town, South Africa, and Milton Keynes, UK: University of Cape Town and Open University.

Ministry Of Commerce People's Republic of China, MOFCOM. (2010). *Country guide to foreign investment and co-operation: Angola.*

Mjimba, V. (2011). *The nature and determinants of linkages in emerging minerals commodity sectors: A case study of gold mining in Tanzania.* (MMCP Discussion Paper No. 7). Cape Town, South Africa, and Milton Keynes, UK: University of Cape Town and the Open University.

Mohan, G., Lampert, B., & Chang, D. (2011). *Chinese diaspora, African development? Chinese business migrants in Angola, Ghana and Nigeria.* Paper presented at the DSA/EADI conference: Rethinking development in an age of scarcity and uncertainty, 19 - 22 September 2011, York, UK.

Morris, M., Kaplinsky, R., & Kaplan, D. (2011a). *'One thing leads to another' – Commodities, linkages and industrial development: A conceptual overview.* (MMCP Discussion Paper No. 12). Cape Town, South Africa and Milton Keynes, UK: University of Cape Town and the Open University.

Morris, M., Kaplinsky, R., & Kaplan, D. (2011b). *Commodities and linkages: Industrialization in sub Saharan Africa.* (MMCP Discussion Paper No. 13). Cape Town, South Africa and Milton Keynes, UK: University of Cape Town and the Open University.

Morris, M., Kaplinsky, R., & Kaplan, D. (2011c). *Commodities and linkages: Meeting the policy challenge.* (MMCP Discussion Paper No. 14). Cape Town, South Africa and Milton Keynes, UK: University of Cape Town and the Open University.

Nigeria National Petroleum Corporation, NNPC. (2009). *National content guideline.* Presentation to investors on the Gas Master Plan, NNPC, Abuja, Nigeria.

North, D. C. (1955). Location theory and regional economic growth. *The Journal of Political Economy, 63*(3), 243-258.

North, D. C. (1966). *Growth and welfare in the American past: A new economic history.* Englewood Cliffs, NJ: Prentice-Hall.

North-South Corridor International Financing Conference. (2009). *Full final report* (6-9 April). Lusaka, Zambia.

OECD. (2009). *African Economic Outlook 2009: Country profile Gabon.* Paris, France: Organisation for Economic Co-operation and Development.

Owusu, J. H. (2001). Spatial integration, adjustment, and structural transformation in sub-Saharan Africa: Some linkage pattern changes in Ghana. *Professional Geographer, 53*(2), 230-247.

Oyejide, T.A. & Adewuyi, A. O. (2011). *Enhancing linkages to the oil and gas industry in the Nigerian economy.* (MMCP Discussion Paper No. 8). Cape Town, South Africa, and Milton Keynes, UK: University of Cape Town and the Open University.

Perkins, D., & Robbins, G. (2011). *The contribution to local enterprise development of infrastructure for commodity extraction projects: Tanzania's central corridor and Mozambique's Zambezi Valley.* (MMCP Discussion Paper No. 9). Cape Town, South Africa, and Milton Keynes, UK: University of Cape Town and the Open University.

Pfaffenzeller, S., Newbold, P., & Rayner, A. (2007). A short note on updating the Grilli and Yang commodity price index. *World Bank Economic Review, 21*(1), 151-63.

Prebisch, R. (1950). *The economic development of Latin America and its principal problems.* Economic Bulletin for Latin America 7, New York, NY: United Nations.

Prescott, D. (2009). *Mapping exercise of mining and local content partnerships.* (Working paper for Harvard CSRI/ICMM/IFC).

Rodrik, D. (2004). *Industrial policy for the twenty-first century.* Mimeo, Cambridge, MA: John F. Kennedy School of Government.

Sachs, J.D., & Warner, A.M. (1997). Natural resource abundance and economic growth. In G. Meier, & J. Rauch (Eds.), *Leading issues in economic development.* Oxford, UK: Oxford University Press.

Sachs, J. D., & Warner, A. M. (2001). The curse of natural resources. *European Economic Review, 45*, 827-838.

Sapsford, D. (1985). The statistical debate on the net barter terms of trade between primary commodities and manufactures: A comment and some additional evidence. *The Economic Journal, 95*(379), 781-788.

Schmitz, H., & Knorringa, P. (2000). Learning from global buyers. *Journal of Development Studies, 37*(2), 177-205.

Singer, H. W. (1950). The distribution of gains between investing and borrowing countries. *The American Economic Review, 40*(2), 473-485.

Singer, H., Cooper, C., Desai, R. C., Freeman, C., Gish, O., Hall, S., & Oldham, G. (1970). *The Sussex Manifesto: Science and technology for developing countries during the second development decade.* (IDS Reprints No. 101). Brighton, UK: Institute of Development Studies.

Spraos, J. (1980). The statistical debate on the net barter terms of trade between primary commodities and manufactures. *The Economic Journal, 90*(357), 107-128.

Sturgeon, T., & Memedovic, O. (2010). *Measuring global value chains: Intermediate goods trade, structural change and compressed development.* (UNIDO Working Paper). Vienna, Austria: United National Industrial Development Organization.

Suliman, K. M., & Badawi, A. A. A. (2010). *An assessment of the impact of China's investments in Sudan.* (AERC Collaborative

Research Project on The Impact of China-Africa Relations). Nairobi, Kenya: African economic Research Consortium.

Taylor, L. J. (1969). Development patterns: A simulation study. *The Quarterly Journal of Economics, 48*(2), 220-241.

Teece, D. J., Pisano, G., & Shuen, A. (1997). Dynamic capabilities and strategic management. *Strategic Management Journal, 18*(7), 509-533.

Teka, Z. (2011). *Backward linkages in the manufacturing sector in the oil and gas value chain in Angola.* (MMCP Discussion Paper No. 11). Cape Town, South Africa, and Milton Keynes, UK: University of Cape Town and Open University.

Terheggen, A. (2011). *The tropical timber industry in Gabon: A forward linkages approach.* (MMCP Discussion Paper No. 10). Cape Town, South Africa, and Milton Keynes, UK: University of Cape Town and the Open University.

UNCTAD/CALAG. (2006). *Creating local linkages by empowering indigenous entrepreneurs.* (African oil and gas services sector survey Vol. 1-Nigeria). Geneva: United Nations Conference on Trade and Development.

UNIDO. (1980). *World Industry since 1960: Progress and Prospects.* Vienna, Austria: United National Industrial Development Organization.

Urzua, O. (2007). *Emergence and development of Knowledge-Intensive Mining Services (KIMS).* (Mimeo, background paper prepared for UNCTAD). Brighton, UK: University of Sussex.

Walker, M., & Jourdan, P. (2003). Resource-based sustainable development: An alternative approach to industrialisation in South Africa'. *Minerals and Energy, 18*(3), 25-43.

Watkins, M. H. (1963). A staple theory of economic growth. *The Canadian Journal of Economics and Political Science, 29*(2), 141-158.

Williamson, O. E. (1985). *The economic institutions of capitalism: Firms, markets, relational contracting.* New York, NY: Free Press.

Womack, J. P., & Jones, D. T. (1996). *Lean Thinking: Banish waste and create wealth in your corporation.* New York, NY: Simon & Schuster.

World Bank. (2009). *Transport prices and costs in Africa: A review of the international corridors.* Washington DC: The World Bank.

Wright, G., & Czelusta, J. (2004). Why economies slow: The myth of the resource curse. *Challenge, 47*(2), 6-38.

Xing, Y., & Detert, N. (2010). *How the iPhone widens the United States trade deficit with the People's Republic of China.* (ADBI Working Paper No. 257). Tokyo, Japan: Asian Development Bank Institute.

Yao, S., Sutherland, D., & Chen, J. (2010). China's outward FDI and resource seeking strategy: A case study on Chinalco and Rio Tinto. *Asia-Pacific Journal of Accounting & Economics, 17*(3), 313-326.

www.ingramcontent.com/pod-product-compliance
Lightning Source LLC
Chambersburg PA
CBHW020742180526
45163CB00001B/320